the Unofficial Guide® to Getting a Divorce

Second Edition

Russell Wild
and Susan Ellis Wild

WILEY
Wiley Publishing, Inc.

To Clay and Addie,
We promised you that even though we'd be living in two
houses, we'd remain a family. We hope that
we've done that. We love you very, very much.
—Mommy & Daddy

Acknowledgements

We would like to thank the many experts who freely shared their advice. You'll see their names throughout the book. We would especially like to thank our two technical editors, Portia Carmichael and Erik Conrad, Esquire, for their hand in making sure that everything we present as fact is, in fact, fact. Thanks, too, to our agent, Marilyn Allen, without whom there'd be no book. And to our editor, Lynn Northrup: You were a dream to work with.

Contents

About the Authors

Russell Wild is a fee-only (takes no commissions) financial advisor registered with the Pennsylvania Securities Commission. He is also the author or co-author of nearly two dozen nonfiction books and more than 300 articles in major national magazines. Way back when, he worked as a credit analyst at a large bank. In college, he studied economics, graduated *magna cum laude,* and went on to get a Master's degree in business administration (MBA), and, years later, a graduate certificate in personal financial planning. He is a member of both the National Association of Personal Financial Advisors (NAPFA) and the American Society of Journalists and Authors (ASJA).

Susan Ellis Wild has been practicing law for 24 years and is currently a litigator with Gross, McGinley, LaBarre & Eaton, LLP, a law firm in Allentown, Pennsylvania. She is President-Elect of the 600+ member Bar Association of Lehigh County, Pennsylvania. Susan has litigated more than 100 cases and has also been appointed by the courts on numerous occasions to act as an independent arbitrator/mediator of cases. She has been admitted to the Bar in Pennsylvania, the District of Columbia, and Maryland, and has appeared in courts in a number of other states.

Susan and Russell were married in Baltimore in 1981. They divorced 22 years later, in 2003. Both live in Allentown, Pennsylvania, several blocks apart. They share custody of one son, one daughter, and a large black poodle named Norman. They can be reached at Russell@globalportfolios.net or Swild@gmle.com.

Almost every married person, at some point or another during married life, considers divorce. For many, it is a fleeting thought during the heat of an argument. For others, it may be a recurring thought that never gets acted upon. And for still others—perhaps those of you who have picked up this book—the fleeting thought became a recurring thought, which eventually became a plan of action. Let's be honest. If you bought this book, borrowed it, stole it, or just picked it up off the shelf to browse through, then you're probably somewhat less than blissfully in love. Well, at least not with your spouse. Perhaps you're shaking with anger at recent revelations about your partner's post-work activities. Or maybe you're just tired of being tired of the marriage, the lack of passion. Maybe you're great friends but lousy lovers. Whatever the reason, if you're considering divorce proceedings, you will find the information in this book to be helpful.

According to official U.S. government figures, nearly half a million marriages end in divorce every year. You may feel like you are headed into an abyss, but it's a crowded abyss, populated by, among others, the authors of this book.

A brief word about us, your authors. We have been married. To each other. For 22 years, to be exact. We have been divorced. From each other. For two and a half years, at the time of writing this book. We have children. We do not advocate divorce, but we recognize it as a reality of modern life. We believe that the divorce process, while never a happy state of affairs, can be gone through with far less anguish than is wrought upon most families. We were among the fortunate in that we accomplished our divorce and we still like each other. Our children are doing well. We've moved on with our lives. And, we think we have useful information to share, not only our information, but information from experts in the field that will be helpful to those of you who have either committed to divorce or are headed that way. We are not only a formerly married couple, but also professionals—a financial planner and a lawyer. In those capacities, we also have valuable information to share with you. We wish you well and hope that the information in this book helps. We also invite you to correspond with us regarding the particulars of your situation. Our e-mail addresses are at the end of the About the Authors page.

What's in This Book?

The Unofficial Guide to Getting a Divorce, Second Edition, provides you with the most useful and up-to-date advice on major divorce issues: what to do about the children and their living arrangements, how to secure fair support for yourself and your children, dividing the marital property. This book also addresses some of the sub-issues of divorce, which are nonetheless vitally important: what to do about the holidays, health insurance considerations, tax ramifications. And, equally important, this book will provide you with valuable financial advice—not only for use during the heated money issues that crop up during negotiations, but for your future financial health.

Within these pages you'll find expert advice from, well, us: a financial planner and an attorney. You'll also tap into the wisdom of numerous experts who know the ins and outs of every step in the process. We'll provide you with the inside scoop on the divorce process from start to finish, based both on personal experience and on the expertise of one of us, a lawyer with more than 20 years of experience.

With the information provided, you'll be on the inside track of the process. You will learn how to minimize your legal costs, come to agreement with your ex, avoid court hearings, and keep your money from Uncle Sam. Just as important, you'll get tips on keeping your children on track (in school and socially), and on keeping your own head together during this stressful time so you can make those important decisions and stay on your toes at all times.

Divorce is the second-highest-ranking cause of stress, after death of a loved one. Little wonder. Entire lives are shaken by divorce. Not only yours and your spouse's, but your children's, your parents, your nieces and nephews, and your friends. We don't mean to increase the burden you are feeling. But it is useful to know that you will not just be tending to your own increased needs for the near future. Your life, and the lives of those around you, will be shaken by this turn of events in your life. Rational thought, lots of support, and the best advice you can get are the things you need right now. It is important to learn from the experts, and to avoid costly trial and error, so that you can get yourself through this as quickly, painlessly, and efficiently as possible.

Here's a general rundown of the easy-access parts of this book:

- Preparation: Options to divorce; making key decisions; choosing an attorney; pre-filing to-dos.

- Process: The initial filing; the discovery process; what happens in court; and reaching resolution.

- Legal Issues: Division of assets; alimony; child support; custody; visitation.

- Coping: Surviving the ordeal; dealing with your emotions; dealing with your ex; dealing with children; and where to go for help.

- Sticky Situations: Handling spouse and family discord; problem solving tips; and dealing with special circumstances.

- Post-Divorce Financial Issues: Handling the legal, financial, tax, insurance, and health-care issues that will arise from your divorce.

In addition to all this information, you'll find a great deal of help in the back of the book. Turn there if you need to consult the glossary, resource guide (including where to go on the Internet), suggested reading, handy checklists, and advice for assembling your divorce team—all of which have been included to help make getting through this process easier. You will find that throughout the book, we're going to encourage you to keep it civil—as much as you can—because through civility and fair play, you're more likely to create a workable divorce settlement in as short a time as possible. Preserving sanity, protecting the kids, and saving time, money, and frustration are the keys here.

How This Book Is Different

This is not a "How I Survived My Divorce" tome. Such books may be inspiring to those who need proof that this whole terrible ordeal can be survived, but such books do not address all the issues you may find yourself facing, because every divorce is different. This book is also not just a cut-and-dried discussion of technical terms that require you to have an advanced law degree. We're not going to talk over your head, nor are we going to scare you with horror stories of noncustodial parents swiping children, homeless divorcees, and a life of welfare and food stamps for the jilted spouse. While we've all heard divorce-court horror stories, the point of this book is that, with proper care and knowledge on your side, it's possible to make this life-changing event a constructive one.

Right now you should be concentrating on figuring out just what you need to make your divorce an event that leads you toward a better future for yourself and your children. This will require that you understand the very real processes of the judicial system, and that you learn the best way to use that system to your best advantage. It also requires that you understand when it is best to avoid the judicial system at all costs. This book will give you that knowledge—the inside scoop on what's going on in the world of divorce law.

In addition to providing you with instruction on the smartest steps to take at each stage of your divorce, we encourage you to develop a sense of acceptance and optimism about your life. We firmly believe you can take definite steps to a positive resolution. But we want you to know this as well: If you have a truly evil ex and you are undergoing the divorce from beyond hell, well, this book is for you, too.

How to Use This Book

The book is divided into parts: legal, financial, emotional, and so on. As you go through the book, highlight helpful points that apply to you and your family and make notes in the margins. Use the checklists provided in Appendix D to help analyze your situation and make a new plan for your life. Browse through Appendix E for some questions you might want to ask your lawyer or your therapist. One piece of advice we'll give you right now: During this stressful period, it's best to leave nothing to memory. In addition, we strongly suggest you get yourself a big spiral notebook and use it to record all of your questions, notes, appointments, and reminders. Vow to write all of your divorce information in that notebook, so that you're never looking for the cocktail napkin on which you wrote down the number of that child advocate. And, if you have that nasty divorce, turn your notebook into a journal that you can refer to when asked the details of his or her many transgressions. Never assume you will remember it all.

Think of *The Unofficial Guide to Getting a Divorce, Second Edition,* as a wise and trusted friend who has been through it before you. All of the experts we've consulted are among the best in their fields, and their advice—gleaned from the sum of their expertise and their inside knowledge of the legal system—is sure to be of great value to you. Best of all, they're not charging you their regular hourly rates.

How to Be a Savvy Consumer

What does being a consumer have to do with divorce? Everything. Think about what being a "good consumer" means. It means shopping around for the highest quality at the best price, making the most of your money. This is as true when you shop around for a lawyer, a financial advisor, or a marriage counselor as it would be if you were shopping around for a car.

The rules of smart shopping include analyzing your options for their advantages, assessing disadvantages, checking past performance and reliability, and making smart money choices. You should research the credentials of your legal and financial advisors at least as carefully as you would look up a new car's ratings in *Consumer Reports*. To check the credentials of the professionals you'll be consulting during the course of your divorce, you should consult your state's bar association and the professional associations of your financial advisor and/or therapist. Read on and we'll tell you how.

You can actually save money by spending a little bit more on your representation. Just as buying a cheap car can cost you more money in the long run when the car breaks down, hiring a cheap lawyer will cost you more in the long run when you have to find new representation or return to court over and over to modify your settlement. But smart consumerism goes beyond researching professional credentials and checking prices. In order to make the most of your investment in your advisors' services, you should cooperate fully, answering all questions and delivering all requested materials and information in order to help your lawyer, therapist, or financial planner to do his or her job to maximum capacity. You can get the most mileage out of your paid partnerships by being a good client.

The experts—and people who've been through the divorce process themselves—agree on the following savvy decision-making ideas:

- **Research your options.** There's no such thing as too much research, when you think of how important the outcome of this process is to you. So commit your time to the process. Since time is a commodity, think of it as investing in your future.

- **Ask questions.** There is no such thing as a dumb question; it's only dumb not to ask for clarification if you're confused. Remember: Your lawyer, therapist, etc. has heard every question and every comment possible. They know you're not an expert in their field, and they expect you to speak up if you're getting overwhelmed.

- **Invest your time in finding the best representation possible.** It makes all the difference in the world, so don't just flip open the Yellow Pages, close your eyes, and point a finger to a name. The first rule of smart consumerism is choosing a high quality "model" at an affordable price.

Once you've got your professional team in place, there is still more you can do to make your divorce go as smoothly as possible:

- **Take your time.** Don't act on impulse or let your emotions rule your decisions. Don't let anyone—including your lawyer—rush you into making any decisions.

- **Don't worry about making waves.** You have to do what's right for you. The easy path is not always the best path.

- **Be organized and on time.** You don't want to waste money backtracking or re-doing finished business.

- **Be realistic about what you want and deserve in your divorce agreement.** Leave your vindictiveness at the door and focus on a reasonable and fair resolution. Save your anger for your therapist or your best friend, and with them, vent to your heart's content.

- **Make sure you understand all fees, and that you keep careful track of what you owe.** Don't just accept a bill for services if you aren't sure what it is you're paying for. Consult with your tax expert about whether any of your legal fees are tax-deductible (some should be!).

- **Be open to advice from experts, but think for yourself.** If something your advisor tells you to do seems unethical or unfair, follow your gut instinct. Remember, this is your case, not hers.

- **Keep in mind: Winning is not the ultimate goal.** Keeping your children and yourself financially secure and mentally healthy is the ultimate goal.

- ***Be proactive!*** Learn about the rules and the paperwork, every term applicable. Don't just sign what's put before you.

How to Keep Your Sanity During the Process

As we've noted, divorce is the second biggest cause of stress that you are ever likely to face in your lifetime. Only the death of a loved one ranks higher. Divorce hits you hard on every level: emotionally, financially, physically, and socially. You may feel as though your entire world has been shaken up, as though you've been torn in half. And you're not alone in these feelings—just look at what some recent veterans of the divorce process have to say:

Jake: "I was so out of it in the initial phase of filing for divorce that I didn't even know what my assets were. My lawyer had to ask me if I had a car."

Lila: "I was not very quick on the uptake when my ex-husband was leaving home. I very foolishly let him take some valuables from our home that I had to fight him in court to get back later."

Bryan: "It cost me a lot of money to change and add things to my initial divorce complaint paperwork that I was too numb to remember in the first place. It wound up adding a few thousand dollars to my legal bill."

Cynthia: "I made the mistake of seeing a "shark" lawyer, who turned what could have been an amicable divorce into the battle of a lifetime. I'm still shaking from the trial, and I will be paying my lawyer's bills for years to come.

To get through this process, you're going to have to find a way to ground yourself, calm your nerves, keep your wits about you, and think straight. Having a good support system is going to be essential—not one of our divorced experts made it through his or her own situation without the help of family, friends, and support groups. All of them emphasize—and we'll cover this in greater detail in Part V—that you have to recognize your value as an individual, not just as part of a married couple, and you have to look at this whole experience as a new beginning, not a devastating ending. You owe it to yourself to tackle this project for your own well-being and your children's long-term happiness. Done well, it can be the dawn of a new era in your life, one in which you are in control of your own happiness.

So now, get ready to learn the essentials of the successful divorce. With *The Unofficial Guide to Getting a Divorce, Second Edition,* on your side, you've gained an advantage.

Special Features

Every book in the Unofficial Guide series offers the following four special sidebars that are devised to help you get things done cheaply, efficiently, and smartly.

1. **Moneysaver:** Tips and shortcuts that will help you save money.

2. **Watch Out!:** Cautions and warnings to help you avoid common pitfalls.

3. **Bright Idea:** Smart or innovative ways to do something; in many cases, the ideas listed here will help you save time or hassle.

4. **Quote:** Anecdotes from real people who are willing to share their experiences and insights.

We also recognize your need to have quick information at your fingertips and have provided the following comprehensive sections at the back of the book:

1. **Glossary:** Definitions of complicated terminology and jargon.

2. **Resource Guide:** Lists of relevant agencies, associations, institutions, Websites, and so on.

3. **Recommended Reading List:** Suggested titles that can help you get more in-depth information on related topics.

4. **Important Checklists:** "Official" pieces of information you need to refer to, such as government forms.

5. **Assembling Your Divorce Team:** Find the best lawyer and money manager.

6. **Index**

Smart Preparation for Divorce

PART I

GET THE SCOOP ON...
Deciding whether to split ▪ Marital counseling,
separation, or postponement ▪ Soul searching ▪
Moving forward

Is This Really the End of the Marriage?

The foundation of any marriage is the human connection—the bond that is formed between two people who have chosen to share their love and their lives. You and your spouse may enjoy many of the same activities, may have brought children into the world together, may still laugh at the same jokes. But if you reach the point where you feel you're losing—or have lost—that deep human connection—nothing else may matter. That's when divorce may start to seem like the best option.

The breakdown of the human connection can happen for all sorts of reasons. In the heat of an argument or during a time of high stress—or perhaps right after bumping into an old flame in the supermarket—it is often easy to leap to the conclusion that divorce is the answer. And it may well be true—but before you start flipping through the Yellow Pages for a lawyer, it's important to look at the big picture, and to try to do so with an objective eye.

Have you really thought this out? Do all of your problems, all the things that have gotten on your nerves over the years, all of your spouse's wrong-doings and alleged wrong-doings, warrant a divorce? Take the time to consider what you really want and need before you enter into that extremely grueling process. Consider, too, whether you are realistically evaluating a future relationship with someone else. Might you not be just trading in old baggage for new? And, of course, if there are children, you need to weigh the likely effects of a divorce on their lives.

In this chapter you'll learn about resources and options available to couples who want to make certain that they have exhausted all options before giving up on a marriage.

Deciding to decide

Only you can decide if divorce is your best, or only, option right now. Of course, you may wish to seek the input of counselors, friends, and family when making this decision. But remember that friends and family will often have an agenda of their own (they may adore your spouse, or they may think your spouse is the devil incarnate). Before you begin the divorce process, *you*, and you alone, need to be fully comfortable that this is the right decision for you

You may decide to see an attorney at that point. An attorney will help educate you on all the legal consequences of your divorce and will help guide you through the process. Some attorneys will also provide moral support. But don't ask your attorney if you *should* divorce. That is not a legal question. And if he or she answers it, find another lawyer.

Ditto for the court. Except in rare instances, it is relatively easy to *get* a divorce (not to be confused with settling financial

 Watch Out!

Divorce isn't cheap. Even an amicable divorce is much more expensive than most people realize. Not only does one house become two, but you'll also have two heating bills, two water bills, and twice as many lawn mowings.

Bright Idea

When your marriage is in deep trouble, you need to focus on communication. Really work to discover the root of your problems and to understand why that fundamental connection between you and your spouse has been weakened or severed.

and custody issues, which are never easy). But it is not the court's place to decide whether you should seek a divorce. You are the one to decide that.

There *are* options to divorce

In the extreme cases of physical abuse or repeated and flagrant affairs, your best option is, of course, to simply *get out*. But these are special cases and need to be handled carefully—more on that in Chapter 14.

The vast majority of divorces are brought on by more subtle problems. You may have seemingly grown apart or lost sight of what once bound you together. What to do in that case? Work like there's no tomorrow to evaluate the problems and try to save the partnership. Marriage is too important to be dumped without a fight.

Some couples find that simply taking time out of their busy schedules to sit and talk, or perhaps to run away for a week to the islands without the children, can work wonders. Other couples decide to separate, which if done very wisely, may help create space enough to figure a few things out without having to actually divorce. Sometimes it helps to have a referee, an experienced negotiator, someone who can coach you through the stickier parts of communication. In short, it may be time to give marital counseling a try.

Marital counseling

The human connection between partners is the heart of a marriage. When that connection starts to crumble, you might need some help in reconstructing what once was.

Watch Out!

Whatever you do, don't even think about divorce if you've been married for 9 years and 11 months! That's because the law, in most cases, allows you to tap into your ex-spouse's Social Security only after you've been married for 10 years.

Counseling may be the answer. But you'll have to take the initiative yourself. Don't look for a therapist in the Yellow Pages. Ask family and friends, or work colleagues if you prefer to keep family and friends out of this, or perhaps your physician for a referral. Make a few calls. Always ask about credentials, experience, and cost.

Licensing of therapists differs from state to state. In some states, just about anyone can call himself a therapist, so be careful. If you choose a psychiatrist (an M.D. who specializes in psychology and emotional issues), ask if that psychiatrist is board certified. Be aware that many psychiatrists do not really provide counseling, but rather, their approach to psychological issues may be through use of drug therapy, which may not be what you need in the context of marital problems. By contrast, psychologists (who are not trained in medicine) generally focus on talk therapy. A psychologist should have a Ph.D. in psychology from a respected university, and should certainly be certified by the state. Don't be shy about asking anyone holding himself out to be a marriage counselor exactly what qualifies him to be so. If he or she resists or seems offended, find someone else.

Set up a first appointment to see if you and your spouse and the therapist "click." Determine if the therapist seems impartial, confident, and competent. If not, don't hesitate to hunt for another. If your spouse refuses to join you in therapy, consider going alone. (More on therapy in Part V.)

What's going on here?
If you've never gone to counseling or therapy, you may be curious to know what's in store. So here's the general flow of events ... On

your first visit, you will be asked some basic questions about your situation—after all, the therapist doesn't know you or the circumstances that led to your marital woes.

If on the strength of your first meeting your therapist can determine that you and your spouse are not at each other's throats, but agrees there are areas of strain and uncertainty in your marriage, that will suggest direction for the therapy. The counseling sessions are likely to be good-natured and without conflict. Hopefully you've come to the sessions as two people who care about each other, but who have discovered that they need a third-party opinion and a nudge in the right direction. That is exactly what the therapist is trained to do.

On the other hand, if you and your spouse walk into the session looking like a Hatfield and a McCoy, with big issues of anger and hurt and possibly even a lust for revenge, your therapist will no doubt have to adopt a different approach—more of a referee or negotiator.

Your therapist's questions may surprise you—some of them may seem to have little or nothing to do with your immediate problems. For example, you may be asked questions about how you and your spouse met: Did you have a whirlwind courtship? To the therapist, that might suggest you didn't know each other very well before you decided to get married. Did you marry because you had to, or because you wanted to? Your answer may disclose areas of hostility that you or your spouse didn't even know existed.

The counselor may also ask about how well the two of you communicated during the earlier stages of your marriage. Maybe some of today's issues were always present, but were ignored while you were in the first blush of romance. In addition, the counselor may want to know about your relationship with your in-laws. If this relationship is troubled, maybe it's setting up conflicts of loyalty for you or your spouse.

If yours is a second marriage, and especially if there are step-children in the picture, the therapist will likely ask many questions about the stepfamily dynamic.

Moneysaver

Since your therapist is charging you by the hour, the easier you make the job, the less you'll be forking out. Preparing a short written biography of your relationship—how long you've been together, a list of your major problems, some information about your family backgrounds—may help shave a few hours off the time the therapist will need to get up to speed.

Many people become frustrated with these kinds of questions. They want to get right to the heart of their present problems, so to speak, and they don't see the point in talking about their first date. Indeed, it's hard for a couple to stick with it while the therapist gathers this important background information. But your therapist knows that the couple you are now has evolved from the couple you were back then.

Identifying old patterns

Early in her marital counseling sessions, Linda was surprised when the therapist asked about one of her old boyfriends, Pete. She'd been with him for six years before they broke up, after which time she eventually met and married her current husband. When Linda talked about the relationship with her old boyfriend, the therapist discovered that Linda had been very dependent on Pete, which led Pete to feel smothered and, in turn, caused Linda and Pete to break up. It's no surprise, then, that Linda's current husband was complaining of feeling smothered as well. This revelation gave the therapist a starting point—an issue that Linda and her husband could now begin to address.

We all develop our styles of relating from the patterns we've seen or followed in the past. This fact, which a good therapist well knows, is something that counseling helps us to discover for ourselves. For example, your notions of what marriage should be like are very much colored by the example of marriage you grew up with. If your parents had an unhappy marriage and you grew up with fighting and verbal abuse in your home, you might be likely to repeat those patterns within your own marriage. Those patterns may not even seem unhealthy or strange to you. Just as likely, you may be unwilling to have a healthy argument with your spouse because you never saw an argument between your parents turn out constructively. Or perhaps you never saw dear old Dad fight with Mom at all, and you are trying to mirror your parents' "perfect" marriage. Understanding the role models that shaped your individual expectations of marriage can help your counselor either debunk or support the lessons you've learned through the examples within your life.

You will also be asked personal questions—questions about how you perceive yourself and your place in the world as an individual. At the very core of counseling is the notion that two people come into a marriage with their own individual identities. These identities may be fairly well adjusted or they may be insecure. By helping you deal with the pasts, beliefs, personal fears, and values held by you and your spouse, the counselor can work with you to see how the pieces fit together now, and how you can make them fit together better in the future.

It may take a few sessions, but once the necessary background information has been gathered, you and your spouse will work with the counselor to identify what is and isn't working in your marriage. This work may be done in one or more of several different ways. You may be asked to fill out detailed questionnaires. You may be given essays to write, or you might be asked to write letters to your partner. You may be given specific topics to discuss, or you may be given the floor to bring up whatever topics are most important to you at the moment. You might even be given exercises to do at home—scripts you can use to foster better communication within your home environment.

The techniques your therapist gives you may take a little time before they start to work. Or they may take a lot of time. Emotional knots that have been tightening for years won't suddenly unravel. Don't get discouraged, however. Remember your

Moneysaver

Every time you consider terminating therapy because it's "too expensive," remember this: The financial expense of therapy is nothing compared to the expense of divorce. Don't quit because of money. If necessary, talk about the financial impact with your therapist, and work with her to find alternatives.

counselor is not a magician. And, since we all generally try to be on our best behavior in front of strangers, you may not be presenting your counselor a clear view of your communication and fighting styles—at least, not at the beginning. So your therapist may not hit on the most effective techniques to recommend right away. Be prepared for the fact that it is probably going to take some time for you and your spouse to become comfortable enough in therapy to open up naturally. The time invested is worth it, however—after awhile you'll begin to find it easier to communicate with your spouse, and thus to constructively address your problems.

When only one will go

What happens when you want counseling, but your spouse refuses to go? This happens often, but before you give up on the counseling option, find out why your spouse is refusing. Here are some of the most common reasons for lack of cooperation:

- **Denial:** Your spouse thinks the problems aren't that major.
- **Defeatism:** Your spouse thinks it's too late to fix the problems.
- **Avoidance:** Your spouse is afraid to face up to what he or she is doing wrong, or is afraid that an honest discussion of problems will cause you pain.
- **Threat:** Your spouse is afraid that talking about the problems will lead to, not away from, divorce.
- **Control issues:** Your spouse doesn't want an outside authority figure to tell him or her what to do. This attitude may

also spring from a lack of respect for the mental health industry.

▪ **Financial issues:** Your spouse may be reluctant to pay for counseling.

You can't force someone to go into counseling if that person doesn't want to—it just defeats the whole purpose. But you can be careful not to overanalyze your spouse's decision. You can stay open to other means of working on your marriage. And even if your partner won't go, you might choose to enter into counseling alone. If you do, you might at least be able to figure out what can be done on your end to help solve your marital problems. There is a danger in this, however—for while individual counseling can give you insights into your own behavior and feelings, it can't address the problems of the entire "machine." After all, the counselor is only getting your side of the story, and can't, therefore, directly help you to work on how you and your spouse interact. If your partner won't agree to work with you in counseling, it might be time to look at your other options.

Separation

Sometimes two people get too close to their problems or begin to take one another for granted. In such cases, a little distance and time spent apart might be all the two of you need to cool off and gain perspective. Well, that's what the common wisdom says. In truth, separations rarely work. They tend to only make matters more complicated. Once the two of you are living in separate houses, paying separate bills, reconciliation becomes a lot of extra work.

Of course, you could look at separation as a kind of "trial" divorce. During a separation, both parties have an opportunity to see what life without the other would be like. For many people, a separation comes as a relief; for others it's extremely unsettling. They miss being at home, being with their children—maybe they even miss their spouse. The old saying "Be careful what you wish for, you just might get it" sometimes comes back to haunt people during a separation, making them realize that the initial decision to live apart may have been ill advised.

On the other hand, some people use separation as a convenient escape from the responsibilities of marriage, one that even gives them permission to have relationships with other people. In such cases, separation no longer becomes a means of cooling down and getting better prepared to work on the marriage. It becomes an excuse to party.

> 66 In many cases that I've seen, a suggestion to separate is merely one spouse's idea of softening the blow of divorce. 99
>
> —Michael Dolan, Psy.D., psychologist and marriage counselor

Clearly, separation can mean different things to different people. It's even common for some couples to shuttle back and forth between living apart and getting back together again, never really making a full commitment one way or another. For such couples, separation and reconciliation become a way of life.

In terms of the law, an informal agreement to separate is very different from a "legal separation." In an informal separation, one party in the marriage may simply pack up and move out on his or her own. A legal separation involves legal action. But no matter what your reason to separate—whether it's because you and your spouse simply want a time to cool off and gain perspective or because you see this as a first step toward making a more final split—you must still deal with all the practical issues that will arise once you decide to live apart. You have to make decisions about visitation with your children, payment of support and/or monthly expenses, division of assets (such as bank accounts and automobiles), payment of debt, covering the mortgage, and the division of future income. To protect your interests, you have to know where you stand not only for the time you're separated, but also in the event that you ultimately *do* get divorced.

Bright Idea

If you feel you must separate, consider doing so under the same roof: you in one room, your spouse in another. It makes reconciliation a *lot* easier than if you are living in two homes. (Of course, older children may question this new arrangement.)

The separation agreement

Regardless of the legal status of your separation ("separation" means different things in different states), all resolutions or agreements arrived at by you and your spouse should be in writing and signed by both of you. This agreement, typically known as a settlement or separation agreement, will serve as the law of your separation and may eventually be used as the basis for a final divorce agreement. Until the two of you are able to agree on terms, a written and signed agreement may be impossible, but in this case, try to record any interim agreements in a written document. Perhaps it has been agreed that one spouse will move out of the family home, but that fact is not to be held against him or her later in the proceedings. Or perhaps there is an interim agreement that the husband will pay a certain sum to his wife for temporary "support," although not court-ordered. Anything along these lines should somehow be documented. If one spouse refuses to sign anything, the other should at least write a self-serving letter or note to the other that sets forth what is happening.

A written agreement protects you, because unless you can prove to the court that your spouse did not meet his or her agreed-upon obligations, such as paying half of the mortgage, your agreements cannot be enforced. No matter how amicable you and your spouse may be at the time you separate, this may change. Without a written and signed agreement, the two of you may find yourself fighting over issues that could have been resolved as part of a fair and equitable contract.

The wording of a separation agreement, like other official documents, can be a little formal, but don't let the legalese frighten you—your lawyer can take you step by step through the document. Also, there is a trend in the law to put documents in plainer English. When you first talk with your lawyer, tell him you want "plain English" documents. Instead of "Husband," the document should refer to the man by name. Ditto for "Wife." Believe it or not, the term "issue of the marriage" refers to children! Ask for the children to be identified by their names. You'll be surprised to find out how much more readable a legal document can be when written in this manner.

Although you and your spouse no longer live together, you generally cannot (and should not) financially abandon each other. For example, where alimony or child support would be applicable in the event of a divorce, this type of support should also be paid during a separation.

Similarly, the spouse who moves out still has an obligation to share in the household expenses, and each of you typically shares in the financial obligations incurred by the other. Before you separate, it's important to understand how you and your spouse plan to divide your income, expenses, assets, and liabilities— including those that arise after your separation. For example, your spouse may incur substantial credit card bills or enjoy an increase in income after you separate. The two of you should address these types of issues, if possible, prior to or in conjunction with the separation.

If you have concerns about your spouse's spending habits (and many separated people do), contact the credit card companies and notify them of the separation and that you will not be responsible for any charges incurred after the date of separation. You should apply for new credit, in your name alone, before you separate, or, if that hasn't happened, as soon as possible after the separation.

Watch Out!

Separation shouldn't become a way of life; some action has to be taken to either save or end the marriage. Living in limbo is not wise or healthy for either of you or for your children. Look at separation as a tool that should be used for a limited time. There may also be important financial, legal, and tax reasons to finalize your status.

You've got work to do

You'll need to lay some ground rules so that the terms of your separation are consistent with both your needs and the needs of your spouse. By all means, get legal advice (turn to Chapter 5 for information on how to find and hire an attorney), and draw up an official agreement on the following issues:

- Who gets custody of the children, and how will visitation be handled?
- Who gets which personal belongings?
- How will you handle paying the mortgage, household expenses, and debts—and especially, meeting the kids' financial needs?
- What about insurance?
- What about contact between the two of you, post-separation?
- What'll you do with the mail?

This last one may strike many people as being a bit trivial, but it often becomes a real hot spot for separated couples. What happens to mail that comes in both your names? How about bills addressed to both of you? The post office may not forward third-class mail (including magazines or journals)—what should you do with those? You will want to make arrangements with your partner to have important items set aside for some sort of regularly scheduled pickup.

Reality check

Separation isn't easy. In some cases, it may prove to be a constructive tool in deciding where your marriage is going to go in the future. The time you spend apart can show how much you really want to be together. On the other hand, as happens in the majority of cases, separation will pave the road to divorce.

Either way, we suppose, the separation has served a useful purpose.

Is this the end?

So, you've tried counseling, and maybe even tried a separation, and things still aren't working out. If all efforts to re-connect with your partner have been unsuccessful, it's probably time to consider the option of divorce. This is a highly emotional decision, a huge life change (probably bigger than you can even imagine) that will affect everyone in your lives. Take it one step at a time. It may be best to begin with exploring the issue thoroughly—both privately and with your spouse.

> **66** It took me a long time to get over the feeling that I had failed. The divorce was especially hard for me because I was the first in my family to get a divorce. Now, I can look back and see that I had made a bad decision to marry, true; but that's nothing I should beat myself up for. **99**
>
> —Cindy, divorced 13 years ago

The list of questions coming up will help you determine whether divorce is the right choice for you. The questions are intended to get you thinking about what you truly want. Remember, however, that you are not the only one who may have questions about the state of your marriage. And your spouse may answer these questions differently than you. Be prepared to probe deeply and honestly, and recognize that this is something that the two of you (and your children) have a stake in.

Watch Out!

It's only natural to feel a little bitter right about now. But nothing is ever just black and white. While you may be angry at your spouse, remember he or she does has some good qualities. After all, you agreed to marry, remember? Be willing to see the gray areas, and try to stay objective while assessing your marriage.

The truthful answers to these questions—asked of yourself and of your spouse—will help clarify whether divorce is truly the best route to take. If nothing else, they will help bring you to a deeper understanding of yourself and your needs. But again, keep in mind that only you can make the ultimate decision that divorce is the best thing for your situation. And there are other considerations to keep in mind. Divorce will have an effect on many aspects of your life.

Because marriage—and divorce—is a two-way street, you really should check with your spouse. How does he or she feel about the issues raised by these questions? Communication, difficult as it may be, is important, even in divorce. But before you bound in on your spouse with a list of soul-searching questions in hand, consider the following ground rules to keep the discussion amicable:

■ Watch your timing. Don't approach your spouse when he or she is tired or stressed.

■ Make an appointment with your spouse to talk. It may be as simple as "Can we talk after dinner? I have some important things to discuss with you."

■ Minimize distractions. Wait until the kids go to bed, or better yet, are out of the house. Turn off the television and unplug the phone.

■ Really listen to what your partner says; keep an open mind and don't interrupt.

Twelve Personal Questions to
Ask Yourself and Your Spouse

1. How am I doing in my life? Am I content within myself?

2. What are the roles and tasks that I consider important in my life? How does my marriage affect those roles, and how would divorce affect them?

3. What gives me satisfaction? Marriage? Job? Caring for kids? Friendships?

4. Where do I want to be right now? In one year? In five years?

5. Are the conditions and needs of my marriage holding me back from what I need? Would divorce move me closer to or further away from fulfilling those needs?

6. Are the problems in the marriage fixable or are they beyond my control?

7. Is there an outside influence that is affecting our marriage that can be eliminated?

8. Can I openly share my frustrations with my partner? If not, why not?

9. Can I forgive my partner for what I perceive as some awful wrong-doings?

10. Do I find my spouse physically attractive?

11. Do I respect my spouse as a person?

12. Is this someone I want to grow old with?

Because this conversation may be the first time you or your spouse have openly admitted to dissatisfaction in your marriage, there is an inherent risk that the responses you receive may come as a shock. But it's generally better to be completely honest now than to let resentment and anger simmer below the surface. By beginning the discussion of divorce in this way, you minimize the possibility of resentment and confrontation further down the road.

Changing your mind

Yes, it's sometimes possible to put the brakes on, even after you've begun the process of a separation or divorce. If necessary, you may have the option of postponement.

Maybe you need a bit of time and reflection to make the right choice. Or, if you or your partner are going through some rough life events (a family member might be ill, or there's been a death in the family, or one of you has just lost a job), maybe the stress arising from these outside events is central to your current marital distress. If such ups and downs of life coincide with a time of marital discord, the resulting turmoil can be all-consuming. If this is true, dealing with your marriage may just have to wait until you're a little more coherent, a little less emotional, and a little better able to think clearly.

> 66 With divorce as easy as it is, and its consequences so hard, people with children need to ask themselves whether they have given a marriage their best shot and what more they can do to make it work before they call it quits. 99
>
> —Hillary R. Clinton,
> *It Takes a Village*

The decision to end your marriage should never be made in the midst of a larger tragedy or upheaval in the family. Couples with larger problems in their lives often transfer their emotions, fears, and frustrations onto their partner. If you're dealing with a family crisis, put off decisions about your marriage until the smoke has cleared.

If you're putting off making a final decision right now, you'll still have to deal with the underlying issues of unhappiness in your marriage. Since you'll be getting back together, you'll need to find a way to coexist. Here are some tips to make this possible:

- Don't pretend there are no problems. Deal with issues in a constructive and communicative way.

- Have a definite length of time for the postponement. Don't leave things hanging indefinitely.

- Notify your counselor or lawyer of the postponement so she knows what your status is.

- Notify your friends and family that you're postponing your decision. Even well-meaning friends and relatives, if uninformed, can escalate tensions between the two of you and push you out of postponement into finalization.

- Notify your children of the postponement. They have a right to know what's going on.

- Use this time to think, to measure the depth of your problems, or to see the good in your spouse and in your marriage. This thinking, of course, may deepen your commitment to divorce, but it is honest consideration, a mature handling of the realities of your partnership.

Even if the divorce process has already begun, if it doesn't feel right, you still have choices. Don't despair. People do cancel their divorce proceedings. The gravity of the process is sometimes enough to convince them that their problems are not insurmountable. If your case has reached the filing stage, your lawyers will contact the judge and inform the court of the new situation. No big deal.

Depending on where you live, you may have to fill out forms stating your reconciliation for the record, but otherwise you'll be free to go home and work on your marriage.

 Watch Out!

Keep in mind that although you can change your mind after filing divorce papers—especially if you did it as a threat or an impulsive act—your spouse may not have a similar change of heart. If you find yourself in this situation, talk to your spouse and perhaps suggest counseling for the two of you.

Of course, counseling can help repair the damage that may have occurred during the aborted divorce—perhaps your lawyers can recommend a good marital counselor. What's important to know is that the process can be stopped, if necessary, right up until the final court date.

Looking ahead

Sometimes, no matter how hard a couple tries, they still find that they can't work things out and a divorce becomes the apparent best answer to their problems. That was the answer for us. And it may be the answer for you.

We hope that this book will help you to see that a divorce does not have to be destructive—in fact, it can be the beginning of a new and better life for yourself, your spouse, and even your children.

In the next chapter you'll learn just what it takes to set up a "successful" divorce—one in which you can avoid behaviors and confrontations that will only lead to misery. Then you'll learn what you need to do to get your affairs in order so that you can protect your interests, what to look for in an attorney, and how to effectively participate in your own divorce.

> ❝ I would never have asked for divorce. Never. But it happened. That's no reason that I should feel ashamed or belittled. No reason to mope. I'm going to live life to its fullest! ❞
>
> —Yvonne, divorced after 12 years of marriage

Just the facts

- The decision to divorce is one that will affect all aspects of your life. It should never be taken lightly.
- Consider marital counseling if you're not yet certain that divorce is the answer.
- A separation may be an act of last resort.

- At every stage of the divorce process you have the option to slow down or change your mind—divorces can be postponed or even canceled.

- The end of a marriage is not the end of your life, and even more important, it should not mark the end of your children's happy childhood(s).

GET THE SCOOP ON...
Setting priorities and goals ■ Breaking the
news to others ■ Laying the groundwork for a
successful divorce

Setting Up a Successful Divorce: The First Steps

Chapter 2

A successful divorce—it seems like a contradiction in terms, doesn't it? How can a divorce be successful? But if you look at the process as a constructive act rather than a grim ending, the idea of "success" begins to make sense. Divorce is, after all, an organized process designed to provide a fair resolution to your marital problems and to ensure a fair level of support and security for you, your soon-to-be-ex spouse, and your children. A successful divorce, then, is one that reaches an equitable agreement that protects the interests of all parties involved.

You might not be ready to think about your divorce in a businesslike way right now. You may be reeling from the shock of this new situation in your life. Even if you're not surprised to be in this situation, you may feel overwhelmed and raw. The idea of treating it like a calm, cool, business dealing might be a bit too much to expect right now. However, you'll soon start to see that although working toward a successful divorce takes many steps, in the end it really isn't

23

rocket science. You can do it. In this chapter you will learn how to make your divorce a positive life change.

You have to start somewhere

Once you decide that divorce is where you're headed, your first step in the process is to ask yourself some key questions. What do you want out of this divorce? What's most important to you? The answers to these questions will create the foundation of your divorce. Before you even think of calling a lawyer, have a game plan. Organize your thoughts so that when you do speak to a lawyer, you have something concrete to present. In the following sections, we'll discuss some of the issues you'll want to consider.

Establish your priorities

Start by getting your priorities straight. If you have children, you will need to consider their best interests above all else. Ask yourself these questions, and then answer them objectively: Which parent is better suited to have primary custody? (Hopefully, you will both remain full-time parents, even though the children may not always be sleeping in one house.) How much child support is needed to adequately provide for them? What kind of custody arrangement will best suit their needs? It is important to remember that you and your spouse are the parents, and if you can work well together (at least on the critical issues pertaining to your children), the two of you can completely control the issues pertaining to custody and support. There is no "rule" that the courts have to make these decisions for you; in fact, the courts will get involved only if the parents cannot work these issues out

---

 Watch Out!

Do not allow your initial assessments to be colored by the presence of an "I'll get you" mentality. This kind of mindset will only cloud your thinking and make resolution more difficult. It will also exhaust you in the long run.

Bright Idea

Yes, you should also take into consideration what is fair for your ex. Remember, the goal here is to create a *successful* divorce, so fairness should be your watchword at all times.

together. If you make such decisions with the children's well-being in mind, then your own priorities will fall into line.

Of course, if your situation is such that you cannot work with your co-parent on these issues, you will need to quickly tap into legal and mental health resources in your area. (More on both later in the book.)

If you do not have children, your main concern should be to secure a fair settlement for yourself—one that will allow you to conduct your new life with some sense of security. You'll need enough cash for right now, you'll need a place to live, and you'll need adequate means by which to support yourself in the long run. Good divorce settlements provide both spouses with the means for continued self-reliance and financial survival. Courts attempt to shape their decisions based on considerations of fairness and true need. So forget about all those media stories of spectacular settlements—a successful divorce is *not* about "winning."

Begin with a plan

Having the right priorities from the outset will help you create a fair and realistic list of goals, so you can decide what you want out of the divorce. It's never too early to get organized. Making a list is always a good way to keep yourself on track. The following questions will help you draw up a complete list of your goals, and it is this list that will help you create your divorce agreement:

- Do you want to keep the house? Even if you both believe that it will eventually need to be sold to fairly divide the assets of the marriage, consider whether one parent can hold on to the house at least during the initial phases of the separation and divorce process to minimize the disruption to the children.

■ Where will the children sleep? Believe it or not, this may be your children's number-one question. They will need consistency and predictability, and for most children, the issue of where they sleep at night is critical.

■ Do you require financial assistance from your spouse? Avoid, for the time being, using the word "alimony." That term is loaded with negative meaning, and while you may eventually be using it for the IRS and other purposes, you should both initially just be thinking about equalizing your economic situations. That may well require one to assist the other financially.

■ What other financial assistance do you think you'll need? Child support? Help paying school tuition? Are there extraordinary medical or dental bills anticipated for either you or the children?

■ Which of your household belongings do you want to keep and which are you willing to let go to your spouse? Don't get hung up on this issue in the first weeks after you decide to divorce. There is plenty of time to divvy "things" up, and they should be of least importance right now. Caveat: *Do not*, under any circumstances, dispose of anything that is of even remote importance to your ex. If necessary, pack things up and store them until the two of you can calmly and rationally divide the belongings. Again, for the sake of the children, try to avoid disrupting the "look" of their home, at least for the first few months.

■ What are your financial assets? Assess and list IRAs, stocks, and retirement plans. Don't even begin to divide them yet. There is time later for that. Just get them itemized.

■ Will you maintain a share of a jointly owned business? If so, how do you want to handle working together after the divorce?

Moneysaver

If you take the time to create a list of goals before you visit a lawyer, you will not have to pay for the time your lawyer would otherwise spend recording your thoughts in his or her office. Better to do it on your own time, before-hand, so you're ready with a workable outline.

Take your time in putting these lists together—put some real thought into the process. If you should hire a lawyer, it's what your lawyer will work with when he or she starts to build your case. Lawyers look for basic elements within the divorce: Will they be dealing with child custody issues? Alimony issues? Are there business dealings that have to be divided?

As we've tried to emphasize from the start, marriage—and divorce—is ultimately about the connection between people. When you first think about divorce, your focus is on you and your spouse, but there are many other people who will be affected by the actions you are about to take.

Breaking the news

Now that you've explored the issues and have a plan in mind of how you want to proceed, it's time to consider all the other people whose lives will be touched by your decision—this is, after all, not just between you and your spouse. Children, especially, deserve to know what's going on, but others may need to be told as well. How you handle telling them will have a major impact on the "success" of your divorce.

Telling the kids

While breaking the news of divorce to children is never a pleasant task, there are ways that you and your spouse can present the news of your impending split in a comforting and supportive way. Keep the following tips in mind:

■ Before you approach your children, you and your spouse should privately discuss what you are going to say, how you are going to say it, and how you will handle the children's reactions. Having a loose script will make the process much easier than going in unprepared. No matter how confused either of you may be, it is essential that that confusion not be imparted to the children at this critical time.

■ Before you speak to the children, it's a good idea to already have some of the details of the divorce worked out, particularly those that directly relate to the children. For instance, you will be able to quell the children's fears about where they'll live if you can tell them right away that you'll both be spending some time with them almost every day, or that they'll be spending weekends at Dad's new place from now on.

■ Both parents should tell the children together, if possible. This lets them know that you have made this decision together, that you've thought it out fully, and that you're both committed to the decision. This simple shared act makes it clear to them that you are serious about the divorce and may help them avoid feelings of divided loyalties. No matter how angry or hurt you may be, do not communicate those emotions to your children during this process. They have enough to process on their own without having to worry about your emotional state.

■ Do not assume that your child knows the reasons for the divorce. He or she may not have witnessed any of your arguments. It's important to spell out the fact that the adults cannot get along anymore, and that you both still love the children—especially because children are likely to assume that the divorce is their fault.

■ Expect interruptions, and allow the child to ask questions as they arise.

- You and your spouse should agree to be respectful to one another during this discussion. If only for this one meeting, you should present a united front.

- Know that children read the underlying messages. They're going to be watching your body language, picking up on sarcastic tones, and interpreting so much more than the words you're saying.

- Be honest. We are not suggesting you need to enlighten your children about your spouse's misdeeds; in fact, you clearly should not. But don't make up stories, either. Telling lies or half-truths at this point undermines your credibility and your child's trust in you. In almost all situations, it is a truth to tell the children that Mommy and Daddy simply cannot get along anymore, and that while they both love you kids, they need to live apart from one another. If the children are very young, you might use the words, "Mommy and Daddy aren't playing well together."

- Do not promise things you can't deliver. If your child asks about issues you haven't yet resolved, don't pretend you know the answer. Simply promise that you'll provide the answer once the issue has been decided, and that you will inform the child promptly.

- Be ready for tears or anger. The children may react out of surprise or fear, and crying or yelling is not uncommon. Be quick to hold them and jointly provide comfort.

Children's first reactions to the news of divorce commonly take one of the following forms:

- We can't let this happen.
- There has to be something you can do.
- What are we going to do?

But kids can come up with some surprising reactions—here are a few, reported by real parents:

- I knew this was going to happen.
- I thought this only happened to other families.
- What are my friends going to say?
- Do Grandma and Grandpa know?
- How could you do this to me?
- You *promised* you would never get divorced.

Experts agree that the one thing kids need at this time is your support. Start by assuring them that they are not losing their parents. Tell them that although you and your spouse are not going to be married anymore, both of you are still—and will always be—their parents. You still love them, and that will never change. Make it clear that parents don't divorce their kids. This is an important issue for kids. They take things personally, wondering what they will lose in this situation. Spell it out for them—they won't lose the love or the presence of their parents—and take that pressure off their young shoulders.

> **❝** Remember this: no matter what the situation, no matter what your child's response: Kids are not adults. They'll have their own set of emotional reactions, and from that perspective, they may not agree that a divorce is the right thing to do. **❞**
>
> —Dr. Paula Bortnichak, family therapist

Remember also that, no matter their age, the children will still need a chance to speak their minds. Give them the time and opportunity to talk about their feelings, their fears, and their concerns. Kids can't always defer their questions until the most convenient time; they ask them as they come up. So allow them the freedom to come to you at any time for discussions. Remember to listen to them. Realize that your kids are upset and frightened. They're trying to sort out this complicated issue just like you are.

> **Bright Idea**
>
> Make it clear to your children that the divorce is *not* their fault, that they had nothing to do with Mommy and Daddy getting divorced. This is a message that warrants repeating, days, weeks, even years after the divorce.

You will undoubtedly see that your child is really struggling with putting his feelings into words. It will become quite clear that your child wants to talk it out, but just doesn't know how. At this time, you need to know what to say to get your child through this. It may help for you to talk to a therapist about how to improve communications with your child. A therapist who is well-versed in how children think may be able to give you some useful insight. At the very least, he or she might be able to give you some specific wording for opening up a dialogue.

If your children are not functioning well in the aftermath of your initial conversation on the subject, and later conversations don't seem to be helping, you might need to seek outside help for them. Look for these signs in your kids to determine whether further help is needed:

- **Personality changes.** Your once-outgoing child becomes withdrawn, moody, and irritable.

- **Loss of interest.** Your child no longer enjoys the things she once loved doing, like a favorite sport or hobby.

- **Withdrawal.** Your child spends more time alone.

- **Mood swings.** Your child cries easily or more often.

- **Disrupted eating habits.** Your child is not eating, or he's bingeing.

- **Changes in sleep patterns.** Your child is either sleeping too much or too little, or your child may resume bed-wetting.

These are serious signs that you should get some outside help for your children. No matter how much you try to let them talk things through with you, your children may feel that they can't because they don't want to upset you. A qualified third party may be just the outlet they need to get it all out. Explain that going to a counselor doesn't mean they're crazy. Kids worry about such stigmas. Say instead that this is just an expert who might be able to help them sort out their feelings and who will let them talk. Some people refer to a child's therapist as a "talk doctor."

A therapist is not the only outside source of support available to your children. There are many people in a child's life: older, trusted relatives; teachers; religious leaders; instructors; even their own friends.

Your children won't be the only ones in their class to experience divorce. They've heard friends talk about the subject, so they most likely have someone their own age to whom they can talk about the divorce. Perhaps your child spends a lot of time at a friend's house, and that friend's parents are divorced. Your child learns by observation of his friend's life that the problem is not insurmountable. His friend may even open his eyes to the benefits: no more fighting between the parents, having two rooms—one at Mom's and one at Dad's—and so on. On the other hand, if your child has a friend who has experienced a tumultuous divorce, you will need to reassure him that yours will be different.

Quite clearly, if your children have close friends they can turn to for support or distraction, it actually helps them to cope better with the divorce. A good friend will talk about her own experience and will share the feelings and fears she had. In listening, your child learns that her own feelings and fears are normal, and that she too will eventually get used to it like her friends did.

 Watch Out!

As with all kids, some can be little demons. To make sure your kid's same-age advisor is feeding him good and helpful information—not tips on "how to make your parents pay for doing this to you"—make yourself available for heart-to-hearts with your kids on a regular basis.

Talking to your parents

It may be hard to tell your parents that you're getting out of your marriage. They, and the rest of your family, are likely to react strongly to the news. Their reaction may be one of shock or disbelief—or, in the case of abuse, adultery, or alcoholism, they may be thrilled that you are finally taking the step to dump your undesirable spouse. It may help to deal with some of the family reactions you face if you realize where they're coming from.

Most of our parents grew up in an era when divorce was uncommon— maybe even unheard of. The older generations married "for better or worse,"

> 66 The divorce was very hard on my parents. They cling to old-world ways and traditions, and divorce was simply not part of the old world. 99
>
> —Maria, second-generation Venezuelan-American

and they meant it. They were conditioned to put up with the problems of marriage, and they had a much stronger adherence to traditionally defined gender roles. Fewer women worked outside the home, and the men "ruled the household." Sure, these are old-fashioned notions to some, but these attitudes might influence your parents' reaction to your news of divorce.

If your parents find it hard to accept your divorce, it may have to do with their current status. Maybe they're older. Maybe they're sick or disabled. Up until now, they may have depended on you; perhaps they were even counting on you—safely married and in a stable home—to care for them in their old age. Having been accustomed to seeing you as being part of a "stable marriage," they may have trouble understanding that your problems cannot be worked out.

And, after all, they *are* your parents. No doubt they're worried about you as well. Will you ever marry again? Will you ever find someone to love you and care for you?

Bright Idea

If your parents insist on involving themselves inappropriately in your divorce, find a different confidante. Try a support group. The perspective of objective third parties whose judgments are not colored by knowing you personally could be helpful. While they will always be your parents, it may be hard for them to remember that you are no longer a child.

Your parents may also be experiencing a sense of failure. Not your failure, though that's what you might expect, but *theirs*. They may very well be asking themselves if this is their fault—if they failed to teach you how to make a marriage work or to persevere. Then again, if your own parents are divorced, they may find it a little easier to accept your decision. They know what it's like to be in a marriage that isn't working. They know how ending it can sometimes be the only answer.

Don't be surprised by any response you get. People don't always know how to express their feelings, especially when faced with something as difficult as a divorce. If you've been married for any length of time your family has no doubt learned to at least respect your soon-to-be ex, if not to love him.

Whatever their reaction to the news, remember that our parents often push our buttons, usually without even meaning to. Having a rational and constructive discussion about the divorce with your parents is probably going to take some work. You'll need to convince them that you have thought this through; that the marriage was just not working, even though you made every effort; and that the only solution was to end it. Here are a few tips to make it a little easier to talk with your parents about the divorce:

- Keep the messy or humiliating details to yourself, however much you might be tempted to divulge the intimate details of the dissolution of your marriage. Exception: If you have always had a particularly close relationship with your parents, and they (or one of them) already knows some of the more intimate details of your marriage, you may find it helpful to lean on them. But, otherwise, remember that they—like your kids—may need some protection from the messy aspects of the split.

- Rule out all intrusive discussion. It's good for you to talk with your parents, but you should maintain some boundaries. Make it clear that some questions are off-limits. Some concerned parents can be pushy, wanting—out of concern for you—to dig in and find out everything. Just say "I don't feel like talking about this right now." It may be reassuring to your older parent to know that you have found an outlet elsewhere—perhaps with a therapist (if you feel comfortable telling your parents that), or with a sibling, or a close friend. Let them know that while you appreciate their support, you are venting with someone else.

- Keep the negative talk about your spouse to a minimum, especially if you have children who will remain in contact with your spouse. Your parents don't need to hear you slam your ex, because that will only make them worry about the children when they see your ex. Remember also that your ex will still be the parent of their grandchildren, and that you want to preserve your parents' respect for him or her so as not to encourage bad-mouthing of your children's other parent.

- Remember that your parents love you and want the best for you.

Telling siblings

Breaking the news to your siblings is going to be difficult as well. While they may not have the same hang-ups as your parents, they will have strong reactions of their own. Again, they may feel relief if you're dumping an abusive spouse, but otherwise there may be pain.

Your change of identity affects them. They want to comfort you and support you, but your new status shakes them up a little. They may worry about how this affects Mom and Dad. What about family parties? What about your kids? What about their own? The idea that little Sam may no longer have Uncle Bob at family gatherings is likely to cause some upset. The entire makeup of your family changes, especially if you're the first member of the family to divorce. Be patient with your brothers and sisters, but also remember that their role in your life may be more conducive to confiding than with a parent. In some cases, your siblings will become your strongest support system. They've known you all your life, and they're likely to be protective of you during difficult times. Lean on your sisters and brothers, just as you'd want them to lean on you during their roughest moments.

You're also likely to be in for some surprising revelations. Now that your marriage is ending, everyone is free to tell you what they *really* thought of your ex. You may hear stories about things your ex did or said that no one ever told you about. These stories can be unsettling. But don't get upset at your family. Know that they're only trying to support you in your decision, or trying to make you feel better about leaving—or having been left. Don't hesitate to tell family members that it's important to you to be spared the gory details of how they felt about your spouse all these years. Explain that it isn't helpful to you to hear negative things about your spouse. You're trying to heal, and reopening wounds isn't going to facilitate that process.

Finally, don't be surprised at unexpected generosity. Siblings may offer to give financial advice or help with the house and kids, or even offer to help out with divorce-related expenses. And while you may not be comfortable asking for financial assistance, keep in mind that your siblings and their children may provide a haven of comfort for you and your children during this difficult process. When you need space, or perhaps time to go over divorce details with your ex, try to arrange quality family time with that other family—the extended one—for your children.

Consider a "press release"

You're going to have to break the news to everyone you know eventually—your co-workers, your friends, your neighbors. Sure, they may hear about it through gossip, but it would be in your best interest to handle the flow of information yourself.

Since everyone must be told sooner or later, it's a good idea to make your own contact list, and make sure it's complete. You don't want to get an anniversary card addressed to you and your ex from some well-meaning but uninformed relative. That day will be painful enough.

As you tell people, you're likely to encounter a fair amount of shock, surprise, and sympathy. Sometimes this will be uncomfortable, but take this as an opportunity to expand your support system. The people you tell may show you great love and concern, calling you often, inviting you out, offering to help in any way. Know that these reactions are genuine and take comfort in that. You have wonderful people in your life. Keep in mind that people will take their cues from you. If you show pain, those around you will hopefully lend support. If you show glee, your supporters will react similarly. If you are just fine with the situation, feel free to tell people that so they don't worry about you. And, if you're not yet ready to be introduced to everyone's cousin from Buffalo who just happens to still be single, say so. The last thing you need right now is unwanted social plans. Tell those people that you will let them know when the time is right!

If you don't want everyone to find out through family gossip, you might want to print out and mail an official announcement. The wording can be as simple as "It is with great sadness that I must share with you the news that we are planning to end our marriage." This saves you from having to go into great detail, and the job gets done quickly.

If you'd like to write something more, you might want to use the following letter as a guide. Of course, what you'll want to tell your close ones will depend on the nature of your relationship to them and the nature of your divorce.

A Sample Letter to Family and Friends

Dear _____,

We write this letter to let you know that we have decided to end our marriage. This separation is completely and totally mutual. All the same, we imagine that some of you will feel awkward about this, but we hope you will continue to consider both of us (and our children) to be your friends.

This is a difficult situation for all involved—for our family, of course, but also for our friends. Our paramount concern is to assure our children of as little disruption to their lives as possible. This includes the assurance that they will still play regularly with their friends, go to their parties, and see both of their parents attend social and school events together. We fully intend for this to be the case, and we hope that you will help us to do that.

We expect the actual separation to be gradual and hopefully gentle on the children. Soon, we will live apart, but the children will see both of us regularly. We have arranged our living situation to keep us in close proximity so as to facilitate this process. Carol will remain at our present address. John, on or about the first of May, will be moving to East Grove. (See new address below.)

The situation is not perfect, by any means, but we will make it as close to normal and comfortable for our children as is possible. We would greatly appreciate any assistance you can give us in that regard.

Please feel free to call either of us with any questions.

Yours truly,

Carol   John
(telephone and address)   (telephone and address)

Watch Out!

Some reactions may surprise you. You might be taken aback at your family's anger at your soon-to-be ex. Don't be shocked if your brother wants to clobber your husband, or your sister offers to try to get your wife fired from her job. The desire for retribution is often strong among those who feel protective of you. Discourage any retribution! It won't help matters.

What do you say at the office? With one significant exception, which we'll discuss in a moment, you are under no obligation to tell your work colleagues that you are going through a divorce. Whether you do so or not should depend largely on the atmosphere of your office. Do you work in a close-knit environment of people you regularly socialize with? If so, they probably already know that trouble has been brewing in your household for awhile, and you may want to share the news with everyone. On the other hand, if you work in an environment that is more impersonal, it would probably be advisable to share the news only with those you are close to. And, if you are in a supervisory position, your news should only be shared with those who have daily personal contact with you: your secretary or assistant, and perhaps a protégé or two. Those people will eventually find out anyway, and if you are having a tough time of it, you should let them know—in the most professional manner possible—that there are changes in your personal life.

It is very important to recognize that your own supervisors will assume, perhaps wrongly, that the impending divorce is going to negatively affect your job performance. Be acutely aware of that, and take the following steps to counter that impression:

1. If you are still at the stage where you cry every day, or are just unable to concentrate and be productive, don't tell anyone at work, and take some personal time off. If for some reason you must share the news, explain that you are having a tough time of it, and that you would like to take leave. Most employers would far prefer that approach to having

you show up for work in a dysfunctional state and spending your days with a tissue box at each co-worker's desk.

2. Once you are past the most severe emotional stage, get back to work, and work hard. Prove to your supervisors that they were wrong about the adverse impact this divorce would have on your work performance. This may actually mean working harder and longer than you previously did. Take comfort in the fact that you won't have to do it for very long. All eyes will be off you once they are satisfied that you are okay with the situation. Working hard will also help distract you from your personal issues and may give you a sense of much-needed fulfillment at this difficult time.

3. Whatever you do, refrain from discussing the details of your divorce with your co-workers while at work. Employers hate nothing more than chit-chat and gossip. Don't let yourself become the subject matter that keeps the water-cooler gossipers busy. Even if you are not actively engaged in the chatter, you will be tainted by the lack of productivity that seems to be arising from your situation. If your co-workers also happen to be close friends upon whom you rely for support, make a point of meeting them after work (or going out to lunch) to discuss what is going on in your life.

4. Be proactive. As soon as separation or divorce becomes a reality, take it upon yourself to schedule a meeting with your supervisor(s) to inform him of the situation. Be clinical in your presentation—no nitty-gritty details! Assure him that the situation is amicable and that you have already dealt with the emotional aspects. (If this isn't true, and you're still in the thick of the emotional phase, ask for understanding and specify a period of time off that you need to take to gather yourself.) Stress to your supervisor that it is very important to you to maintain a stable work life and that you will do everything possible to separate work from the domestic situation. In other words, turn your supervisor into your ally.

The one person at work who must be told of your situation is the human resources manager (or person who holds the equivalent role if your organization does not have a formal HR person). This is because the fact of a separation or divorce can affect your insurance status and/or your tax status. When you tell the human resources director your news, ask for confidentiality. He or she has an obligation to respect that request.

The elements of a successful divorce

Now that you've taken care of the preliminary business of setting priorities, developing goals, and informing the people in your world about your upcoming divorce, it's time to take one last look at the big picture. Your ultimate goal is to turn this difficult experience into a constructive life-change—to have, in other words, a "successful divorce." A successful divorce includes many elements, all of which contribute to helping you reach a fair agreement with a minimum of confrontation. A successful divorce...

- Is timely and efficient—the divorce doesn't drag out for years.
- Is based on open communications between parties, so that both sides are heard and understood.
- Indulges no behavior that leads to an escalation of tensions.
- Involves the ability, by both parties, to leave hurt feelings and anger out of the decision-making process.
- Seeks a fair financial settlement, not retribution.
- Prioritizes the right values, such as putting the children first.
- Involves a certain amount of give-and-take.

Taken together, all these elements contribute to a fair and equitable agreement that both sides can accept. But not all divorces work out this way. Unsuccessful divorces happen when people fall into certain common pitfalls that make an equitable and amicable settlement impossible and cause needless pain and expense. The hallmarks of an unsuccessful divorce are as follows:

- The divorce process is long and drawn out.
- Tension and fighting are allowed to continually escalate.
- Communication is lacking between the divorcing parties.
- Retribution, not resolution, is the motivating factor.
- The children are used as pawns in the negotiations or as messengers between noncommunicating parents.

These elements will result in a miserable divorce—one that fails to achieve a fair settlement for all parties involved. Clearly, your goal should be to do what is necessary to have a mutually satisfactory divorce—a successful divorce, so to speak.

The road ahead

At this point, you may feel like you're looking down an endless road. You're about to begin a journey to a place you may not want to go. You may have preconceived notions about the divorce process, and these can sometimes be forbidding. You may have many questions—some minor, some monumental. And you no doubt have plenty of concern about not just the divorce process itself, but also about how you will cope in your new, post-marriage life. We'll be discussing the actual divorce process in great detail in Part III, and in later chapters we'll take up the issues of coping, but for the moment let's take a brief look at what's down the road for you.

If, like many people, this is the first time you've had to cope with a divorce, you may fear that you're facing years of negotiations, a messy court battle, and unrelenting personal attacks. Or, based on what you've seen on television and in the movies, you might have an unrealistic expectation that the entire affair can be cleared up in a week's time, once your shark of a lawyer makes it clear to the other side that you should get it all. Whatever your preconceptions or misconceptions, it is vital to get a realistic perspective on the process of divorce so that these expectations do not scare you unnecessarily.

So, what's it *really* going to be like? The answer to this question is different for everyone. We're happy to say that our divorce started amicably and remains so. But a lot depends on the circumstances of your marriage, the number of sticky issues you'll have to deal with—such as child custody and spousal support—and the particular circumstances of your breakup. A case involving children and property will usually take longer and be more difficult than a simple split between two people who have been married for a year and have no assets to divide; although, amazingly, this isn't always true. Each divorce is unique, just as each marriage is. Challenge yourselves to defy the odds and to actually accomplish a civilized split. You will reap the benefits for years to come.

> 66 The hardest thing about this is not knowing what the future will bring. The next hardest thing is the feeling that the past has been a waste. 99
>
> —Marc, in the process of divorce

Of course, your spouse's behavior will make a difference in how your divorce will proceed. Here you may be able to make an educated guess about how things will go. After all, you know how your soon-to-be-ex reacts and how he or she communicates. Is your spouse stubborn and vindictive, or fair and level-headed? Given the nature of divorce, the personalities of the people involved generally determine the course of the process. You probably can accurately predict what it will be like to work with your spouse on such an important issue as this, especially at a time when emotions are high. In this sense, you know more than your lawyer does. After all, you know what to expect from your spouse—it's the rest of the process that has you feeling unsure. But with this special knowledge of yours, you can at least predict with a certain degree of certainty some likely outcomes.

Bright Idea

The word "ex" is filled with negative connotations. If you and your divorcing spouse are also parents, consider referring to each other in public as "my co-parent." It's much nicer. In writing, the use of the term "former spouse" is less harsh than "ex-spouse," for some reason.

If the two of you can agree upon the terms of your divorce, you're not likely to have to face a dramatic court trial. Instead, what you're likely to be up against are multiple negotiation meetings until you can reach a fair settlement. Your lawyers, if there are lawyers involved, simply file the resulting settlement agreement with the court. No gavel-banging, no witnesses. We discuss the details of negotiating a settlement in Chapter 8.

One question that's probably at the top of your list is "What's this going to cost?" Unfortunately, this is one question that we can't answer with any exact figures. The cost of a divorce depends on the scope and duration of the case, as well as the state in which the divorce is filed. But we can tell you this: It's not going to be cheap. If you think about your expenses as an investment in your future, however, they may be easier to take.

Many people blow huge amounts of money on lawyer's fees. Hopefully you won't. Many attorneys demand several hundred dollars an hour, so as the clock ticks during your meetings and negotiations, the tab increases accordingly. In Chapter 5 we will address ways to keep your legal costs down.

Time to get started

If both you and your spouse maintain communication, respect, and the right priorities throughout your divorce process, you'll find that you can create the foundation for successful, secure futures and for the protection and nurturing of your children. These are the goals of the successful divorce, and they should always be at the forefront of your mind as you chart your course. If you keep these basic concepts in mind as you set your priorities, you'll see that you really can have a successful divorce. In the next chapter, we'll deal with the first practical steps you'll need to take to prepare for the actual divorce.

Just the facts

- Getting your priorities straight is the first step to a successful divorce.

- It's never too early to start forming a plan and setting your goals.

- Your children and other loved ones need to know what's going on—take care in telling them about your split.

- Keep the elements of a "successful divorce" in mind and you can make this experience a constructive one.

GET THE SCOOP ON...
Do you really need to hire a lawyer? ▪
A checklist for an amicable divorce ▪ Getting
help from other pros ▪ Staying focused on
long-term goals

Making the Best of It

In the previous chapter we discussed the first steps in setting up a successful divorce. This chapter assumes you have followed some or all of that advice, meaning you have established your priorities and have at least considered a plan for the coming months that deals with the logistics of who is going to live where and how the bills are going to get paid. If you haven't already told friends, co-workers, and extended family of your impending divorce, you at least have a plan for doing so. Hopefully, you and your spouse share a commitment to working toward a peaceful and civilized divorce. If all of this has happened, congratulations! Some of the hardest steps are already behind you. Now is the time to move on to the next part of the process that will enable you to minimize costs and avoid mental anguish, while still moving forward with your respective lives.

Following the initial shock of realizing you are about to become part of that statistical 40 to 50 percent of married people who eventually become divorced, you probably went through a period of emotional ups and downs—alternately feeling sad, angry, hateful toward your spouse, thinking you would never find anyone as wonderful as your spouse, and back to angry or hurt. While those emotional swings will probably continue for quite some time, you should soon settle into a state of acceptance that will be marked by a need to move on with your life. In this situation, "moving on with your life" is not just a trite and overused expression, but a true description of exactly what needs to occur at this juncture. Whether you were the initiator of the divorce or the one who feels wronged by it, the need to move on is equally important for both of you.

If you can feel that you are in control of the situation, you will fare better overall. And the best way, at this point, to feel in control is to *take* control of the separation and divorce proceedings. You may ultimately find that you need to hire a lawyer, either as a litigator or simply to put the finishing touches on your divorce. But at this stage, you and your soon-to-be ex need to take joint control and figure out just how much you can accomplish on your own.

You may not need a lawyer

We want to stress that we do not hate lawyers. One of us *is* a lawyer. The other is the son of a lawyer. Notwithstanding all of the long-running lawyer jokes out there, we really do believe that the law is a noble profession, and that there are far more good lawyers out there than bad ones. In most divorces, lawyers serve an essential role of counseling and advocating for their clients. In some divorces, unfortunately, the wrong choice of lawyer can serve to escalate hostilities and turn what could have been a relatively painless divorce into a process that makes protracted oral surgery look like fun.

Thankfully, though, most divorce lawyers are highly ethical and good at what they do. Having seen it all in their years of practice, they may be able to give you not only solid legal advice, but also tips on managing other aspects of your life during the divorce process. In Chapter 5, we will explore methods for you to use in finding just the right lawyer for your situation and your personality. For now, let's talk about why you might not need one, at least during the early stages of your divorce-planning process.

The law moves slowly

A fully litigated divorce (one in which no amicable arrangements are worked out) and all aspects of the divorce—custody, support, and the final divorce decree—are decided by the court system, and can take from one to three years, sometimes even longer, to finalize. We know what you're thinking: three years?! But keep in mind that the pace of your divorce in a litigation setting will have to be governed by the pace of the particular court system you are in, and that while your divorce may be the most important thing in *your* life, it plays third or fourth fiddle to the other pressing matters pending before the court. All criminal matters take priority over any other case in the judicial system. Civil cases (including but not limited to divorce proceedings) are always second string, and of those, the older cases get heard before the newer ones. So, if you are just entering the court system with your divorce, be prepared for a long wait while the stale cases that are already in the system wind their way through.

> 66 It is the trade of lawyers to question everything, yield nothing, and talk by the hour. 99
>
> —Thomas Jefferson

Now you may be starting to think about how to avoid that delay. You should be asking yourself how you can possibly "move on" with your life if you can't even get this divorce process behind you quickly.

The fact is, that one to three years the average litigated divorce takes generally consists of less than one week of actual court time. The remaining months consist of the opposing lawyers preparing allegations against the other side, seeking and delivering information through the discovery process, negotiating, meeting with experts to develop their client's case, and so on. And, of course, all that effort costs a lot of money and takes a lot of time.

Are you a candidate for a lawyerless divorce?

If you already know that you are dealing with a spouse who is irrational and hasn't had a cooperative spirit about anything since the day he or she was born, you may want to skip this chapter and the next and go directly to Chapter 5. But if you have a spouse who is a reasonable human being, consider the practical approach of working things out without lawyers for the immediate future. Even if your otherwise-reasonable spouse has been acting temporarily insane in the initial stages of separating, assume that he or she will resume a reasonable attitude once the emotional aspects settle down, and that the two of you will be able to work through some of these issues without legal counsel.

Rarely do both spouses come to a simultaneous realization that they need to work together, with a spirit of cooperation, throughout the divorce process. In fairness, many couples have no clue that they can handle much of the work themselves. But in any event, one party will usually need to take the lead. Otherwise, what often happens is that events stall after a decision is made to separate, with neither party certain whether he or she should leave the home, pay a bill, find a lawyer, or even whether it is acceptable to go out on a date. The answers to all of these questions are unique to the two people getting a divorce, and no one else can answer them for you. But there are questions that must be asked—no matter how difficult they are—and that must be answered to the satisfaction of both parties.

 Moneysaver

If you and your spouse can sit across from each other at the kitchen table and make a list of your objectives and plans, you will save countless hours of legal and court time in the long run. If there are a multitude of issues facing the two of you, confine each kitchen table session to one issue.

What's the first step?

Let's assume you are the one who is going to initiate the idea of a cooperative divorce. We suggest you follow these steps, in order, to maximize your chances of securing your spouse's willingness to participate:

1. Approach your spouse with the concept that the two of you should not squander your life savings on legal fees and court costs associated with this divorce. This is usually one area that both parties can agree on, and at this point, incremental agreements are good and will pave the way for bigger and more important agreements later. If the two of you are unable to have a civilized conversation at this point, consider sending your spouse an e-mail or written note to make the first overture.

2. Mention that you have been reading about methods to save money on legal fees and to work out divorce issues together. Stress that *you* do not want to do battle. Aside from this book, look for magazine articles or items on the Internet that support an amicable resolution. Offer to share those materials with your spouse. If you find a particularly helpful article or passage in a book, make a copy and leave it for him.

3. If you do not get an immediate positive response from your spouse, leave the issue alone for a few days. It may take time to sink in that this can be done harmoniously. Often, a reluctant spouse will come around after a single visit to a lawyer's office, where legal fees over the next year are projected.

4. When your spouse indicates a willingness to move forward amicably, don't rush into the substantive discussion. Suggest that a specific date and time be set, hopefully within a few days, to sit and talk. Obviously, it should be a time when the children will not be present. Set aside at least an hour for that initial discussion.

5. Create a checklist of items that need to be discussed, using the list in the following section as a guide. Don't expect to cover all of the items in the first session unless you and your spouse have an unusually amicable situation.

6. Refrain from bringing up the subjects that are on your checklist, except when you have actually agreed to meet and talk about them. Don't drag discussions of overdue bills or visitation issues into everyday conversation, especially around the children. Remind each other that you have set aside a time and place for discussion of the difficult issues.

Checklist for an amicable divorce

There are certain issues that are common to virtually every divorcing couple, and then there are issues that will be unique to your situation. The following checklist is designed to guide you in creating the framework for your own constructive discussions, and will hopefully lead you to think of other issues that may be unique to you. Depending on how far along you are in your separation, some of the questions may either be premature or may already have been dealt with.

- How long are we going to continue to live under one roof?

- Which of us is going to move out, and when? Where will that person go?

- What are our current bills that need to be paid?

- What bills do we anticipate in the next 60 days?

- Do we need to take action with regard to any of our joint bills that we will need forbearance on because money is tight? (Creditors are far more willing to work with you and make special payment arrangements if you contact them before the bill is overdue.) Which of us is going to contact that creditor?

Bright Idea

Every time you and your spouse meet, take notes for your shared use. Alternate between you as to who will record the issues that were discussed, and any results. Next time you meet, take a few minutes to go back over what you accomplished at the last meeting.

■ As of what date do we agree that we are formally separated? (This is an important question with legal significance, as most jurisdictions require a mandatory separation period before a divorce will be granted. When one party moves out of the house that date is obvious, but if you are not going to immediately have a physical separation, you may still be able to start the clock ticking by agreeing that you will no longer live together as husband and wife as of a certain date. While this generally requires separate bedrooms, it is not always necessary. If you have unique circumstances, you may wish to consult an attorney regarding the laws of your jurisdiction governing separation dates. If both parties can agree on a specific date that the separation commenced, no court will ever challenge it.)

■ Are we ready to start seeing other people? (Caution: This topic is included in this checklist only to be considered as a point of discussion. You alone must determine whether your situation is ripe for this kind of dialogue. If you just told your spouse last week that you want a divorce and he was shocked by the news, now is not the time to ask this question. On the other hand, if you have essentially been living as roommates for the past two years and it was just a question of who was going to ask first, then perhaps this question is timely.)

■ If there are children, how are they doing? Do they need assistance from a trusted relative, friend, member of the clergy, psychologist, or medical professional?

Watch Out!

If you find your spouse is misusing the information you share during these sessions, or turns the information against you in the heat of an argument, discontinue the discussions until there has been a change in his or her attitude. You will soon be able to tell whether your discussions will be productive or just turn into another opportunity to argue.

- Are we reinforcing for the children, each and every day, that they are still our children, that we are still their parents, and that we will always love them?

- Do the children understand that the divorce is not their fault?

- Do they feel as though they can talk to either of us about any issues they are having?

- And to each other: How are you doing? (Remember, although you no longer want to live together as a married couple, you presumably have common ground having been married for a certain number of years. You have shared history and you probably know each other better than anyone else does. Don't abandon one another as friends just because you've decided to divorce. While you probably don't want to get into in-depth discussions of your new dating life, there is nothing wrong with sharing some of your concerns or emotions. Just make sure that both of you understand that the purpose is to remain friends, and that the discussion is not intended to lead to a renewal of your romantic relationship. If boundaries are a problem for one of you, stay away from this question.)

- When should we set aside a time to meet to discuss long-term issues such as our retirement planning, our children's college funds, sale of the house, and so on?

Professional assistance other than lawyers

Often, both members of a couple want to work amicably toward a resolution, but find themselves incapable of doing so one on one. The history between them, the recent tensions culminating in a separation, money issues, extramarital relationships—all can contribute to an inability to work things out together. If this is the case, and you still believe the two of you as rational and reasonable human beings should be able to work out the details of your divorce without litigation, consider seeking the assistance of a trained mediator (see Chapter 4), a member of the clergy (especially if you have been regular attendees at a house of worship), or a psychologist or marriage counselor.

Emotional help

Psychologists and/or marriage counselors are uniquely situated to assist you with the process of separating. While you may think of a psychologist as someone to go to only when you are trying to *save* the marriage, these professionals are thoroughly trained in human dynamics and have encountered a multitude of marital situations. If the two of you have been seeing a counselor together prior to the separation, you may be able to continue seeing that individual and simply ask him or her to switch gears to help you work through the divorce with a minimum of anguish, and with the clearly stated goal of ending the marriage as painlessly as possible. In this situation, you should specifically ask the therapist if he or she feels comfortable doing this and is committed to the notion that you are not there to save your marriage, but to end it amicably. If you have not been seeing a marriage counselor, or for whatever reason do not want to go back to one you have been seeing, find a well-qualified therapist who has credentials in the field of marital issues. You might ask family and friends or your doctor or minister for a recommendation. You can also call your state's psychological association.

A therapist—one who specializes in children—can also be helpful in getting your kids through this stressful time. Years ago, seeing a "shrink" had all sorts of bad connotations. Today, fortunately, that has changed, at least in most parts of the country. All the same, use some discretion in deciding who is privy to your family's weekly visits to the therapist.

Financial help

If the main area of contention between you and your spouse is the division of assets, you—preferably the two of you together—should consult a financial expert who can suggest the best division of assets. (See Appendix E for tips on finding a good financial expert.)

What are your ultimate goals?

We don't mean to suggest that doing things amicably will make divorce easy. It is never a simple affair, and it takes a great deal of determination to do the work involved in coming to a final resolution. Many times it may seem easier to just hire a lawyer and let him or her slog through the mechanics of reaching a settlement agreement. But it bears repeating: The more the two of you do yourselves, the happier you will be with the outcome. As with any difficult task, there are methods of compartmentalizing the chores at hand and making them slightly easier to handle.

If you're having trouble staying focused on your long-term goals, it may help to write them down or print them out on your computer and post the list somewhere you'll see it every day. While you will have many intermediate goals during the divorce (becoming financially independent, starting to date others, etc.), your long-term goals should be fairly simple and very broad. If you have children, your primary goal must be to preserve their happiness and stability and to ensure that they always feel loved. A secondary goal (or primary, if you do not have children) must be to keep yourself mentally healthy, stress-free (or as stress-free as is possible in today's society), and physically healthy. If you can get your spouse to agree on these goals as his or her own goals as well, so much the better.

Each time you feel frustrated or exhausted from the process of trying to work toward an amicable resolution, remember that the ultimate goals you have set out have a much better chance of being achieved if you can avoid the nastiness and delays inherent in litigation. The goals should help to keep you on track. Have faith that if you and your spouse are able to achieve a resolution that you have worked on together, the chances of acrimony and disagreement later, in the post-divorce years, will be that much less. Think of your child's wedding day, perhaps many years hence, and how nice it would be for each of you to be present, perhaps with a new spouse or companion, and to be able to share in the happiness of your son or daughter's big day. Visualizing such future events may help to get you through the practical matters that must be taken care of today.

Just the facts

- You may be able to expedite your divorce by handling it outside of court, without lawyers.

- Assume the best of your spouse and work together to negotiate a peaceful separation.

- An amicable divorce hinges on good communication.

- Lawyers aren't the only professionals who can help you. Consider consulting a member of the clergy or a psychological counselor.

- Set clear long-term goals for yourself: What do you want your life to look like from here on out?

When War Seems Imminent

PART II

GET THE SCOOP ON...
What to ask your lawyer ▪ Protecting yourself ▪
Keeping good records ▪ Protecting your financial
assets ▪ Stopping short of going to court

Before You See an Attorney

Your own situation will dictate how quickly you should get yourself to an attorney. As a general rule, you should see an attorney for at least a consultation as soon as you have made the decision that you are going to separate or divorce. It is important for you to have a basic understanding of the divorce laws in your jurisdiction, and to understand how the financial aspects are likely to be handled, before you take any steps that may harm you in the long run.

It is not essential at this early stage, however, for you to formally retain a lawyer who will represent you throughout the divorce. In fact, you should probably be wary of any lawyer who wants you to fork over a huge retainer fee at that first meeting and is ready to file suit immediately. What you really need right now, except in exceptional situations, is information—not litigation.

What's a lawyer for?

At this early stage in the game, you need to obtain from your lawyer a basic understanding of your rights with regard to where you live, your children, and basic financial support. For example, it would be extremely unwise to move out of the family home without first consulting an attorney. In some jurisdictions, doing so may be considered an "abandonment" of the home (which may entitle your ex to remain in it indefinitely), and an abandonment of the family (which may work against you in a future custody battle).

You might also feel more secure about shifting bank accounts and assets if you speak with a lawyer first. Do not sell or trade any piece of property without talking with a lawyer first, although you can safely remove up to one-half of liquid bank accounts and move the money to an account in your own name, even without consulting a lawyer. If you plan to take more than one-half, get legal advice first. By the same token, if you believe your ex is going to dispose of or conceal assets, get immediate legal advice on your right to sequester some portion of those assets in your own name. In other words, in the early days of your divorce process, gather information and seek legal counsel, but do not rush to the courthouse.

Controlling legal fees

No matter what your emotional state is at this early stage, you are presumably concerned about what this divorce is going to cost you in dollar terms. Be aware that almost all lawyers charge on an hourly basis, but don't be misled into thinking that you will only get a bill for *hours* that are spent. What hourly billing

 Bright Idea

Stay focused and organized by making a "divorce to-do" list for yourself. Record tasks from this book or your consultation with a lawyer, and prioritize according to urgency. Keep the list constantly updated.

really means is that they are charging for every *minute* they spend on a legal matter. What that also means is that you should not ask your lawyer to be your personal organizer or therapist. Clients who show up in lawyers' offices with mounds of loose receipts and bills, and proceed to dump the whole pile on their lawyer's desk, end up with little to show for it except huge legal bills.

Getting organized

You, and you alone, are the best person to sort through your bills, stubs of paper, checks, and the like. You should ask your lawyer what categories of expense are important (food, shelter, medical, tax records, etc.), and then you must do the hard and mundane work of organizing and calculating. Be well-organized, and you will save many dollars on your legal fees and have a greater likelihood of accuracy. The chance of error in estimating your expenses is greater if someone other than you compiles them. Your attorney has no way of knowing whether you are omitting a significant expense, whereas you are likely to notice its omission during the organizational process. Finally, you may find this to be good experience for the future—you may find expenses that need to be curtailed or reduced, you may realize that certain waste is occurring, and you may come across items from which you can derive income (for example, medical expenses that have not yet been submitted to health insurance for reimbursement).

Safety first

Before you even begin to worry about anything else, you must give first priority to any security issues that may exist in your home. If domestic violence is part of your marriage, as it is in all too many homes, you must do everything you can to protect yourself and your children. If you feel you are in immediate danger, forget about seeing a lawyer for now. Instead, report the violence immediately to the court or to the police. In either case, you are turning to people who are well trained in responding to a domestic violence complaint and who can provide you with the guidance and protection you need.

Take precautionary measures

Whom you should contact depends largely on the nature and frequency of the abuse. If you are living with someone who has been violent in the past but is not currently abusive, you should consult with your attorney about the best methods of proceeding with your divorce while protecting you and your children from possible abuse during the divorce process. Sometimes, the news that one spouse wants a divorce precipitates an act of violence, and you may be able to protect yourself against that by arranging to have divorce papers or a letter from a lawyer served while you and your kids are away from home, visiting a relative or trusted friend.

If you wind up going to court to file a complaint against an abusive spouse, know that all court systems are now well equipped to handle such cases efficiently and at low cost. Typically, an abused party will simply fill out a form in a courthouse office, describing the type and frequency of abuse, and identifying the abuser. A caseworker will then be assigned to help the abused party navigate the court system. (Note that lawyers are generally not required as part of this process, at least not initially.) Often a hearing will be scheduled on the same day as the form is filed, at which time the abused party will go before a judge and testify about what has happened. The abusive party will not be present at that time.

A temporary restraining order (sometimes called a "Protection From Abuse" Order, or PFA, in lawyer's lingo) will be issued based solely on the word of the testifying party. Typically, such orders are effective for 10 days, during which time the alleged abuser is banned from the marital home and from having any contact with the victim and/or children. The person in need of protection must keep the order on her person at all times, in the event police are called to intervene. If such an order is shown, the police will automatically arrest any person who has violated the terms of the order.

Moneysaver

Visit the local courthouse and ask for forms and any guidelines for divorce proceedings. As much as possible, become familiar with the legal process. You are almost guaranteed to save money on your legal bills if you familiarize yourself with the process and forms.

Under the protection of the court

Once the immediate threat of physical violence has been dealt with by the police, the court will hold a more in-depth hearing, at which your spouse will be present and permitted to testify. He or she may bring legal counsel, particularly if an attorney has already been engaged in connection with divorce proceedings. Again, it is not essential for the abused party to have counsel present, but it may be reassuring to do so. After the hearing, the court will address the issue on a more permanent basis and may issue a final restraining order. Such an order may prohibit one spouse from returning to the home, or it may require the spouse to visit with the children only under supervision. Violation of a restraining order is generally punishable by jail time. In most jurisdictions today, the legal system favors the rights of the abused over the abuser.

If your divorce or separation arises directly out of an act of domestic violence and the subsequent issuance of a restraining order, the court will often grant some immediate financial protection in addition to securing physical safety. This protection may include an order for interim child and/or spousal support, pending a more detailed analysis of the situation. For example, the courts are aware that if a spouse and children are financially dependent on an abusive spouse, the dependent spouse may be afraid to seek legal help because of fears of being penniless. In this type of situation, in addition to ordering that the abusive spouse stay away, the court will generally order immediate temporary child support and/or spousal support to ensure that the victim(s) can pay bills.

Watch Out!

Become very proactive if your ex is an abuser. Contact the domestic violence resource centers in your community immediately for tips and assistance before even mentioning divorce to your spouse.

Seeking shelter

Unfortunately, restraining orders are simply pieces of paper, and some violent offenders do not respect the authority of the court order. If this is your situation, further steps will need to be taken immediately. Locks can and should be changed. If necessary, leave town, at least temporarily. Seek out a shelter that specializes in abuse situations. Such shelters often offer a wealth of information about housing and self-help that is completely free of charge. Do not be embarrassed to seek them out. Those shelters exist for the sole reason that there is a need in the community, and the people who work in them have seen and heard it all.

The importance of keeping records

During the divorce process, important decisions will be made about custody, property division, and the allocation of responsibility for debt. As a general rule, with regard to financial issues and issues involving children, the more hard evidence that is available, the better the result, whether you formalize your settlement agreement through lawyers or in court. One way to ensure that you can prove your claims is to keep detailed and accurate records. This does not just mean financial records, although those are certainly vital. Depending on your situation, you may want to keep records of visitations with the children, noting times they were picked up and dropped off, what activity was engaged in with the children, who was present, and any hassles with your spouse that you encountered during the process. Of course, if custody and visitation are not contentious in your situation, and we hope they are not, then this may not be needed.

Records pertaining to the children

If you already know or anticipate that you are going to be in a custody fight, you should arm yourself with as much hard evidence as possible that will attest to your suitability as the custodial parent. Your lawyer will be able to use this evidence in presenting a case to the court for your custodial rights, so meticulous record-keeping and collection of data is essential. Here are some steps to take:

1. Purchase a daily calendar planner, notebook, or other system you are comfortable with and begin keeping a daily record of all the things that need to be done in caring for your children. Depending on your children's ages, it may be as detailed as documenting their daily hygiene activities (diaper-changing, tooth-brushing, baths, etc.) or it may— in the case of older children—deal with less basic issues (discussing social problems at school, helping with math homework, shopping for prom dress, transporting to athletic events, etc.). Record which parent assisted with or took care of each of these activities. You will use this record should you need to demonstrate that you assume most, if not all, of these essential chores.

   You might find it helpful to set up this record in the form of a daily schedule that shows what needs to be done for which child at what time during the day, and which parent completed the task. (Note that this exercise can and should be followed even if you and your ex have not yet formally separated, but expect to.)

2. Keep a record of disciplinary events. If you believe that your spouse uses excessive or improper disciplinary techniques, you should keep detailed notes of any such events that occur. Or, if your child has behavioral issues, keep track of what discipline has to be meted out, why, and who handled the discipline.

3. Keep a record of the children's schoolwork. Include any input you have received from teachers regarding your child's performance when he or she is staying with you versus how your child does in school when staying with your spouse, presence (or absence) of your ex at any school functions or parent-teacher conferences, etc. Courts regard a parent's involvement in the children's education as vital in determining custodial arrangements, and the more involved you can show yourself to be, the better.

Records pertaining to alimony or support

Regardless of how amicable your divorce is, you must immediately start keeping a weekly or monthly record of your personal income and expenses. Even in the most harmonious of divorces, usually one spouse ends up paying the other child support, spousal support, or both. Good record-keeping is vital on both sides. For the receiving spouse, it is important to have a realistic assessment of your own needs, and to be able to provide documentation of those needs to your ex, your lawyer, and/or the court. For the paying spouse, your outflow—the expenses you have every month—will be important in determining the level of support you will pay to your ex. For either spouse, we recommend keeping a highly detailed spreadsheet or log of your daily, weekly, and monthly expenses.

> 66 When my wife threatened to sue for sole custody, I was able to show my lawyer a detailed journal [in which I wrote] of all the times she let them down, or let her anger rule her emotions with them, including once when she hit our son. My lawyer was able to convince my ex's lawyer not to sue for custody based on this journal. 99
>
> —James, recently divorced

Watch Out!

Beware the spouse who hides financial records. Prior to your separation, if you are the party initiating it, or as soon thereafter as possible, secure copies of all bank statements, credit card bills, and so on for individual and joint accounts and put them in a safe place.

You must also keep records of significant changes or events, such as the transfer or expenditure of significant amounts of money, the receipt of bonus monies, inheritances, etc., whether received or paid by you or by your ex. Third-party records such as bank statements are the best kind of evidence from the court's point of view. They are highly accurate and come from an unbiased source. However, even if you don't have such records, jot down what you think your ex received (or what he received last year) in the way of a bonus, or an estimate of any money she may have been gifted by her parents. While not precise, these records will at least form the basis for an inquiry into the actual amounts received or paid.

Cover your assets

In anticipation of filing for divorce, it is not uncommon for one spouse to drain bank accounts or accumulate huge debt on credit cards. You may be the one doing that, or you may be the one stunned when you find out the other has done so. Such tactics are often recommended by lawyers, often with full justification (as with a nonwage-earning spouse who anticipates that when she files for divorce, her ex will immediately cut her off from all funds, and will cancel her credit cards). In such a situation, a lawyer might well—and fairly—tell his client to anticipate her needs for the next few months, and to charge up the credit cards for such needs in expectation of being penniless until the court enters a support award. The downside of such advice is that it usually escalates the tensions and hostilities and ensures a bitter start to the divorce, even though the lawyer may have been completely reasonable in counseling his client to take such action.

Believe it or not, some people have no idea what assets or liabilities they have. One spouse always handled the checkbooks, the credit card accounts, the investments, bill-paying, etc. It was his (or her) job. Well, if these accounts were also in your name, they're your job as well. It's imperative that you become fully informed of your assets and liabilities so that you know what you're dealing with on the financial end of your divorce. Get copies of everything you can get your hands on, and seek out the assistance of someone with knowledge who can help you understand these documents.

Credit cards

Credit card debt: It's the American way, right? A significant percentage of married couples rack up thousands of dollars in such debt during their marriage, and unfortunately, that debt is still there and must be taken care of upon divorce. Regardless of *who* actually incurred the debt or what it was incurred *for*—or, for that matter, regardless of whether the card is in one or both names—if the debt was incurred while you were married, the obligation for payment belongs to both of you. However, who actually ends up paying off those credit cards will depend on the total financial picture, and who receives more assets and has more income. But remember, just because your wife is a spendaholic who buys Fendi bags rather than putting the maximum into her retirement accounts does not mean that she will be penalized in the

> 66 Margin? Until I got divorced, I thought a margin was the space on the side of a page. I had no idea that my husband had been doing something called margin buying with our investments. We were in big debt, and I was half responsible for it. 99
>
> —Racquel, divorced four years

Watch Out!

If your spouse has children from a previous marriage, he or she may start fun-neling marital assets to those children, actually putting assets in their names, prior to your divorce. If you suspect as much, discuss it with your attorney. Those assets may be retrievable.

divorce distribution. Again, the general rule is that any purchase made during the marriage is a "marital debt." (Note that there are a few very limited exceptions to this rule—for instance, debts incurred by one spouse during a "fling" with a paramour, or unjustifiable charges run up by a spouse in anticipation of split-ting up.)

However, you can protect yourself after the separation. If you know in advance that you are going to be separating, take steps to get credit in your name alone. The minute you sepa-rate, notify most of the credit card companies to cancel the cards that are jointly held. Do not completely cut off all credit cards, leaving your spouse with none, particularly if your spouse is incapable of getting credit in her own name due to low or no earnings. Doing so is an act of war.

(Ideally, the couple will agree to cancel most of their joint accounts and will keep open only one or two accounts as neces-sary to cover expenses related to the children and essential upkeep of the home, etc. We recognize, however, that this is only possible in an amicable and cooperative atmosphere, and most of the comments in this chapter assume that your situation is not this harmonious.)

Most importantly, notify *all* credit card companies, in writ-ing, to take your name off the joint accounts going forward, and that you will not be responsible for any debts incurred from that date on. Then cut up those cards and never use them again. If you do that, the credit card company will not be able to look to you to pay any new debt incurred (although the court may nonetheless order you to pay some portion, depending on what

Bright Idea

If you don't have a credit card that is solely in your name, get one *before* you separate. Depending on the circumstances, you may find that you have to temporarily use credit for ordinary living expenses.

the bills were incurred for, and whether your ex had any other means of support from you during the separation).

Bank accounts

Unfortunately, it is not uncommon for a spouse who is planning to separate to unfairly invade the bank accounts and leave the other virtually destitute in the initial weeks of the separation. If you didn't see the divorce coming, you may not even have had the opportunity to anticipate this action. In such situations, court action may be required to seek reimbursement of some of the money. At a minimum, an immediate petition for spousal support should be filed.

If you are the spouse contemplating divorce, plan ahead. Don't be greedy, but sequester some assets in your own name. Generally, an attorney should be consulted in advance, but be wary of any sharks who tell you to take it all and hoard it, leaving your spouse penniless. Such advice is a harbinger of long and nasty divorce litigation, and you would be well advised to seek more rational legal advice. Unless you believe your spouse is hiding assets, or will do so during the divorce process, it is generally best to only transfer one-half of any jointly held funds to a bank account that is solely titled in your name. Generally speaking, an equal division of liquid assets is fair and will not give rise to adverse action from the court at a later date.

Ideally, if the couple is able to work together toward a common end, joint funds should be used during the separation to pay for the mortgage on the home where the children are living, their clothing and medical expenses, any tuition bills, etc. Furthermore, you may agree to pay the costs of the divorce process from joint funds, such as appraiser's bills to determine the value of the home (for purposes of allocating that asset during the divorce), court costs, mediation, and the like.

Other assets

Most of your property is ultimately going to be divided as part of your divorce. Some of the property, such as furniture and household items, will be divided as you separate, or during the months that follow. We strongly advocate that the separating couple work out the details of this splitting of personal property (such as furniture and household items) between themselves, without involving lawyers or the courts. Except in very rare circumstances, the value of such items does not warrant spending any money to work out how they will be divided. Generally, the division of such property should be based on purely practical considerations (for example, split the towels and the dishes so that neither party has to run out and spend money on such basics in the early days of the process). Save your battles for the more important items—the division of the valuable art collection and the investment accounts.

Some types of property, such as pensions, IRAs, real property, or business interests, cannot easily be divided at the beginning of your divorce. Both sides, however, must take steps to protect their interest in them. To the extent possible, assets should be frozen and kept intact until a final divorce resolution.

Gathering information

Unless you already have a good working knowledge of all your accounts and resources—you're the one who always handled the family finances during the marriage—it is important to start

 Bright Idea

If you have concerns that your spouse is going to run off with all of the bank accounts and liquid assets, take steps to protect yourself. Remove one-half the balance of joint bank accounts and deposit in an account in your own name.

gathering household financial information early. Start now to take note of the monthly bank statements, bills, and expenses.

Even if you believe that your spouse will be completely fair with regard to money, you must still take steps to educate yourself about the family financial situation. First, any information you gather will help to reassure yourself that you are being treated fairly in the final settlement. Moreover, you are going to have to assume this role for yourself once you are divorced, so you might as well start now. The sheer number of records involved in running your household may come as a surprise to you. In addition to bank statements, you should locate and copy the following:

- Tax returns
- Business records
- Investment account statements
- Tax bills
- Receipts
- Canceled checks from checking accounts
- Savings account passbooks
- Credit card statements
- Expense account statements
- Safe-deposit box activity records
- Children's bank account statements and passbooks
- Medical records
- Phone bills

In short, you should re-create or copy any information that directly or indirectly concerns the family finances. This is of

 Watch Out!

If you fear that your ex will dissipate joint investment accounts, contact the financial institution and ask that a freeze be placed on the accounts, or that you be notified before any trading or withdrawals are allowed.

Bright Idea

Any financial records kept on your home computer should be copied onto a disk, and a printed copy made. Keep both in a secure place, such as a safe-deposit box.

extreme importance if your spouse is much more sophisticated than you in financial matters, or if you fear that there will not be an honest disclosure of all assets and liabilities of the marriage.

Stopping short of court

Once you've fully explored your priorities and secured the safety of yourself, your children, and your finances, you may think that you're ready to charge ahead with the divorce. However, there is one more issue that you should consider. While the public's perception of most divorces is that they are long, drawn-out affairs that ultimately end in a heated trial before a judge, the reality is that most are long and drawn-out, and then end with a

66 Parents who chose litigation must continually litigate. If Johnny needs new braces, it's back to the lawyers. 99

—Keila Gilbert, Philadelphia-area mediator

whimper as both parties come to their senses and settle their differences. Unfortunately, that usually only happens after way too much money has already been spent on lawyers. Instead of waiting to reach the courthouse steps, consider saving both of yourselves a significant amount of time, money, and anguish, and approach the divorce process reasonably right from the start. If you and your spouse can work together cooperatively, you may be able to resolve your differences and issues through a variety of alternative methods—mediation, arbitration, "do-it-yourself," and uncontested divorce. Now is the time to at least explore whether any of these methods will work for you.

Mediation

Mediation is a method of resolving your differences without involving the court and adversarial attorneys. A neutral qualified third-party mediator will foster communication between you and your spouse.

A mediator is not a marital counselor. Instead, he or she will assist in resolving the issues that arise as a result of separation or divorce. The mediator will deal with such issues as early spousal support, child support, or payment of interim bills. The mediator will try to fashion an agreement between the spouses that addresses present and future problems. The mediator's goal is to forge a compromise between separated spouses, avoiding the adversarial nature of an attorney-led divorce.

In mediation, issues are discussed rather than litigated. Both spouses will meet with and be encouraged to openly discuss all the issues that arise as a result of separation or divorce. A mediator does not tell the parties how to resolve their differences, but rather leads them toward finding their own resolution, which may later lead to a separation or settlement agreement.

For mediation to work, both spouses must be fairly equally informed about their finances—there is no "discovery" process as is provided by the courts. Mediation assumes that the parties already know most everything they need to know in order to resolve their issues, although in some cases, the mediation process can be used to facilitate the exchange of information. Unless both have sufficient knowledge of the family finances, it is highly unlikely that mediation will result in a just and proper agreement. Both spouses must deal in good faith and be willing to compromise in order for mediation to be successful. If the circumstances of

> **❝** Mediation or litigation? That depends [on] what you want. Do you want to send your kids to college, or do you want to send your lawyer's? **❞**
>
> —Keila Gilbert

Bright Idea

Remember that your mediator is not a counselor or therapist. Conduct your mediation sessions as you would a business meeting, with an agenda and checklist of what you wish to accomplish. Be attentive and follow the mediator's advice. Save the emotions for counseling sessions.

trust and honesty exist so that a neutral mediator can be used effectively, this option can save considerable expense and will alleviate much of the emotional distress that is generally associated with the divorce process.

Even divorces that start out acrimoniously may benefit from involvement of a mediator later in the process, once emotions have quieted, all issues have been explored, and financial information has been exchanged.

Choosing a mediator should be done as carefully as choosing a lawyer to represent your interests. Ask the mediator about his or her credentials, and look for education, references, number of years the mediator has been doing this work, and membership in a professional organization.

When you and your spouse first meet with your mediator you will explain the conditions surrounding your divorce and discuss the major issues between you.

Once you've established the areas you need to work on, your mediator will help you keep your communications on a cooperative basis as you discuss your issues, one by one, for as many sessions as it takes to reach an agreement acceptable to both of you. After one or two sessions, expect to hash out the nitty-gritty details of each issue that confronts the two of you. The goal is to reach an agreement that spells out specifics on issues such as custody, visitation, division of assets and liabilities, and support payments. If that agreement can be reached, the mediator will work with the two parties to come to an actual understanding, embodied in a written contract, about what your respective rights and obligations will be in the future. If you are successful in reaching an agreement, you will each then take a copy to your respective attorneys, who will tweak the terms of the agreement and finalize the process.

Arbitration

As with mediation, arbitration can be faster and cheaper than going to court. However, it is much less common. Arbitration refers to a process by which your lawyers mutually select a neutral party, almost always a lawyer who has considerable experience in domestic relations law, to hear the evidence pertaining to your separation and divorce. The arbitrator then conducts a proceeding which has somewhat less formality than a courtroom trial, but which is designed to elicit the facts and evidence that you would present to a judge. The parties and their lawyers generally agree that the arbitration process will be binding. In this context, the arbitrator is acting as a quasi-judge, not as a mediator trying to bring the two of you closer together in resolving your differences. Arbitration may follow mediation, or may occur in situations where it is clear that mediation is not likely to be successful (due to the character of the divorce proceedings and individuals involved), but where the parties want to save some expense and expedite the process. Generally, arbitration is somewhat less expensive than engaging in a full-scale trial before a judge, and proceeds at a faster pace; individual arbitrators do not have an overflowing docket of cases to be decided, as does a judge.

> ❝ I've been a divorce lawyer for more than 20 years. I've found that when I have a client who is successful in reaching a resolution through mediation with an ex, the likelihood of post-divorce conflict and relitigation of issues is much less. Both parties feel as though they have had their say and have had input into the final product—the separation agreement. ❞
>
> —Bill F., divorce attorney

Bright Idea

If your lawyer recommends arbitration, ask him who the arbitrator will be, what his or her costs are, and the likelihood of a satisfactory outcome at an earlier date than a trial. If you are not satisfied with the responses, you may be better off with the more conventional process of having your case decided by a judge.

For all you do-it-yourselfers: *pro se* divorce

In cases where the issues are simple and both sides have mutually agreed upon the terms of the divorce, you may want to represent yourself rather than hire a lawyer. This type of divorce is called *pro se* (a Latin term meaning "for yourself"), and it's generally an acceptable idea if the following conditions are present:

- You have been married for a short period of time, you don't have many assets to divide, and/or you agree how they should be divided; *or*

    You have been married for a longer period but have an unusually harmonious divorce situation, *and* (in either event)

- You do not feel at a disadvantage to your spouse in terms of the emotional or economic aspects of your divorce, *and*

- You have a basic understanding of your rights in the divorce process.

When these conditions exist, there may well be reason for you to save substantial legal fees and attempt to "do it yourself." You may have gotten the idea from the Internet or divorce software kits that provide you with all the legal forms necessary. But while this may *sound* like an easy way to divorce, taking matters into your own hands can be dangerous.

First, you need assurance that your spouse isn't consulting legal counsel on the side. If one spouse has an unfair advantage, doing it yourself simply does not make sense. For example, you may overlook a major issue in the divorce that later requires you to hire a lawyer to try to undo your agreed-upon do-it-yourself divorce. Not only will you then spend legal fees for the corrective action, but your chances of undoing a deal that has been done is much less than if you had simply gone to a lawyer in the first place.

Even if you and your spouse are able to work out the terms of an agreement without any lawyers' involvement, it is still advisable for each of you to hire a lawyer for the very limited purpose of reviewing your agreement and giving you input, even if the two of you have ironed out the details. Be aware, however, that in most states it is either impermissible or highly inadvisable for one lawyer to represent both parties in a divorce situation—even where the situation is uncontested—and that you will probably need to consult two different lawyers to finalize your deal. If this is your situation, both you and your spouse need to make it clear to the attorneys involved that you are not looking to escalate the legal proceedings, that you expect the lawyers to act in accordance with your harmonious approach to this process, and that you are consulting him or her only to make sure you have not acted imprudently in some aspect of the agreement.

Some issues that you and your spouse should specifically discuss with lawyers, even if you are doing this yourself, include:

- Tax ramifications (discuss with your financial advisor as well)
- Pension and retirement plans
- Life insurance issues
- Debt repayment
- Children's long-term plans, including education, weddings, religious ceremonies, etc.
- Estate planning after divorce

No contest?

You may not be comfortable "doing it yourself," but if you've reached the point where you and your spouse agree on the substance of a settlement of all issues, you should be able to obtain what is generally referred to as an uncontested divorce. The significance of an uncontested divorce is:

- You do not have to have a trial or hearing on disputed issues.
- The granting of the actual divorce decree will be expedited.
- You should be able to save money on legal fees that will not be incurred in connection with protracted proceedings on various issues such as support, custody, and so on.

An "uncontested" divorce is no less binding than a fully litigated divorce—it's just cheaper and less emotionally taxing.

In the next chapter you will learn what you need to know to effectively choose a lawyer, whether you are gearing up for the divorce trial of the century or are in basic agreement with your spouse about most of the issues. The issues and responsibilities of handling a divorce are daunting to most people, and good legal advice is essential. All lawyers are certainly not created equal, and even among the best of divorce lawyers, finding the one who is best for your particular situation is imperative. Chapter 5 takes you step by step through the process of finding and interviewing prospective lawyers and gives you a few tips on how best to establish a good lawyer-client relationship for the tasks ahead.

Just the facts

- Securing the safety of yourself and your children should be your first priority.
- Meticulous record-keeping is essential and will support your claims in court.
- Take steps to ensure that marital assets don't start to mysteriously disappear.
- Evaluate your situation to determine whether you and your spouse are good candidates for the money-saving mediation process, or some other process that avoids going to court.

GET THE SCOOP ON...
The attorney's role ▪ How to find a (good)
attorney ▪ Cultivating a successful lawyer-client
relationship ▪ Fees, retainers, and other payment
concerns ▪ Making your final decision

Choosing Your Lawyer

Unless you're an attorney yourself, and perhaps even if you are one, a big question in your mind is likely going to be how to find a "good" attorney. You may know attorneys either socially or in connection with a past legal transaction such as a real estate settlement. You probably "know of" other lawyers—those who advertise, those who are well known because of their high-profile cases in your community, those who are parents of kids in your child's school whom you've happened to meet from time to time.

Even if you (and your spouse) have decided to try to handle the bulk of the divorce process yourself, you should consider retaining a lawyer on a limited basis with a clear understanding that you are going to do the legwork, but will use that lawyer to review your work and make sure it complies with local filing requirements. (Not all attorneys will agree to this kind of arrangement but there are enough out there who will, so if you are going to handle the details on your own, look for a lawyer who is accommodating.)

Chapter 5

83

In all cases, a divorcing party needs a clear understanding of what the law is and what his or her rights are—not the information that you gather from your friends about what happened in *their* divorces, and not just what you pick up from the Internet (although that is a good starting point for information), and not even just what you pick up from books like this one, however well researched they may be. You need the input

> **66** Don't misinform your
> Doctor nor your
> Lawyer. **99**
>   —Benjamin Franklin

and advice of a lawyer in your own locale who can give you the big picture (what is the law governing in your case), and the little picture (what are the courts in your area like, what do the judges expect, how long will it take to wind through the local court's docket system, etc.).

What does the lawyer do?

There are a lot of lawyer jokes out there, and a tremendous amount of anti-lawyer sentiment. This is not the platform for discussing whether the legal profession has contributed to the overall decline of the United States (as some politicians would have us believe), or whether as a group they provide valuable services to people who are often vulnerable and downtrodden. For purposes of this book, the important issue is why a lawyer may be valuable to you as a soon-to-be-divorced person.

Obviously, as a lawyer myself, I (Susan) have a unique and perhaps biased perspective. I know a couple of lawyers to whom I would not send my worst enemy. But I also know many, many lawyers who are caring and compassionate, and will advocate for their clients as though each client was their most important one. I firmly believe that in any matter that requires technical expertise, in which you—the consumer—are likely to feel emotional and vulnerable, it is in your best interest to find a respected member of the bar who can keep you grounded and realistic, and can fight your battles for you.

Trying to navigate the judicial process without a lawyer is like trying to build your own house without a contractor. You may be able to get the permits from your local municipality on your own, you may be able to get the hole dug for the foundation, and you might even be able to get the foundation poured with some assistance from friends, but are you going to be able to install the complex electrical wiring and plumbing systems? And, if you build that house on your own, with input from family and friends but no professional help, are you going to be happy with the result?

The best lawyer for you may not be the best lawyer for someone else, even if that other person is getting a divorce. There are specific things you must know about the attorney and things you must ascertain when you first meet with him or her. We hope that this chapter will help you find just the right lawyer for you.

So, what does a *good* lawyer do? Good lawyers for any legal matter are smart, attentive, keep themselves abreast of developments in their area of the law, are responsive to their clients, show empathy, and, most important, are highly ethical. Beware of any lawyer who starts the divorce process by encouraging you to withhold information, or who generally makes you feel uncomfortable when you deal with him. Similarly, beware of any lawyer who immediately talks of "taking [your spouse] to the cleaners." Chances are you will be taken to the cleaners by your lawyer at the same time.

> 66 Discourage litigation. Persuade your neighbors to compromise whenever you can. As a peacemaker the lawyer has superior opportunity of being a good man. There will still be business enough. 99
>
> —Abraham Lincoln

Of the desirable characteristics for your lawyer to have, there is no single attribute that is most important. While it is obviously essential to have a lawyer who has an excellent working knowledge

of the law, it is just as important to find a lawyer with whom you
have a good rapport. That wealth of knowledge is almost useless to
you if the lawyer you are paying money to doesn't share her expertise with you. Here is a general outline of the functions a lawyer
should perform in the early months of representation, in roughly
chronological order from your first meeting:

- Meet with you and hear your story. The lawyer should ask
  fairly detailed questions about the state of your marriage;
  what caused the breakup; your children, their ages, and
  how well they are doing with the new state of affairs; your
  marital finances (in general terms); and whether there are
  any safety issues that need to be taken into consideration.
  This initial meeting with the lawyer should touch on all of
  these issues, but don't be concerned if you feel that there
  is still much ground to be covered. The first meeting is as
  much about whether the lawyer and client have a "comfort
  zone" together as it is about the specifics of the divorce.
  The first meeting should end with a firm date set for the
  second meeting, at which time more specific information
  will be obtained.

- Initiate contact with the other side. If your spouse does
  not yet have a lawyer, yours will discuss the manner in
  which he should be put on notice that legal proceedings
  are imminent. Some people decide to tell their spouse
  themselves that they have retained legal counsel and that
  divorce papers are coming. Others, perhaps for safety reasons or just because of a general discomfort with breaking
  the news, ask their lawyer to write to the ex and initiate
  discussions. If your spouse is already represented, your
  lawyer will advise your spouse's lawyer that you are now
  represented. You should have no direct contact with your
  spouse's lawyer at any time.

- Give you a checklist of items and information that you
  need to compile. If you have already done the homework

Watch Out!

Resist the temptation to contact your spouse's lawyer if you do not have one. Do not think you will be able to "convince" him or her that your spouse is to blame for everything. Lawyers are not permitted to speak with individuals who have their own lawyers, but if you are unrepresented, the lawyer is ethically permitted to do so. But remember: He does not represent *you*, he represents and is working *for* your spouse.

set out in the earlier chapters of this book, most of your information will have been gathered and you will simply be able to turn it over to the lawyer. Remember our earlier advice about presenting the information to your lawyer in a well-organized manner, both to ensure that your case is properly understood and to save yourself legal fees.

▪ Once your materials have been received, the lawyer should give you a plan of how she would like to proceed with the case, and will make recommendations to you as to next steps for securing (or paying) interim support and determining visitation and custody.

▪ After the pressing issues of support and custody are determined, at least on a temporary basis, the lawyer should provide you with a more global plan for resolving your entire divorce. Depending on the complexities of the finances and how adversarial you and your spouse are, the global plan may envision months of discovery (see Chapter 7) followed by hearings, or it may start with a plan for early settlement of the case. Either way, the big picture can only be determined by your unique set of facts.

How to recognize a top-notch attorney

There are some specific traits or assets that all good divorce lawyers must have. Some of these will be difficult for you to ascertain on your own, but we will provide you with guidance a little later on how to find out if your lawyer possesses these attributes. Here are the essentials:

- **Experience and expertise.** You do not necessarily need a lawyer who has been in practice for 20 or more years. But you also do not want the guy who just graduated from law school last May and is anxious to handle his first divorce case. Check out the framed diplomas on the office wall to see when this lawyer graduated. Be blunt. Ask how many years he has been in practice and how many divorce cases he has handled.

- **Knowledge.** There is obviously no way for you as a layperson to quiz your lawyer on what she knows about divorce law, nor are we suggesting you do so. However, the lawyer should be able to quickly and confidently answer questions about virtually any aspect of divorce, and when in court, should possess a good command of the law and be able to articulate it in front of a judge. You will quickly ascertain if your lawyer is unqualified. This is not likely to occur, as very few lawyers attempt to practice outside an area in which they are unqualified. Not only do they want to avoid a malpractice claim, but there also are stringent rules governing the legal profession, and they do not want to run afoul of their state's licensing board.

- **Ethics.** Your lawyer must be committed to the principles of absolute confidentiality between the lawyer and client, and must always act in an ethical manner with opposing counsel and the court. The lawyer's failure to do so will eventually harm you and your case. Look for candor, honesty, and openness in his dealings with you.

- **Accessibility.** Your lawyer must be available to you. This does not mean you should have unfettered access 24/7, and don't expect it. If you persist in calling your lawyer on her cell phone every Saturday night, you will quickly find yourself in "least favored client" status. On the other hand, you should receive regular communications from your lawyer by phone, letter, or e-mail. Any or all of these methods are acceptable. Your phone calls to your lawyer should always be returned within 24 hours, and if for some reason the lawyer is not available, you should hear back from an assistant who will take your inquiry and let you know when you will hear from the lawyer.

▪ **Personality.** A good lawyer does not need to be your best friend. But you should feel comfortable with him, and you should never be made to feel patronized. You should never feel that you have to apologize to your lawyer for needing his time. Ideally, you will have a comfortable rapport and mutual respect with the lawyer. Anything less—or more—is inappropriate.

Where can I get one of those?

Finding a good attorney is far more important than, say, finding a good florist. As we mentioned at the beginning of this chapter, you probably know, or know of, several lawyers. But how do you find the one who is best for your divorce? Here are some guidelines:

▪ Call your local County Bar Association and ask whether they maintain a law directory that shows areas of expertise. Although the bar association will not recommend a lawyer to you, they may have a local guide that is more detailed than the Yellow Pages, or a statewide lawyer's directory. If you don't have access to the local bar association, go to a public library and ask for the same information.

▪ Once you have a list of lawyers in your area who are divorce practitioners, make a complete list of them and keep notes on that list. Then follow these steps:

1. Go to www.martindale.com. This is the bible of lawyer directories and is fairly easy to navigate. Type in each lawyer's name and your city and state. You will be

redirected to a page devoted to that lawyer's credentials: where he or she went to law school, any honors
received, year of graduation, areas of specialization or
expertise, etc. This resource will save you from having
to "interview" the lawyer on such specifics.

2. Talk to lawyers who do not practice divorce law. Ask
them for their recommendations from the list you have
already compiled. Call the attorney who handled your
will or your real estate closing. If he gives you only the
name of his partner or another lawyer in his firm,
specifically ask him about some of the names on your
list. (Although, if you liked the lawyer who handled
your real estate deal or will, consider using one of his
partners. Chances are that one good lawyer experience
will lead to another, as most law firms have a "personality" that may work well for you.)

3. Ask nonlawyers for their recommendations, but take the
information you receive with a grain of salt. We cannot
stress enough that a lawyer who was great for one person
may not be the lawyer for you, especially if that divorce
was much different from your own. But get the information from friends and colleagues, and pay particular
attention to comments about the lawyer's accessibility,
responsiveness, and manner in which she handled herself in court. If all of these were positives, they probably
will be for you too.

Lawyers who advertise

You may find it interesting to know that lawyers were not even
permitted to advertise until 1977. Prior to that time, all states
had laws prohibiting lawyers from advertising on the theory that
it was unseemly for a noble profession to be engaged in advertising its services. The sentiment seemed to be that advertising
reduced lawyers to the ranks of car dealers, exterminators, and
retailers, and that any lawyer worth his salt would not need to

advertise. It was a throwback to the days of long ago, when there were no more than a handful of lawyers in any given town, and most of them were on a first-name basis with every citizen. In those days, every lawyer was capable of handling any area of the law—criminal matters, bankruptcies, wills, divorces—they were all handled by the same guy.

Now, of course, the ranks of lawyers have swelled in direct response to the huge demand for legal services nationwide. No longer are you likely to rub elbows with the only esteemed lawyer in town as you sit through church services. As more lawyers enter the profession and the profession itself becomes more special-ized, the more reason there is to get the word out about which lawyers specialize in a given area.

In 1977, the United States Supreme Court squarely addressed the prohibition imposed by a state bar association (*Bates v. State Bar of Arizona*) on lawyers' rights to advertise, and held that it was a violation of the First Amendment (freedom of speech) to pro-hibit lawyer advertising. Since that time, all state bar associations have modified their rules to permit advertising, although with strict criteria. (For instance, it is generally not permissible for an attorney to advertise a "success rate" because that is considered misleading.) Although advertising among lawyers was slow to catch on and many still refuse to engage in it, there is nothing fundamentally wrong with lawyer advertising.

You may have seen those ads on television—a lawyer sitting behind a mahogany desk, law degrees framed and hanging on the wall, promising you a win in court. An 800-number flashes on the screen, and a list of legal specialties rolls by faster than you can read it. Or maybe you've seen display ads in the news-paper advertising special rates for "quick, easy divorce cases." They may even provide a coupon or quote a flat fee. Beware of such ads. The best use of lawyer advertising is simply to find those attorneys who work within a particular field. Come-ons in the form of coupons, flat fees, and 800 numbers are generally not a good way to find a reputable lawyer.

Watch Out!

An aggressive approach to soliciting clients may be a sign that a lawyer is a businessperson, not a lawyer. He or she may be interested in volume rather than quality. Beware the lawyer who engages in the "hard sell."

There is a lot of work involved in choosing a good divorce lawyer, but since it is one of the most important steps in the entire process, it's worth every minute of effort. Make it a project to spend a good amount of time making phone calls, asking questions, and getting referrals. This is one of the most important investments you will make, and the right decision will have a great deal to do with the outcome of your case.

How to work with your lawyer

You can't just dump a bunch of files in your new lawyer's lap and expect him to successfully navigate your divorce. It doesn't work that way. There are certain things your lawyer can and should expect from you:

- **Candor.** You must be open and honest with your lawyer. One of the most difficult problems lawyers face is when clients fail to divulge a damaging fact (such as an extramarital affair or shady financial dealings). Your attorney can help with damage control if you share the information early on, but finding out later from your spouse's attorney may be too late.

- **Timeliness.** Your lawyer expects you to be on time to meetings and conferences. Never fail to show up, and don't cancel at the last minute.

- **Cooperation.** If your lawyer asks you for a list of your assets, you must provide the necessary information. Your lawyer needs to work *with* you to best serve your interests.

- **Realistic expectations.** Your attorney expects you to have a decent grasp on reality, to know what you are and aren't likely to accomplish in your case.

- **Firmness of decision.** No lawyer wants to work with a client who is going to waffle through the process. Make sure you know what you want. If you're seeking a postponement, say so—your lawyer will know how to handle that. But persistent foot-dragging on your part will cause problems, and delays on either side will cause both parties' legal bills to grow. This is not the lawyers' doing, and you will be expected to pay for the additional time spent as a result of the delays.

- **Respect of boundaries.** Remember that your lawyer is your advocate and your bridge to the court system. Don't expect her to become your confidante, your therapist, or your financial planner. There are other people who will happily perform these functions for you. Don't become the client from hell, the one who shows up without an appointment, hoping to get in to see the lawyer to unload a box of papers, or just to cry on the lawyer's shoulder.

The ideal attorney-client relationship is a partnership, one based on a willingness to listen, communicate, and work hard together to accomplish your goals.

 Bright Idea

Ask your lawyer if e-mail is an acceptable means of communicating during your case. You may find it easier to tap out your questions about certain issues immediately while you are thinking of them rather than playing telephone tag. The lawyer can then respond when he has the time to give you his attention on the issue, and his written response will be something you can refer to, rather than having to rely on your recollection of a brief telephone conversation.

How much will I pay?

Regardless of your financial position, you should have a choice of lawyers within the bracket you can afford. If money is an issue, and it usually is, you may need to immediately forget about retaining the best-known divorce lawyer in town. (You may want to forego him or her anyway, as such lawyers are often too busy to give you the quality service and attention you will need.)

Go back to that list of lawyers we asked you to compile earlier in this chapter. As you start to inquire about them and place calls to their offices, don't hesitate to ask what their standard hourly fees are, how much they require in the way of a "retainer" (more on retainers later), and how much they charge for less experienced attorneys and paralegals in their office to do some of the legwork (see Cutting Costs later in the chapter). Keep notes of this information to use when you finally make a decision among the qualified candidates on your list. Often, hourly rates vary dramatically even within the same community, and the fact that one attorney charges considerably more than another should *never* be considered a sign that he is better than the one who charges less.

What affects the price tag?

First and most obviously, the issues involved in your case will determine how much you can expect to spend. A divorce between two people who have kids, millions of dollars in assets, and a shared business will require greater effort and generate higher expenses than one between a recently married couple

 Moneysaver

Don't be deterred from shopping around for a lawyer because you don't want to pay an initial consultation fee to someone you may not end up hiring. Many lawyers will give you a half-hour of their time for free. Others will charge you a nominal fee for that first visit but will apply it to your total fees if retained.

with few assets and no children. Are there larger issues of adultery, bankruptcy, child abuse, or violence in the home? This too may take more time and expense than a simple, mutual parting of ways. Experts may have to be called in to testify, medical tests may have to be performed, and witnesses may have to give depositions. As a rule, the more that's involved in your case, the higher the final price.

Second, what is your lawyer's overhead factor? Sole practitioners often can run their offices much more efficiently than lawyers who practice in groups and therefore may charge less per hour. On the other hand, the particulars of your case may justify hiring a lawyer who has in-house colleagues to assist—again, if you have a complicated divorce, you will need more legal support. The costs of fine lobby furniture, multiple young lawyers, computerized legal research, huge staffs, and benefits for all of them will drive up the cost of practicing law. And guess who those costs get passed on to? Don't assume sole practitioners are less able to do the job well. Often, they are attorneys who have simply decided that they want to stay close to their practice and their clients and do not want the hassles of working in a larger firm. The sole practitioner may be exactly the right fit for you. But, by the same token, don't automatically shy away from a law firm because you are afraid of the cost. Be upfront about your ability to pay and your expectations, and let the lawyer tell you what the cost is likely to be.

Expenses beyond your lawyer's fee

There are a number of items totally outside your lawyer's control that will cause your total legal bill to mount. These include fees paid to experts (forensic accountants, private detectives, mental health experts, etc.), court costs (filing fees, special fees attached to certain hearings, etc.), stenographer's fees (for deposition transcripts), and court-imposed fines that may be levied against you if you fail to comply with a court order. Apart from this last item, your lawyer should be able to give you a rough estimate of

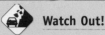 **Watch Out!**

Beware of legal bills you do not understand. In all cases, a good lawyer should provide a descriptive bill that can be easily understood, or at least, will take the time to explain the bill to you. (You should not be charged for any time incurred in explaining the legal bill.) If you have paid a retainer upfront, ask for a monthly accounting of how much has been used, and for descriptive details on what has been done.

what the total "costs" (as opposed to fees) will be when you first hire him. Ask for all legal bills to fully describe these costs so you know exactly what you are paying for. In some cases, portions of the expert fees may eventually be tax-deductible, so for that reason also, you will want full details on them.

Cutting costs

While you want the best lawyer your money can buy, be open to the idea of having others in the lawyer's office work on your case. For example, a well-trained paralegal generally bills at less than half the hourly rate of the attorney. Divorce work is particularly well suited to the use of paralegals because it is document-intensive and requires a great deal of detail work. Paralegals frequently perform these functions better than lawyers do, and for a fraction of the cost. When meeting with prospective lawyers, ask about their use of paralegals and then ask to meet the one who will be assisting on your case. Another big advantage to paralegals is that they, unlike lawyers, are rarely out of the office, so you can usually reach them by phone.

You should also make it clear to your lawyer that you want to save on costs as much as possible. Don't be shy about reminding him of this regularly. Lawyers are used to such reminders and will not hold it against you that you want to keep your costs down. By reminding your lawyer periodically, you will create a mental note for him to follow in working on your case. If a function can be performed by a paralegal, the lawyer is likely to ask her to do it rather than doing it himself. Likewise, if you are open to the idea of doing much of your own legwork, tell the lawyer just that. Make it clear that you will be happy to review your spouse's discovery responses, ferret out important information, or highlight salient points. This is a particularly good moneysaver if your spouse's lawyer barrages your lawyer with reams of paper in an attempt to conceal his or her financial dealings. If your lawyer doesn't use a paralegal, ask to take on a quasi-paralegal role with regard to your own case.

Another potential area of cost-savings is to ask your lawyer to obtain fee information from the experts who are going to be used in your case. If an accountant is needed to provide a valuation of your spouse's business, for example, don't allow your lawyer to automatically hire the guy he always uses, with whom he probably has a very nice reciprocal referral arrangement that benefits them both financially. Instead, ask for a list of potential accountants whom your lawyer would recommend, and if you are inclined, interview them yourself. Or, if you have an accountant whom you personally have used and have been pleased with, so much the better. Inform your lawyer you expect that accountant to be used as the expert in your case. Chances are there will be significant money savings, since the accountant will already know you and be familiar with at least part of your financial situation. Keep in mind, however, that if the accountant has handled finances for both you and your spouse, he will not be able to handle your divorce accounting needs due to a conflict of interest.

The most important thing you can do to cut your legal bill is to be very aware of what the projected fees and costs will be, and to question your lawyer if the bills seem to be mounting faster than had been projected. Be pleasant but firm and make it clear that you do not want duplication of effort and that you are not willing to pay for unnecessary work to be done. A good lawyer will be responsive to these concerns and will heed them.

Different types of fees

There are different types of expenses in any legal proceeding. Here is an overview of what fees you can expect in a typical divorce case:

- **Initial consultation fee.** This is the fee charged for the very first visit to the lawyer before you have officially hired him. Some lawyers do not charge for an initial consultation, but will generally limit the free time to half an hour. Some will charge their regular hourly rate and expect you to pay for the amount of time you spend. Still others will have an "introductory" rate—generally in the neighborhood of $100 for an hour or less.

- **Hourly rate.** Virtually every lawyer nowadays charges by the hour. It is essential that you know what your lawyer's hourly rate is, as well as the hourly rates of anyone else in his office who will be working on your case. Expect to pay a much lower hourly rate for a younger lawyer who might assist on the case, and even less for a paralegal. Hourly rates vary greatly from region to region and there is no way for us to give you a range of acceptable rates. However, in compiling your list of attorneys, you should see a pattern in the rates charged by all of them. Avoid any that are clearly far above or below the pack. Keep in mind that you should never have to pay for work performed by the lawyer's secretary, such as returning phone calls to you or walking across the street to the courthouse to file papers.

- **Retainer fee.** Once you have officially hired (or "retained") your lawyer, she is likely to require a retainer fee. This is generally a lump sum of money that is paid in advance and placed in a lawyer's escrow account, with monthly billings then drawn against the retainer fund until depleted. Most lawyers have a "standard" retainer they require before work will commence, and it probably will vary depending on whether the case is anticipated to be relatively easy or complicated. Some lawyers request a "refresher" to the retainer once it is depleted if there is further work to be done. If the case concludes before your retainer runs out, you are entitled to a refund of any unused portion.

▪ **Contingency fees.** A contingent fee is one where the lawyer takes a percentage of money won at trial or through settlement. If nothing is recovered, nothing is paid to the lawyer. You will not encounter such fees in the divorce setting; they are prohibited in all states in domestic relations cases.

Example 1 on the next page shows a sample copy of a fee agreement similar to one you might see when you are negotiating with an attorney. Note that it's general enough to accommodate any one of the several different fee options we've just discussed.

Get it in writing

Your relationship with your lawyer is a business arrangement that must be committed to writing. In fact, most states now require lawyers to have written fee agreements with their clients. That fee agreement can be presented to you on a general purpose form, like the one in Example 1, or it can deal only with the specific type of fee arrangement you and your lawyer have worked out. Example 2 is another example of a written fee agreement that includes more specific provisions than those in Example 1.

Example 1: Attorney's Fees

The attorney's fees in this matter will be set as follows:

( ) Hourly rate at $_____ per hour for the following attorney: [Separate itemization for each additional lawyer or paraprofessional who will be working on the case.]
( ) Estimated fees in the range of $_____ to $_____

( ) Retainer required: $_____

This office will bill you:
( ) Monthly on _____ of each month
( ) Upon completion of case
( ) Other arrangement: _____

ALL BILLS ARE PAYABLE UPON RECEIPT. IF YOU DO NOT PAY WITHIN 30 DAYS OF RECEIPT, YOUR ACCOUNT WILL BEGIN TO ACCRUE INTEREST CHARGES.

RETAINERS:
Retainer of $_____ is to be applied:
( ) Toward fee and out-of-pocket expenses
( ) Toward fee
( ) Toward out-of-pocket expenses
( ) Retainer is refundable
( ) Retainer is nonrefundable

COSTS AND EXPENSES
Typical out-of-pocket expenses for this matter may include:

( ) Costs such as court costs, filing fees, process server fees, deposition costs, sheriff or clerk of court fees, investigator's fees

( ) Abstracting charges or title insurance premiums, clerk's recording fees

( ) Photocopying, telephone charges, postage, and travel costs

( ) Other: _____

Estimate for costs and expenses, not including attorney's fees:

( ) Expected to range between $_____ and $_____

NOTE: This is an estimate for your convenience, not a guarantee.

If the above properly sets forth our agreement, please sign below and keep one copy.

Return the original with a check for your retainer fee in the amount of $_____.

If we do not receive the signed original of this agreement (you retain the copy) and your check within _____ days, we shall assume that you have obtained other counsel and shall mark our file CLOSED and do nothing further. Thank you.

Dated: _____

Signed: _____

Attorney

The above is understood and agreed to by me:

Dated: _____

Signed: _____

Client

Example 2: Attorney's Fees
(Specific Breakdown)

RE:

Dear _____:

We are pleased that you have asked our firm to represent you in your legal matter. This letter sets forth the understanding concerning our representation of you.

1. You hereby agree to pay our firm a deposit of $_____ toward fees for legal services. This agreement is effective upon our receipt of your deposit. The time expended in your initial consultation will be charged against the fee deposit and the balance will be credited to your account for services to be performed, and costs to be incurred, in the future.

2. We feel that the most equitable basis for our fee is to determine how much time is spent on your matter. It is impossible to determine in advance the amount of time that will be needed to complete your matter. Our billing is based on an hourly rate of $___ per hour for a partner; $___ per hour for associates, depending on their level of experience; $___ per hour for paralegals; and $___ per hour for law clerks. This hourly rate will prevail until further notice, after which, due to rising costs and overhead expenses, the hourly rate will be subject to increase in accordance with the then-existing hourly rate schedule. Fractions of hours are computed in periods of not less than .2 of an hour and the interruption of other work is taken into consideration in our billing system. If some of the work

on your matter can be done by an associate or law clerk whose hourly time rates are substantially lower than mine to the extent that their time is utilized, the overall fee will be lower. You will not be billed for clerical or secretarial time. For the preparation of certain documents, you will be billed on a flat-rate basis rather than a time-expended basis.

3. We will bill you monthly, using our regular billing format, on a time-expended basis. By your acceptance of this Agreement, you give us permission to draw against your deposit and to apply the drawn funds as payment on account of your bill. If and when your deposit has been exhausted by applications toward your bill, then all future bills become payable upon receipt. We reserve the right to terminate our attorney-client relationship for nonpayment of fees or costs when due.

4. Attached is a copy of a sample of one of our bills. You will be billed in a similar form. In the event you wish a more detailed bill, it can be supplied to you; however, we will be required to make an additional charge since our rate is based upon a computerized billing system using this format. Also, in the event you have any objections or questions about our bill, please contact us. If you do not object or question the form of our bill within 10 days of receipt, we will assume you are satisfied with its amount and detail.

5. "Costs" are our out-of-pocket expenses, such as filing fees, transcripts, photocopies, long-distance phone calls, telefax charges, and, if necessary, appraisals and accounting fees. We may ask for an additional deposit to cover

costs, in addition to your initial deposit, if we deem it appropriate.

6. As much as possible, we shall keep you informed as to the progress of your matter. We shall send you copies of all papers coming in and going out of our offices, including correspondence and other documents, which we believe will be of interest to you. If we are unavailable when you telephone, your call will be returned with reasonable promptness. There will be times when we will be in court, or at meetings, or in conference, which will preclude me from returning your telephone call as quickly as we both might like, but we shall do our best to return your telephone calls as soon as we can.

7. While I will be primarily responsible for the legal services to be provided, one of the strengths of our firm is the assistance and support available from the other lawyers of the firm, each of whom maintain a particular expertise. At times it may be necessary or appropriate for one of the other lawyers in the firm to handle a portion of your matter. I will make such determinations based upon my availability and the nature of your matter.

8. Every reasonable effort will be made to handle and conclude your matter promptly and efficiently according to legal, ethical, and local practice rules, standards, and customs. Because of the unpredictability of changes in the law, because unanticipated facts and events often occur, and because of other unknown or unanticipated factors,

we cannot and do not warrant or guarantee the successful outcome of your matter, or the amount of time it will require.

9. In addition to our right to withdraw for nonpayment, we have the right at our discretion to withdraw from the matter if you have misrepresented or failed to disclose material facts to us, if you fail to follow our advice or cooperate, or for any other valid reason. Likewise, you may discharge us at any time for any reason. In these events, you will be required to pay for our time expended to release our file(s) and other information to you or a substitute counsel as well as any costs for copying the file and any other reasonable charges related thereto. Any portion of your fee deposit remaining thereafter will be returned to you within 45 days.

Please signify your acceptance of these terms by signing the enclosed copy of this letter and returning it to my office.

Very truly yours,

_____

Attorney

ACCEPTED this _____ day of _____, 2005.

_____

Client

Interviewing prospective counsel

As you look for a lawyer, arm yourself with a list of "interview" questions and ask the same of all the lawyers on the list you have compiled. (See Questions to Ask Your Attorney in Appendix E for a complete list.) Then compare and contrast what each attorney has to offer and choose the one who best fits your needs.

You might also photocopy the list of questions and use it to record notes as you interview attorneys, whether you do so by phone or in person. If you feel uncomfortable about taking notes in front of the lawyer, do it immediately after leaving his office. Compare your notes before making a final choice as to a lawyer. Before making a final decision about an attorney, ask yourself the following questions:

- Was he willing to take the time to explain things fully?

- Did she talk down to me?

- How much time did he give me? Did he seem rushed?

- Did she focus on me and my needs and listen carefully?

- Was he well-spoken?

- Were my billing questions answered completely and satisfactorily, or did she seem to resent that I asked about such things?

- Did he have a "leave it all up to me" attitude?

- Did she seem to empathize with my situation?

Early on, ask yourself whether you have any preference about your lawyer's gender. In today's times, never assume that

Bright Idea

While you're there, check out the lawyer's office. Is it organized or are there piles of papers all over the place? Are the "In" and "Out" boxes overloaded? The lawyer doesn't have to have an elegantly appointed waiting room or mahogany paneling, but the office should be neat, well supplied, and conducive to an efficient workday.

a male lawyer will garner more respect from the court, because that is highly unlikely. All judges in virtually every jurisdiction now encounter both male and female lawyers on a daily basis. The real test for whether your lawyer will have the court's respect is whether he or she is well prepared, organized, and knows the law. So don't eliminate a candidate on the basis of gender, unless you feel that you will feel more comfortable with one or the other. But even if you are predisposed to one, at least interview a couple of lawyers of the opposite sex. You may find yourself pleasantly surprised by the rapport you feel with the opposite gender. In the final analysis, the important thing is that you are comfortable with, and confident in, your attorney.

When you're done interviewing...

Once you've found the lawyer you want, call or e-mail him and tell him you are ready to proceed. Make it clear that you want to settle the financial arrangements and get started with your case as quickly as possible. Set the tone for your future relationship by being professional and letting him know you will do whatever is necessary to start the process and cooperate as it continues. Set up a time to meet again, and at that time, expect to spend a couple of hours or more reviewing what needs to be done and mapping out a strategy.

A word about conflicts of interest

There are two cardinal rules for lawyers. The first is that all matters between the attorney and the client are to be kept confidential, and only the client can waive that confidentiality. The second is that no lawyer is permitted to undertake the representation of a client that would cause a conflict of interest in his relationship with another client, even if the lawyer no longer represents that other client. So, if your ex has consulted a lawyer and has shared any details whatsoever with him, the lawyer will not be able to represent you in the divorce, even if your ex didn't end up formally retaining the lawyer!

The first thing you will be asked when you schedule an appointment with a lawyer is your spouse's full name, as well as your own. The reason for this is that every law office does "conflict checks," using various methods to ensure that a lawyer does not violate this conflict of interest rule. If your ex previously consulted with a lawyer whom you call, you will probably be told that the lawyer cannot see you. His office may not be specific about why, as the lawyer is walking a tightrope in his obligation to your spouse and his need to politely decline to see you. Technically, he is not even permitted to tell you that he saw your spouse, even for a consultation, but if a lawyer's office declines for unspecified reasons to see you, you can probably assume this is the reason.

You may have seen this conflict of interest scenario at work in television dramas, where a soon-to-be-divorced person may "conflict out" all of the best lawyers in town by seeing each of them just for a consult. In so doing, he will have precluded his spouse from retaining any of them as her own lawyer. This is an extreme example and rarely occurs in real life, but if you live in a particularly small town, or have a strong preference for a specific lawyer, it behooves you to get to him first.

Moving on

Now that you've hired your lawyer and had your first few meetings, the actual process of the divorce will begin. In Part III you will get the lowdown on the various stages of a divorce, from the initial filing through trial. This process can seem intimidating—there are so many forms and the terminology is so foreign, with so much information to keep in mind—but if you break the process down into steps, it will be somewhat easier. Read on for a one-step-at-a-time tour through the divorce process.

Just the facts

- Choosing the right attorney involves a combination of finding someone smart and knowledgeable with whom you have rapport.

- Evaluate potential attorneys fully and remember to ask about billing practices and meeting schedules.

- Be an involved client. Don't just turn the reins over to your lawyer and hope for a good result. The best results come about with good lawyering and extensive client input.

- Attorney bills should be read over carefully. Feel free to ask questions. Make sure you fully understand what you are paying for.

Welcome to the U.S. Court System

PART III

Filing for Divorce

Chapter 6

You've made your decision to divorce and you've broken the news to your spouse. Hopefully the two of you have at least had some preliminary discussions about finances, children, and future living arrangements. Or perhaps you haven't told your spouse, perhaps out of fear of what the reaction may be, but in any event, you've decided to get the ball rolling. You're ready to file for divorce.

We hope you have found a lawyer you feel comfortable with. Or, if you and your spouse are unusually amicable, you may have decided to attempt to do it yourself. Whichever route you've chosen, the very first legal step in the divorce process is *filing a complaint*.

The paper trail

A "complaint" (sometimes called a "declaration," a "petition," or a "bill of particulars"—they all generally mean the same thing) is the document filed with a court seeking a final dissolution of the marriage. It informs all parties concerned of the reasons for the divorce (generally known as the "cause of action" or the "grounds for divorce") and sets forth some basic background information regarding you, your spouse, and the conditions of your marriage.

In past eras, marriages could only be dissolved for reasons pertaining to "fault" of one party; for example, adultery, abuse, or abandonment. The more recent trend, which started in California in the 1970s, has been toward "no-fault" divorce, which does not require either spouse to be painted as a womanizer, a harlot, or a generally awful person, but rather, requires only a demonstration that the marriage is basically over, and that the parties are no longer suited to live as husband and wife. Often people are alarmed when they first view a complaint that their own lawyer has prepared to file with the court, or when they are on the receiving end of such a document, as the nonfiling party. Be aware that lawyers must fit your particular circumstances into a document that complies with the rules of the court and local laws, and that the complaint may appear unduly formal or harsh to you upon first glance. To prepare you for what you are likely to see, Example 1 shows a typical complaint for divorce citing the fault of one party, the husband (defendant) in this case.

Does it matter who files first?

Ideally the filing of the divorce papers will happen within several months after you have decided to end your relationship. There is generally little point in dragging out the process, although there is also no need to rush into things if you still believe there is hope of saving the marriage. Often people believe that it is important to be the person who files first in a divorce action. In most jurisdictions, however, it does not matter which spouse files first—the courts do not give an advantage to a party simply because he or she has beaten the other to the courthouse, so don't let that be your impetus. It is far more important that your divorce process be well thought out and deliberate, rather than rushed and vindictive. In some cases, you and your spouse can even file jointly. But whoever files the complaint, there are some general rules of procedure that have to be followed.

Example 1: Sample Complaint for Divorce Citing Fault of One Party

JANE DOE
    Plaintiff
vs.
JOHN DOE
    Defendant   Complaint

Plaintiff, Jane Doe, resides at _____, says:

1. She was lawfully married to John Doe, the defendant herein, on _____, in a religious ceremony.

2. She was a bona fide resident of the State of New Jersey when this cause of action arose, and has ever since and for more than one year next preceding the commencement of this action continued to be such a bona fide resident.

3. The defendant, John Doe, resides at _____.

4. The defendant has been guilty of extreme cruelty toward the plaintiff starting in _____ and continuing until this time. Particularly specifying some of the acts of extreme cruelty committed by the defendant, the plaintiff says:

(a) Defendant demeans and insults plaintiff. He often criticizes plaintiff in front of the children.

(b) Defendant constantly demands to know the whereabouts of plaintiff. He has become obsessive and paranoid.

(c) Despite the fact that defendant earns a good living, he refuses to spend any money on the family, but all too often needlessly spends money on himself.

By reason of these acts, it is improper and unreasonable to expect plaintiff to continue to cohabit with defendant.

More than three months have elapsed since the last act complained of as constituting plaintiff's cause of action. The acts of extreme cruelty committed by the defendant within a period of three months before the filing of this complaint, as above set forth, are alleged not as constituting in whole or in part the cause of action set forth herein, but as relating back to qualify and characterize the acts constituting said cause of action.

5. _____ children were born of the marriage, namely _____.

6. There have been _____ previous matrimonial actions between the parties.

7. Personal property was legally and beneficially acquired by the parties, or either of them, during the marriage.

8. The plaintiff is unable to support herself and the minor children of the marriage.

WHEREFORE, Plaintiff demands judgment:

A. Dissolving the marriage between the parties;

B. Equitably distributing property which was legally and beneficially acquired by them or either of them during the marriage;

C. Compelling the defendant to support the plaintiff and the minor children of the marriage;

D. Compelling the defendant to pay the legal costs and fees incurred by the plaintiff with regard to the within action;

E. For such further relief as the Court may deem just and equitable.

CERTIFICATION OF VERIFICATION AND NONCOLLUSION

I, Jane Doe, do hereby certify that:

1. I am the plaintiff in the foregoing Complaint.

2. The allegations of the foregoing Complaint are true to the best of my knowledge, information, and belief.

3. Said Complaint is made in truth and in good faith and without collusion, for the causes set forth therein.

4. To the best of my knowledge and belief this matter is not the subject of any other action pending in any Court, nor is any such proceeding contemplated at this time.

5. To the best of my knowledge there are no other parties who must be joined in this action.

6. I certify that the foregoing statements made by me are true. I am aware that if any of the foregoing statements made by me are willfully false I am subject to punishment.

Signed: _____

Dated: _____

Grounds for divorce

Different states have different names for what is commonly called *grounds for divorce,* but there is a great deal of similarity in the various causes of action recognized by most states for a divorce to be granted. As we mentioned earlier, historically most states required that there be a "fault" basis for a divorce, usually adultery or cruelty. Even when states started to recognize general incompatibility as grounds for divorce, there was an accompanying requirement of a lengthy period of time of separation (usually three years) before the divorce could be granted. Now every state recognizes some version of *irreconcilable differences* or *incompatibility* as a basis for divorce, but the length of time required for the parties to be separated prior to the entry of the divorce decree still varies from state to state. In essence, a divorce based on irreconcilable differences permits a divorce to be granted for no other reason than the parties want one.

As long as the husband and wife are in agreement about the grounds for the divorce, the court will not question the accuracy or legitimacy of the reasons given. For instance, if the parties agree that they have lived apart for the requisite amount of time and sign documents attesting to that fact, the issue will be treated as true with no further inquiry needed. If, however, one party to the divorce disputes the underlying basis, the court will hear testimony and will be required to make a factual finding as to whether the required grounds for divorce have been met.

The "irreconcilable differences" basis for divorce is generally what is meant when the term "no-fault" divorce is used. As is evident from the name itself, "no-fault" implies that neither party to the marriage is at fault in causing the breakup of the relationship. All states require either that the parties actually live apart for some period of time—or, if still living together, that they have ceased to act as husband and wife—before the divorce can be granted. This is a highly technical requirement, and one which you must either research yourself or obtain legal advice on so that you are certain to meet the criteria. For instance, in New York, the only form of "no-fault" divorce that can be granted is after the parties have lived apart for at least one year after signing a separation agreement. The amount of time they may have lived apart prior to signing the agreement does not count toward the one-year requirement. New York has traditionally had the most stringent requirements for entry of a divorce decree, and until recently, did not recognize "no-fault" divorce at all. Instead, a party was required to allege and prove fault of the other, such as abandonment or adultery.

Other states recognize fault grounds for divorce ranging from bigamy to "incurable insanity" to "unnatural sexual behavior" to alcoholism or drug abuse. These grounds for divorce remain on the law books of each jurisdiction, but their use has become less and less frequent as the general trend toward no-fault divorce continues. Over the years, the courts and legislatures have recognized that little is to be served by forcing an estranged husband

Watch Out!

Do not file divorce papers with the goal of venting your anger and frustration, or in an effort to hurt or embarrass your spouse. These papers are used solely to set in motion the process by which you will begin resolving the issues that surround you and your family. Using them for retribution is highly inadvisable.

and wife to hash out the details of their marital distress in a court of law. There are no winners in such battles, and in particular, the former spouses and any children suffer terribly from such disputes. Only in a truly unusual circumstance should such grounds for divorce be needed in today's society.

The details

Traditionally, all aspects of a divorce proceeding were handled in one bundle, usually at a single hearing (or trial) before one judge. Thus, if your parents or someone else you know divorced many years ago, you may have a vague recollection of all matters having to do with the divorce, including child custody and financial support, being wrapped up at the same time. Now, however, most jurisdictions recognize that it does not make sense to tie all of these issues together. For instance, it is imperative for issues having to do with child support and custody to be decided as early as possible during the separation. This often means that the husband and wife will appear before a court officer other than a judge, present their respective positions on support and custody issues, and that the court officer will enter an interim order. If either party is aggrieved by this order, an appeal to a judge follows and further testimony and hearings may be ordered on the subjects. In the meantime, however, there are interim guidelines for the parties to follow until a final order can be entered.

Likewise, while the issues pertaining to child support and custody are being ironed out in one branch of the courthouse, the parties and their lawyers can be hashing out the details of the equitable distribution of their property in another branch, often before yet another court officer who is highly experienced in the details of division of marital assets. And then, finally, when all of the financial and child-related issues have been resolved, and after the statutory waiting period has been met, a judge will enter a divorce decree, which will "incorporate" all aspects of the parties' agreements up until that point, or, if they have not agreed on anything, will incorporate the orders which have been entered prior to the divorce decree.

This is a simplification of the actual process followed in most jurisdictions today, but is intended to illustrate that parties no longer are required to have every detail resolved before any of the issues can be finalized. It's not unusual today for the parties to have a final resolution on child custody and support, yet no agreement on division of their own bank accounts until a later date. Similar issues, such as sale of the family home and division of the proceeds, or paying off accumulated marital debt, are also often resolved much later in the divorce proceedings than the more urgent issues of custody and child support.

No-fault, fault, and the division of assets

Under the more traditional model, where one judge heard all issues at one time, the fault of one party was inextricably inter-twined with decisions having to do with financial support. Therefore, it was inevitable that the party to blame for the breakup of the marriage was often penalized in the division of assets. As recently as a decade ago, it was not unusual for a spouse who had committed flagrant adultery to receive far less than half the marital "pie" upon final divorce, or to pay more in alimony than a similarly situated individual who had not com-mitted adultery would. Today, however, since the issues are usu-ally handled separately, and because it has been recognized that the courts are not the right place to punish "sins," the trend has been toward a division of assets that is based on need and earn-ing ability—"equitable distribution," in other words—rather than to tie the division of assets to any fault that led to the breakup of the marriage. Since the issues are now generally

Watch Out!

Do not allow yourself to be influenced by a spouse's threats of "taking you to the cleaners" because of some transgression on your part which led to the breakup. Most courts will not permit that to happen.

heard before different court officers and/or judges, at least in the preliminary stages of the divorce proceedings, it is far easier for this to be accomplished than in the days of one judge hearing the whole sordid story at one time.

Actions and reactions

Although all states now permit some form of "no-fault" divorce, your lawyer may nonetheless want to include certain fault allegations if they are appropriate to your situation. For instance, it is not uncommon to allege several alternative grounds for the divorce. Your divorce complaint may cite the fact that the two of you have been separated for more than one year, if that is the requisite time requirement in your state. The same complaint may also claim that your spouse has engaged in cruel and inhuman treatment that makes the marriage unbearable to continue. Or it may allege that your spouse has committed adultery that has not been forgiven by you. While such legal complaints are becoming less and less common, your lawyer may have a good reason for including the fault grounds for the divorce, particularly if your ex's conduct was outrageous or continued for a lengthy period of time. (For instance, if your lawyer is going to make a claim that you will need increased support for some period of time so that you can undergo extensive psychological counseling stemming from your ex's mistreatment of you, it will be necessary for your lawyer to outline that mistreatment.)

However, be aware that your spouse's reaction to the divorce proceedings will, in some part, depend on the claims you are making in your legal papers. Do not use the process as a means of vindication or retribution. Question your lawyer about the

Moneysaver

Resolve your emotional battles outside the courtroom. Don't use the divorce process as a means to exact revenge on your spouse. Your legal bills will mount, and your total resources will vanish if you do.

reasons for including fault grounds in your divorce complaint, and ask him or her what you can expect to gain from doing so. If no sound reason exists to include those allegations, and if the no-fault rules of your state will accomplish your goal of getting a divorce, consider eliminating the fault grounds. Remember that inclusion of such items will only escalate the hostilities of the divorce proceedings and benefit no one, including you. Hostilities result in battles, which result in drained emotional and financial resources...not a good situation for anyone. Strive for the least acrimonious divorce possible, no matter how distressed you may be that you are getting divorced.

"Service" and other legal particulars

Once the divorce complaint has been drawn up, it must be "served" upon the nonfiling party (see Example 2). "Service" simply means that the opposing party is presented with the complaint so that deadlines for response can be set. Once "service" has been accomplished, the person receiving the papers has a set period of time to respond to the allegations, usually by a date specified in the divorce papers.

The method by which divorce papers are served often influences the tone of the divorce proceeding itself. Do not have your spouse served at his place of employment by a uniformed law enforcement officer unless you want to set the stage for a long and ugly battle. On the other hand, if you have reason to believe your spouse will avoid being served, you may wish to take steps to hire a professional process server. Such individuals are familiar with games played by people who don't want to receive court papers, and they are well equipped to deal with those tactics.

Example 2: Sample Text of an Acknowledgment of Service of a Divorce Complaint

JANE DOE
                   Plaintiff
vs.
JOHN DOE   Acknowledgment of Service
                   Defendant

   The undersigned hereby acknowledges service of a copy of the approved summons and complaint in the above captioned matter on this _____day of _____, 2005.

Appearance

Once the divorce papers have been served, the clock starts ticking. The person who has filed the complaint is usually known as the *plaintiff* or *petitioner*, and the other party is typically called the *defendant* or *respondent*. The defendant has the right to respond to the allegations and address the issues of the case and has several options by which to do so. He may simply acknowledge receipt of the papers without admitting or denying the allegations. Instead of addressing the allegations, the respondent may just ask for the opportunity to be heard on the issues of custody, support, and equitable distribution. This type of response is generally known as an *appearance* (see Example 3).

 Moneysaver

Professional process servers charge for their services. Speak with your lawyer about saving this expense by having the papers mailed to your soon-to-be ex or his or her lawyer, using whatever form of mail is permitted in your jurisdiction. If the divorce is completely uncontested, you may even be able to have the document delivered to your spouse, with an acknowledgement of receipt signed by him or her.

Example 3: Sample Appearance Document

JANE DOE
      Plaintiff

vs.

JOHN DOE   Appearance
      Defendant

    Defendant, John Doe, hereby enters his appearance in the above captioned action and wishes to be heard regarding the issues of custody, visitation, support, and equitable distribution.

Signed: _____

Dated: _____

CERTIFICATION OF VERIFICATION AND
NONCOLLUSION

    1. I, John Doe, am the Defendant in the foregoing Appearance to which this Certification is annexed.

    2. The allegations of said Appearance are true to the best of my knowledge and belief. The Appearance is made in truth and good faith and without collusion for the causes set forth.

    I certify that the foregoing statements made by me are true. I am aware that I am subject to punishment if any of the foregoing statements made by me are willfully false.

Signed: _____

Dated: _____

Filing an appearance is usually the least adversarial and least expensive method of responding, and is often appropriate in cases that can be resolved without aggressive legal tactics. If an appearance is filed, the court will be able to grant the divorce based on the grounds contained in the complaint. That does not mean, however, that all issues pertaining to custody and support will be conceded by the person filing the appearance. It simply means that there will be no contest on the issue of whether a divorce should occur and on what basis.

Alternatively, the defendant may wish to address some of the issues raised in the complaint. For instance, if the divorce complaint contains untrue allegations of adultery or cruelty, you should deny these claims in a written document that is generally known as an *answer*. The answer permits you to deny any wrongdoing, or at least to dispute any claims that have been inaccurately presented.

Counterclaim

In addition to either admitting or denying the allegations contained in the divorce papers, you can respond to a complaint for divorce by asserting your own allegations in what is called a *counterclaim* (see Example 4). A counterclaim can be used to allege fault against the spouse who initiated the divorce action, although these days it is less often used for that purpose due to the prevalence of no-fault divorce. More commonly, the counterclaim is used by the responding spouse to set forth his or her own claims for support or custody of the children. You'll need to consult with your attorney to determine whether a counterclaim is warranted in your situation.

 Moneysaver

Do not rise to the bait and feel compelled to file a counterclaim just because your spouse has filed a divorce complaint. Your rights can usually be adequately protected even without a formal counterclaim. Ask your lawyer to keep unnecessary court filings to a minimum.

Example 4: Sample Answer and Counterclaim Responding to the Divorce Complaint Presented in Example 1

JANE DOE
    Plaintiff

vs.

JOHN DOE
    Defendant   Answer and Counterclaim

Defendant, John Doe, by way of Answer to the Complaint, says:

1. That he admits the allegations in paragraph 1.
2. That he admits the allegations in paragraph 2.
3. That he admits the allegations in paragraph 3.
4. That he denies the allegations in paragraph 4.
5. That he admits the allegations in paragraph 5.
6. That he admits the allegations in paragraph 6.
7. That he admits the allegations in paragraph 7.
8. That he denies the allegations in paragraph 8.

WHEREFORE, the defendant demands judgment:

(a) Dismissing the Complaint of the Plaintiff;

(b) Denying all relief requested by the Plaintiff; and

(c) For such other relief as the Court may deem necessary and proper.

COUNTERCLAIM

Defendant-Counterclaimant, John Doe, by way of Counterclaim against the plaintiff, Jane Doe, says:

1. The defendant-counterclaimant was married to the plaintiff herein in a religious ceremony on _____.

2. The defendant-counterclaimant was a bona fide resident of the State of New Jersey on the date this cause of

action arose, and has ever since and for more than one year next preceding the commencement of this action continued to be such a bona fide resident. The defendant-counterclaimant resides at _____.

3. The plaintiff resides at _____.

4. The plaintiff has been guilty of extreme cruelty toward the defendant-counterclaimant. Particularly specifying some of the acts of extreme cruelty committed by the plaintiff, the defendant-counterclaimant says:

(a) Plaintiff told defendant-counterclaimant that she no longer loved him and in fact, probably never really loved him;

(b) Plaintiff stays out late at night and refuses to account for her whereabouts;

(c) Plaintiff has become violent toward defendant-counterclaimant. Specifically, following an argument regarding plaintiff's whereabouts, she hit defendant-counterclaimant.

By reason of these acts, the defendant-counterclaimant's health and mental state have become affected and it is improper and unreasonable to expect the defendant-counterclaimant to continue to cohabit with the plaintiff.

More than three months have elapsed since the last act complained of as constituting the defendant-counterclaimant's cause of action. The acts of extreme cruelty committed by the plaintiff, as set forth, are alleged not as constituting in whole or in part the cause of action set forth herein, but as relating back to qualify and characterize the acts constituting said cause of action.

5. _____ children, namely _____, were born of the marriage and they currently are in the custody of both parties.

6. There have been _____ previous proceedings in this or any other Court pertaining to the marriage and its dissolution.

7. Property was legally and beneficially acquired by the parties, or either of them, during the marriage.

8. The plaintiff has adequate means of support for herself and to pay for her own fees and costs.

WHEREFORE, Defendant-counterclaimant demands judgment:

A. Dissolving the marriage between the parties;

B. Awarding the parties joint custody of the minor children of the marriage;

C. Requiring the plaintiff to pay the legal fees of the defendant-counterclaimant in the within action;

D. Equitably distributing all property subject to same;

E. For such further relief as the Court may deem just and proper.

Signed: _____

Dated: _____

Default

When a respondent fails to answer the divorce complaint in any fashion, a divorce may still be granted by default; however, it will generally take more time than if both parties participate in the proceedings. For example, some states permit an uncontested divorce after three to six months of living apart. However, even if you and your spouse have lived apart for the designated period of time, if the other party does not appear in the action the court cannot treat the divorce as uncontested, and will instead follow the rules for contested divorces based on living apart for a longer period of time (often two to three years). So, if you are faced with the situation of having a spouse who simply refuses to respond or acknowledge service of the divorce papers, you may be faced with having to wait a longer period of time—unless you can prove to the court that your spouse has been properly served and was given adequate time to answer the allegations of the complaint, and that there is no legally valid excuse for failure to respond. In such cases, you may be able to have the court enter a divorce by default.

Interim relief

The wheels of justice, unfortunately, turn ever so slowly. If you and your spouse have not been able to achieve a workable interim set of rules during your separation, you will need assistance from the courts in obtaining support and coming to a workable and fair custody and visitation schedule. However, your needs will probably be more immediate than the court's timeframe for a full hearing on these issues. If this is the situation, your attorney may need to file a request for interim or immediate relief. These requests are generally called *motions for pendente lite* (pronounced "lee-tay") *relief,* meaning "relief pending final resolution" (see Example 5). Examples of situations where pendente lite relief is appropriate include those where one party has little or no earning power yet continues to have day-to-day expenses that must be met, and a spouse who refuses to pay support; or a situation where one party has no financial resources to hire an attorney and needs a distribution from the marital assets, or a payment from the spouse, in order to engage a lawyer. In such a case, the court may grant financial support pendente lite, or may order an award of attorneys' fees to be paid pendente lite.

 Watch Out!

All court orders must be obeyed, even if a party feels he or she has been treated unfairly. Failure to comply with the order will eventually result in a contempt order being issued, which may be punishable by monetary fines, jail time, or both.

Example 5: Sample Notice of Motion for Pendente Lite Relief Demanding Child Support and Alimony, as Well as Continued Insurance Coverage, Prior to the Final Resolution of a Divorce

JANE DOE
      Plaintiff

vs.

JOHN DOE   Notice of Motion
      Defendant

TO: John Doe
SIR:

     PLEASE TAKE NOTICE that on _____, at 9:00 in the forenoon or as soon thereafter as counsel may be heard, the undersigned attorney for the plaintiff shall move before the Honorable _____, at the _____ County Courthouse, _____, ____, for an Order:

     1. Compelling the defendant to pay $_____ as child support, directly to plaintiff, for the support of the parties' minor children.

     2. Compelling defendant to pay $_____ as alimony, directly to plaintiff, for the support and welfare of plaintiff;

     3. Compelling defendant to maintain medical insurance coverage for the benefit of the minor children.

     PLEASE TAKE NOTICE that in support of this notice, Plaintiff's Certification is annexed hereto.

     Also please take note that a form of Order is annexed hereto.

Signed: _____

Watch Out!

You don't want Marvin Milktoast for an attorney, but you don't want Dirty Harry, either. If your lawyer seems like a barracuda and all you and your spouse want is an amicable divorce, pull back the attorney's reins and insist that he handle the case in a nonconfrontational manner. If he resists or continues to bare his teeth at court hearings or meetings, find another lawyer.

Requests for pendente lite relief must be made in writing to the court, usually verified by affidavit or notary seal, with a detailed description of the immediate problem and the relief that is sought. For example, you may wish to explain that you are dependent upon your spouse for support, that the mortgage payment is due, and that you are left without adequate means to buy groceries. Or you may wish to explain that you're caring for two small children and need child support payments to cover their expenses, including day care and medical insurance (see Example 6).

After you file your papers, your spouse has an opportunity to rebut your petition. For example, if you have petitioned for the court to order that your spouse provide financial support, he or she may respond to your petition by suggesting you could obtain employment, or that you are not properly budgeting yourself. Once both sides have filed statements affirming their positions, the court may allow or request oral argument—that is, it may ask that your attorneys make an oral presentation based on the written submissions. Generally, the court will only hear from your attorney; you are not expected to argue your position. After consideration of all the papers and arguments, the court will structure a resolution and order that you and your spouse abide by this resolution until further order (see Example 7).

In this example, the court will most typically ensure that your children are adequately supported, that the mortgage continues to be paid, that the car and credit card payments are made, and that all assets that must eventually be divided between you and your spouse are protected and not unfairly

Example 6: Certification in Support of the Motion for Pendente Lite Relief Appearing in Example 5

JANE DOE
    Plaintiff

vs.

JOHN DOE   Certification
    Defendant

I, Jane Doe, of full age, the plaintiff in the above referenced case, make this Certification in support of my Motion for Pendente Lite Relief, and hereby certify:

1. My husband and I have been separated for the past two months. Last month I filed for divorce.

2. Since our separation, my husband has refused to contribute toward the expenses of the house, including necessary expenses incurred on behalf of our two minor children.

3. My husband works full time. I am not employed. Without support from my husband, my children and I will not be able to meet our monthly bills.

4. Further, my husband is provided medical coverage by his employer for the benefit of our children. However, he told me that he was going to cancel the coverage unless I split the cost with him.

I, Jane Doe, hereby certify that the above statements made by me are true. I further certify that I am aware that I am subject to punishment if the above statements made by me are willfully false.

Signed: _____

Example 7: Court Order Mandating Payment of Child Support and Alimony and the Maintenance of Insurance Coverage for the Children as Petitioned for in the Motion for Pendente Lite Relief Appearing in Examples 5 and 6

JANE DOE
   Plaintiff
vs.
JOHN DOE   Order
   Defendant

  THIS MATTER being presented to the court on the application of _____, Esq., attorney for the plaintiff, and it appearing upon a reading of the certifications by the parties and having heard oral argument by counsel; and for good reason shown;

  It is, on this _____ day of _____, 2005;

  ORDERED, as follows:

  (1) That on the first day of each month, beginning on _____, the defendant shall pay directly to the plaintiff the sum of $_____ as child support.

  (2) That on the first day of each month, beginning on _____, the defendant shall pay directly to the plaintiff the sum of $_____ as alimony.

  (3) That the defendant shall maintain medical insurance coverage as provided by his employer for the benefit of the minor children. Defendant shall be solely responsible for the cost of said insurance.

Signed: _____

diminished by you or your spouse. In framing a decision, the court must try to divide the total available income in a manner that solves the immediate problem; for example, payment of the mortgage. But the court will not anticipate future problems or issues—if your situation changes, you may have to petition the court again and seek further relief.

Issues relating to the children's welfare will generally be very cautiously handled on a pendente lite basis, and courts are not likely to upset the status quo on an interim basis. The main reason for this is that pendente lite determinations, because of their early and efficient disposition, do not generally involve full hearings on every facet of an issue. Rather, the court will attempt to fashion a workable and fair interim solution until a more thorough hearing can be held. However, because of this procedure, there is little time for a full exploration of issues. Since child custody concerns often require expert testimony or independent psychological evaluations, which most likely will not yet have been performed, the court is unlikely to make any radical changes to the children's living arrangements, schooling, or similar matters. Until there has been time for psychological evaluations or other expert reviews, the court is likely to order primary physical custody of any children to remain with whichever spouse is in the marital home to preserve the children's sense of stability and avoid any abrupt changes in their schooling requirements. At the same time, however, the court will want to keep both parents on equal footing and will usually order extensive partial physical custody with the other parent to enable him or her to have ample time with the children. The court will conduct much more extensive hearings later, which will address all aspects of the custodial situation, each parent's fitness to be custodial parent, and any special issues a child may have, before entering a final custody and visitation order. But for purposes of pendente lite relief, the court will attempt to maintain the status quo as much as possible.

Watch Out!

Nothing hurts your case more than withholding information from your lawyer. Without full knowledge of the situation, your attorney cannot effectively represent your interests. One of the worst things you can do is fail to tell your attorney the full and honest truth.

It is important to understand that the court, at this point, is merely addressing the immediate concerns that face your family during the divorce process. For example, your spouse may be showing up at your house on a sporadic, unannounced basis to see the children, and this may be causing you problems. In such a situation you may request that the court establish regular visitation days or times so you and the children can maintain some type of regular schedule. Without much consideration, the court may order alternate weekends or a similar arrangement just to establish a workable arrangement.

In some states, as soon as the divorce papers are filed the court may grant automatic temporary "reliefs" without any need for you to petition. For example, in some jurisdictions the filing of divorce papers has the effect of automatically restraining both spouses from selling, transferring, or borrowing against any of their marital property. The parties may also be restrained from taking a child out of state or canceling or transferring life insurance policies. However, most states do not have these automatic restraints. Make certain you know your state's position on these issues and file any applications you may need to protect your interests and the interests of your children.

How long will it take?

Every divorce lawyer gets the same question when retained by a new client seeking a divorce: "How long will this take?" And every divorce lawyer gives (or should give) the same answer: "It depends." While there are certain definable factors that can help your lawyer determine how long the divorce process will take, such as the court's docket, usual length of time for divorce proceedings in your state or county, and so forth, the fact of the matter is that the pace of your divorce is largely dependent on you and your spouse, and your ability to work amicably toward a resolution.

Because a divorce involves two parties, who are generally at odds, neither one will be able to control everything that happens. Either spouse can greatly influence the tempo and tone of the divorce. If one spouse is anxious to resolve things amicably while the other fights every issue down to the division of the toothbrushes, there is very little that the reasonable party can do to avoid a difficult and expensive divorce. Either spouse generally has the right to contest any issue that affects him or her, the children, the marital assets, and any other relevant concern. As a result, the court normally will not decide a contested issue without at least some type of hearing or presentation of evidence with regard to that matter. The more issues that are contested, and the higher the stakes, the more the court will be involved, the more it will cost, and the longer it will take.

In Chapter 7 we will discuss the negotiation of a settlement, but for now, keep in mind that it is almost always better to compromise and resolve than to disagree and go to court.

One way to help avoid a bad outcome is to make sure you take an active role in your divorce. This sounds simple, but in times of intense emotional distress, many of us are tempted to throw all our difficulties into our lawyers' laps and expect them to solve the problems. It is imperative that you insist on being made aware of all discussions, negotiations, and other aspects of

 Moneysaver

At the initial meeting between your legal team and your spouse's, it helps to state that both sides are interested in a timely resolution to your negotiations. Both sides have much to gain by completing the process swiftly, so setting such a standard helps to establish both sides' willingness to cooperate.

your divorce as they happen. You should not merely hear the conclusion of a negotiation, but rather, you should play an active part.

Privacy issues

All conversations between you and your attorney are confidential and cannot be disclosed without your consent. This is known as the *attorney-client privilege.* The privilege belongs to you, not your attorney. What this means is that only you can waive the privilege—only you can authorize disclosure of anything discussed between you and your lawyer. Your lawyer cannot, under any circumstances, share such information with another person without your consent. However, only those discussions that are solely between the two of you are protected by privilege. If any third party (other than another employee of the same law office) is present, the attorney-client privilege is lost. This is an extremely important fact to keep in mind when meeting with your lawyer. If you bring your mother or your best friend to a meeting with the lawyer, no privilege exists, and the court and your spouse's lawyer are entitled to learn what was said during that meeting.

Moreover, your divorce proceeding is not a private matter, much as you think it should be. Generally speaking, court proceedings are open to the public. This does not mean that anyone off the street will be able to obtain your court file and divulge confidential information. However, except for some issues that involve children, your case is generally heard in an open courtroom in front of strangers. Do not be alarmed by this. Generally, there are few observers to proceedings as dry as a domestic dispute. Notable exceptions include celebrity divorces and ugly fault divorces, but otherwise, few people will have an interest in sitting through a divorce proceeding. Note also that issues pertaining to children are often conducted in a closed courtroom, and you may want to request that your lawyer ask the judge to do this if there are special issues involved.

Discuss any concerns regarding private issues with your attorney
to ensure that your interests, and your children's, are protected
to the fullest possible extent.

With the filing of the divorce complaint and the response
(with or without a counterclaim), the divorce process has
begun. Now you must turn your attention to how to handle the
division of responsibilities, assets, and liabilities that will be necessary when you and your spouse split up. This requires that
both you and your partner are equally knowledgeable about
your household circumstances. To ensure that this knowledge is
equally available to the two of you, a procedure known as "discovery" is available. In Chapter 7 you will learn about this
process, what it's there for, and how to most effectively use it.

Just the facts

- A divorce can be started by either you or your spouse.

- Causes of action can assert either fault or no-fault.

- In addition to either admitting or denying the allegations
  contained in the divorce papers, you may wish to file your
  own claims or counterclaim.

- If specific relief for a particular issue is needed prior to
  the final divorce, you can file a motion with the court for
  immediate resolution.

- Your lawyer must keep all of your information strictly
  confidential.

GET THE SCOOP ON...
Disclosing basic information ▪ Interrogatories
and depositions ▪ Subpoenas ▪ Obtaining
an expert's opinion ▪ Adhering to the
discovery schedule

The Discovery Process

An essential part of the litigation process—in divorce cases and otherwise—is known as the *discovery* phase. In fact, the discovery phase will probably take more time than any other aspect of your divorce proceeding. "Discovery" is just that— an opportunity for litigants to "discover" what information the other side has. In criminal cases, discovery permits the person accused of a crime to find out what information the prosecution has against him. In civil cases, including divorce, the discovery process is somewhat less sinister—it simply enables each side to find out certain things that may be helpful to their presentation of the case.

So, for instance, if you have insufficient knowledge about your husband's sources and amount of income, you are permitted in discovery to delve into such issues and to demand that he produce information, under oath, as to his earnings for a reasonable period of time. You may also demand that documents be furnished, such as paycheck stubs, 401(k) statements, commission reports, etc. Or let's say you are seeking full custody of your children because of a drug habit that your spouse has, or you believe she has. You have seen all the signs of drug use, but have nothing to use to prove it. You can, in the discovery process, seek medical records, drug treatment information, prescription records, etc. In other words, in order to settle all of the issues material to your divorce, the discovery process will enable you (and your spouse) to obtain greater access to information than you might not otherwise have without the court's assistance.

The need for basic information

Gathering information through discovery is an essential part of the divorce process. Even when both spouses want to resolve all issues amicably, some discovery may be needed to ensure a fair and equitable agreement—even if only to confirm certain understandings and justifications that form the basis for your settlement proposal. Either spouse may need assurances as to some of the basic facts before feeling comfortable in reaching a final settlement.

For example, before an agreement can be reached, each party must have a complete understanding of the marital finances, including such items as the value of real estate, pension plans or other assets, wages, debts, expenses, costs of insurance, day care, school, and a multitude of other items. Although both spouses may already have a good idea as to the values of these items, confirmation is helpful to either spouse. Often one spouse has managed the household finances prior to divorce and has a significantly better understanding of the family's total financial picture. Through discovery, both parties have the

 Watch Out!

All information that you provide in the course of discovery is given under oath, even if it's just in the form of a written statement that you are providing truthful information. Any falsehoods are subject to the penalties of perjury. Do not succumb to the temptation to "fudge" the information you give in discovery.

Moneysaver

You should draw up at least the initial list of items for your attorney to seek from your spouse by way of discovery. You have better knowledge of the particulars of what to look for, such as special bonuses he receives from his employer, and you will save legal fees with every bit of work you do yourself.

opportunity to level the playing field. Its procedures are designed to uncover any and all information needed to resolve any issue regarding the divorce.

When a divorce is filed, many states automatically require the filing of a document to disclose basic information about the family unit. While the actual content of such forms differ from state to state, the following list shows some of the information you may be required to furnish. This list serves as a good starting point for formulating your own discovery checklist.

In addition to the general disclosure document, both spouses may be required to provide copies of all federal and state income tax returns, W-2 statements, 1099 statements, self-employed schedule C statements, recent pay stubs, bonus information, and any other financial information that is relevant to the divorce, and more specifically, to the financial aspects of the divorce. If the court does not require these items to be submitted, they should be requested during discovery, as they may shed

> ❝ One of my main frustrations when we were married was that he withheld financial information from me. I never knew how much he earned. I sure as heck wasn't going to enter into a final settlement agreement until I had some assurance that I had an accurate picture of his earnings. Once I received copies of the paycheck stubs and W-2s from his employer, I felt much more comfortable with the terms of our settlement. ❞
>
> —Julie, recent divorcee

The Basic Information List

1. Name and address of parties
2. Name, address, and birth date of child(ren)
3. Person with whom child(ren) resides
4. Name and address of employer(s)
5. Name and address of health insurance company(ies) and type of coverage
6. Name and address of life insurance company(ies) and policy information
7. Income as reported in last five years of income tax returns (joint and individually)
8. Present earnings of each spouse
9. Description of all deductions from paychecks, including taxes, medical insurance, life insurance, pension plan, savings plan, wage execution, voluntary retirement fund payments, loan payments, and all other deductions
10. Budget of monthly expenses, including:
    - Rent or mortgage payment
    - Other mortgages
    - Car payment(s)
    - Utility bills (don't forget water and sewage, an often-overlooked item)
    - Rental or homeowner's insurance
    - Parking fees
    - Real estate taxes
    - Household repairs and maintenance
    - Garbage removal
    - Snow removal and lawn care
    - Telephone
    - Service contracts on equipment
    - Cable TV
    - Plumber/electrician

- Equipment and furnishings
- Automobile insurance
- Automobile registration and license
- Gas expenses
- Commuting expenses
- Food at home for self and children
- Household supplies
- Prescription drugs
- Nonprescription drugs
- School lunches
- Restaurants
- Clothing
- Dry cleaning and commercial laundry
- Hair care
- Domestic help
- Medical out-of-pocket expenses
- Dental expenses
- Medical insurance premiums
- Sports and hobbies
- Camps and vacations
- Children's private school costs
- Miscellaneous children's expenses (piano lessons, tutor, etc.)
- Baby-sitting and day-care expenses
- Entertainment
- Newspapers and periodicals
- Gifts and contributions
- Payments to nonchild dependents
- Prior existing support obligations
- Life insurance
- Savings/investments
- Debt service

11. Values of assets and liabilities, including:
    ■ Real estate
    ■ Bank accounts and certificates of deposit
    ■ Vehicles
    ■ Tangible personal property
    ■ Stocks and bonds
    ■ Pension, profit-sharing, retirement plan(s)
    ■ Businesses, partnerships, professional practices
    ■ Whole life insurance
    ■ Other assets
    ■ Mortgages on real estate
    ■ Long-term debts
    ■ Revolving charges
    ■ Other short-term debts
    ■ Contingent liabilities

useful light on some of the financial issues. It may be that after truthful disclosure of each party's financial status, an amicable resolution can be reached, particularly if lack of knowledge of the other person's assets and earning potential had been a stumbling block in reaching an agreement.

Interrogatories

Apart from the basic disclosure that may be required by your jurisdiction, interrogatories are the most common form of discovery. These are written questions served upon a party by the opposing party. The questions are formulated by lawyers and are generally fairly standardized for the situation. In other words, all divorce cases will have a basic set of questions that are asked. Any unique situations require supplemental questions to be added to the basic set. The party served with the interrogatories must provide written responses under oath. If false information is willfully provided, the responding party is technically subject to the penalties of perjury, although perjury prosecutions are very rarely instituted out of this process. Nonetheless, any falsehoods given in the course of discovery may severely hurt the responding party's status in the litigation, as his or her credibility will be seriously undermined. The set of interrogatories are generally accompanied by an introductory statement that sets forth the requirement that they be answered under oath. Answers to interrogatories generally form the starting point for further inquiry during the discovery process.

Interrogatories can delve into any issue that is relevant to the divorce. Although the language of an interrogatory may be rather formal, the actual questions are quite basic. The following is a list of some of the actual questions that are typically asked in a divorce proceeding:

1. Where do you live?

2. Do you own or rent? How many rooms are in your home, and how are the rooms used?

3. Who lives in the home with you? Give names and the relationship of each resident to you.

4. Are you currently employed? If so, give the name and address of your present employer(s), the date you started working there, your duties on the job, and your weekly pay (gross and net). A copy of recent pay stubs (usually three to six months' worth) will be required to document salary, as will a copy of the W-2 form(s) on file with current employers.

 Moneysaver

Save legal expense when responding to requests that are directed to you by your spouse's lawyer by furnishing complete responses with photocopied papers (such as bank statements). If you don't do the legwork, your lawyer will have to—and you will ultimately pay.

5. If you've been with your present employer(s) for less than three years, or if you held other jobs as well during any of the past three years, provide the same information for each such employment as requested in the above stated interrogatory.

6. Does your employer provide you with any insurance? If yes, list each type and plan, together with the benefits to which you are entitled. Provide the nature and value of such coverage.

7. Does your employer provide you with free or subsidized meals, transportation, or other such fringe benefits? If yes, provide the nature and value and basis of valuation of each such benefit.

8. Does your employer pay for any expenses you incur? If yes, provide the gross amount paid by each employer for each year during the past five calendar years and list each payment you received and the nature of the expense incurred.

9. Do/did you receive any other income during the current year and/or during the past five calendar years? If yes, list the type of income and the source from which you received it, and indicate whether that income was included on your federal and state tax returns during the past three years.

10. Does anyone owe you any money? If yes, provide the name and address of each debtor, the amount of the debt, the date the obligation was incurred, the date it will become due, and the conditions for payment of the obligation.

11. Identify all checking accounts in which you had power of signature within the past five years. Provide the name and address of (each) bank, the account number(s), the date you opened the account, the date you closed it (if applicable), the name the account is in, and the name(s) of any other people with legal right or interest in such accounts. Identify any other person who had power of signature on

any such account, and provide a copy of the check registers and monthly statements for each account.

12. For savings accounts, money market accounts, or certificates of deposit in which you had power of signature within the past five years, provide account information, as well as a list of deposits to the account(s) and the source of the funds deposited, a list of withdrawals, and a copy of any bank books or statements for the accounts.

13. Identify any life insurance or annuity policy, or any life insurance program, in which you have an interest.

14. Identify any safe-deposit boxes maintained by you or in which you had power of signature in the past three years.

15. If you have submitted any financial statement for credit purposes or for any other purpose within the past three years, describe the reasons for such submission and to whom it was submitted, and attach a copy to your answers to interrogatories, if available.

16. If you have made withdrawals or transfers of funds from any account held jointly with your spouse since the time this divorce proceeding commenced, identify all such withdrawals or transfers with specificity.

17. Are there any funds, real property, investments, or other assets that you claim should not be subject to division between you and your spouse in this proceeding? If yes, describe all such assets fully and state your justification for holding such assets apart from the general division of property.

18. Is there any property titled solely in your spouse's name to which you claim a share? If yes, describe that property, including an estimate of the total equity you hold in it and the portion of that equity that you believe should go to you, and the reasons you are claiming a share.

19. Provide the names and addresses of everyone who may serve as a witness to the allegations you are making in this divorce proceeding. Indicate each person's relationship to you.

20. Have you received any gifts or inheritances during your marriage? If so, detail all such gifts or inheritances.

21. Disclose all of your current debts, the parties to whom they are owed, and the circumstances in which the debts were incurred.

22. (Questions about physical or mental health history, if applicable.)

23. (Request for authorization for the release of medical records, if applicable.)

24. Have you used any prescription medicines during the past three years? If so, include details on the types of medication and the conditions for which they were prescribed.

Interrogatories should be very detailed so as to maximize the amount of information obtained in response. Although some states have limits on the number of interrogatories that can be asked in one proceeding, the questions can be carefully framed to elicit the important information you are seeking. If there is an issue as to whether one spouse is unable to work for medical reasons, the specifics of the medical condition and any restrictions on activities should be asked. If a claim for alimony has been rebutted by the spouse's claim that he cannot pay support due to recent job loss or reduction in earnings, seek particulars of that situation and ask for complete details on efforts made to secure new or improved employment.

 Watch Out!

You should assume that every interrogatory asked by your lawyer of your spouse will be turned around and asked of you by his attorney. Do not ask questions that you yourself are not willing to answer.

It is not unusual to receive incomplete or evasive information in response to interrogatories. Although your spouse may have provided substantive information to his or her attorney in response to the interrogatory, the answers themselves are generally prepared by someone in the attorney's office who has experience in crafting responses to provide as little information as possible. If the information is truly insufficient, there are methods that can be employed by your lawyer to compel more complete information to be provided. Alternatively, your legal team may use the information in the interrogatory answers as a launch pad to prepare for a deposition.

Depositions

Unlike interrogatories, which are reduced to written form and are submitted to your spouse for written response, depositions are conducted face to face, with the attorneys asking questions of the witness. The person whose deposition is being taken is a "deponent." If the deponent is your spouse, his lawyer will be present, and your lawyer will have the opportunity to ask him questions in greater detail than provided by interrogatories. If the deponent is a witness other than one of the spouses, he will be given the opportunity to have an attorney present, although that is often not necessary if the deponent is simply being asked factual questions about the two parties to the divorce, their finances, or other matters that have no real bearing on the deponent. The deposition generally takes place in one of the two lawyer's offices, and no judge is present. As with interrogatories, all questions asked at a deposition must be answered under oath.

Because the oath is given in person by a notary public (usually the court stenographer), the deponent may take the obligation to tell the truth more seriously than he or she did when answering interrogatories. This obligation is usually reinforced by the attorney who is asking the deposition questions in a brief introductory series of questions that are asked of the deponent. For example, after a few comments about the nature of a deposition,

---

Sample Notice of Taking of Deposition Document

JANE DOE
     Plaintiff

vs.

JOHN DOE
     Defendant

      NOTICE OF TAKING OF DEPOSITION ON ORAL EXAMINATION

To: John Doe

     PLEASE TAKE NOTICE that in accordance with all applicable Rules of Civil Practice and Procedure, testimony will be taken by deposition upon oral examination by a person authorized by the State of _____ to administer oaths on _____ at _____ at _____, with respect to all matters relevant to the subject matter in this action, at which time and place you will please produce the following [for instance, in a deposition notice to an accountant, all work papers and records pertaining to the couple's past years' tax returns might be requested here]:

Signed: _____
Attorney

Dated: _____

---

the attorney may ask the deponent something along the lines of "Do you understand that you are giving testimony here today that is equivalent to testifying in a courtroom? Do you understand that you have taken an oath to tell the truth?" Such questions are designed to reinforce the obligation to tell the truth, and when asked by a skillful attorney, will usually have the effect of slightly intimidating the deponent, which is exactly what is intended.

Although the deponent will likely have been "prepped" by her attorney in a pre-deposition session where the attorney coaches her about what is likely to be asked and how to respond, one of the primary advantages of a deposition over other forms of discovery is that the deponent is expected to answer questions on the spot, without benefit of a private conference with her attorney after every question and before every answer. While it is permissible to take occasional breaks during the deposition so that the deponent can rest or confer with her attorney, it is not permissible for the deponent to be coached by the attorney after a question has been asked. Moreover, the longer a deposition lasts, the more anxious the deponent usually is to have it end, which often results in a freer flow of words. Typically, a deponent will be extremely cautious at the beginning of the deposition but will grow more confident with the process as the hours pass. Often, the most valuable information is obtained toward the end of the proceeding when the deponent's guard has been let down. Good attorneys are well aware of this pattern and will gear their questioning accordingly.

Generally, depositions can be taken from any persons who have direct knowledge about a contested issue in the divorce proceeding. For example, if one spouse is a salesman who claims that his wages and commissions have been drastically reduced, coincidentally, at the same time that a divorce action was filed, the employer (or appropriate representative of the employer, such as the bookkeeper) may be deposed in order to ascertain more information about the circumstances of the supposed reduction in income. As a general rule, parties to a lawsuit are entitled to depose any person who possesses information that is not only relevant but also necessary in order to fully investigate and present the case.

Watch Out!

Depositions are very expensive to conduct. A lawyer will generally spend several hours preparing for the deposition, and the deposition itself may last several hours. In addition to the lawyer fees, a court stenographer will record the deposition, and that cost is usually substantial. Therefore, a deposition should not be conducted unless truly necessary for the development of facts; and even then, only after all preliminary information has been otherwise gathered.

Despite the advantages of depositions, they are not used in all discovery actions, primarily because of the expense involved. Often the information sought can be obtained through other forms of written discovery that have the advantage of being less expensive, and sometimes more reliable, if the information sought can be obtained from a party or entity with no vested interest in the outcome of the case.

Hand it over: document productions and subpoenas

In litigation, it is best to have "hard evidence" in the form of a document that establishes critical facts. For instance, business records, bank statements, pay stubs, stock certificates, tax returns, appraisals, and the like are all tangible evidence of the value of certain assets or earnings. A party to a divorce action is entitled to seek these and other documents by way of what is generally called a *request to produce* (if directed to a party to the divorce) or by way of a *subpoena* (if directed to a nonparty, such as an employer or banking institution). This type of discovery may be especially important in instances in which one party, to the exclusion of the other, possesses records or documents that are relevant to the issues of the divorce. For example, if one spouse has always prepared the tax returns and then filed them away, sequestered from the other spouse's access, a request to produce will require him to furnish complete copies. Similarly, if one spouse took all responsibility for banking matters during the marriage, the other may be significantly prejudiced by her lack of records and/or information about the bank accounts. These records too can be obtained by a request to produce.

The following are general examples of documents typically sought in a request for production of documents:

1. Lease or mortgage documents

2. Employment contracts

3. Insurance policies, including life, health, disability policies

4. Expense vouchers submitted to an employer

5. Tax returns for the past three to five years

6. Copies of all check registers and bank statements for all checking accounts in which either spouse had any interest or authorization to sign checks or make withdrawals during the past five years

7. Copies of all bank books or bank statements for all savings accounts, certificates of deposit, money market, or similar accounts in which either spouse had any interest or authorization to make withdrawals during the past five years

8. Copies of any policies or annuity contracts or similar in which either spouse had any interest during the past five years

9. Copies of any financial statements prepared or submitted to any company or institution, for credit or other purposes, within the past three years

10. Copy of any report of any expert who was engaged in connection with the divorce

11. Copy of any will or trust by which either spouse received an inheritance or by which he or she received or will receive any income or principal, or in which he or she has any remainder interest

12. Pertinent medical records

13. A copy of the spouse's current résumé

In contrast to a request for production of documents, a subpoena can be used to compel a nonparty to produce documents that are relevant to the divorce proceedings. A subpoena is issued under court order and basically commands the person or institution to which it is directed to produce certain items. Although this sounds formidable and expensive, a subpoena can be easily obtained by your lawyer from the clerk of your courthouse without any involvement by a judge (unless the subpoena is disregarded or defied, in which case the court's powers of enforcement can be employed).

Getting an expert's opinion

Aside from child custody, which is by far the most important issue to be decided in a divorce proceeding (see Chapter 10), the most common dispute has to do with the worth of various assets that are to be divided upon the conclusion of the divorce. To resolve this type of issue you may need to obtain an expert opinion (often called an *appraisal*).

...On real estate

The most common dispute has to do with the value of marital real estate, usually the family home. Often one party is staying in that home and the other is entitled to be compensated for no longer having that property. Such a valuation is generally obtained from a real estate broker or licensed appraiser.

...On the value of a business

If a business ownership interest is involved, it is often very difficult to accurately estimate its fair market value. In these circumstances,

 Moneysaver

As a general rule, real estate brokers, because they want to list a house for sale, provide higher estimates of fair market value than real estate appraisers, who are truly impartial and paid to do nothing more than provide an accurate and detailed appraisal of value.

one spouse may need to hire a forensic accountant to provide a valuation of the worth of the business interest.

...On medical issues

Where a claim for support is made based on a medical condition or disability, a medical expert may be retained to help prove (or disprove) the claim. Generally, the most reliable medical expert is one who has actually treated the person who is alleged to be incapacitated or disabled; however, the opposing party may seek a second opinion from an impartial medical expert who can provide an opinion based on medical records, and sometimes, an independent medical evaluation of the person who is claiming to be disabled.

...On employment issues

Another common example of expert discovery is in the case of a spouse who is seeking support as a result of inability to obtain employment. In these instances, an employment expert may be necessary to either prove or disprove the claim. This is generally a vocational expert who will render an opinion based upon a spouse's education, work experience, ability, the job market, and other relevant factors.

The expert's role

Any expert to be used in a court proceeding will be required to prepare a report stating his findings and conclusions. The expert may then be deposed or asked to render a follow-up report to more specifically address certain issues or address new issues. Eventually, the expert will testify in court if the parties are unable to reach an agreement based on the expert's report. If experts are required, their fees will often be the single most expensive part of the divorce process, as they generally charge on an hourly basis and will charge a premium for any time spent in court.

Watch Out!

Be aware that some experts are just hired guns. There is a network of such experts who, for a fee, will testify to virtually any set of facts. The courts are generally aware of who these hired guns are, and often will disregard or minimize the testimony from such individuals. If you have a hired gun on your side, you may have wasted your money. Insist that your lawyer hires only objective experts with strong credentials.

The discovery schedule

Some courts establish a discovery schedule to be followed during the divorce litigation. The schedule provides time limits, for example, to serve and answer interrogatories, take depositions, or render expert opinions. For example, a schedule may provide for the following discovery:

1. Service of interrogatories: 30 days after filing of the answer to the complaint

2. Respond to interrogatories: 30 days after receipt

3. Depositions: Completed within 90 days following receipt of answers to interrogatories

4. Expert evaluations: Completed within 120 days thereafter

5. Completion of all discovery: 180 days from filing of answer to the complaint

Not all states issue formal discovery schedules, but instead have rules and regulations that dictate the type of discovery and time periods involved with each method. In any event, over the course of months rather than years, you should be able to obtain all information necessary to resolve your case or to present it at trial. The hope is that sometime during the discovery period you and your spouse will be satisfied that you have obtained all necessary information and as a result can resolve all issues without the need to involve the court. During discovery, unless one party involves the court as a result of the other's bad faith or failure to cooperate, the court will in large part ignore the case and allow the parties to come to their own resolution. However, if a party does not properly respond to discovery requests, the other party can file a "motion to compel," asking the court for an order that compels compliance within a certain period of time. Often, if the noncompliance is willful, the court will order an award of attorneys' fees in favor of the party who had to seek the court order. Most judges loathe having to become involved in the discovery process and will quickly tire of parties whose noncompliance forces the court to become involved.

If your divorce is relatively simple and uncontested, make an itemized list of the areas that warrant additional information, and ask your lawyer to confine her discovery to those areas. Make a point of telling your lawyer that you do not want the wheel reinvented, but rather, that you want a fair and efficient divorce, and that she is not to over-utilize the discovery process.

In a complicated divorce, discovery can take months to complete, but the process can eventually provide the parties with sufficient information on which to inform themselves about their own position, as well as their spouse's position. From this point, the parties, together with their attorneys, are often able to reach an amicable agreement on the settlement of financial and parental issues. If not, they may discover information that will assist in presenting a stronger case to the court. In the next chapter, we discuss the steps involved in formulating a proposal for settlement and techniques to assist in negotiating a reasonable settlement. And, in the event that settlement negotiations

 Moneysaver

Extensive discovery means an expensive divorce. Use only those techniques that are necessary, and ask your attorney for a discovery roadmap that will illustrate what he hopes to learn and how he will get it. If you believe that you and your spouse can cooperate to resolve most of your issues, discovery may be a wasteful and time-consuming exercise.

are not fruitful, you'll get the scoop on just what is involved in bringing your divorce to court.

Just the facts

- Both spouses may obtain information from the other regarding all issues of the divorce.

- Many states require the automatic filing of an informational document that discloses basic data.

- If one spouse does not fully respond to discovery requests, the other party can ask the court to compel a proper response.

- Most courts will establish a discovery schedule to be followed during the divorce proceeding.

- Although discovery is a valuable tool to be used by a spouse who has insufficient information about the marital assets, it is expensive and should be reserved for situations that warrant its use.

GET THE SCOOP ON...
Negotiating the terms of the divorce ▪ What to
expect if you go to trial ▪ Courtroom tips ▪
Settling out of court ▪ The final settlement
agreement ▪ Modifying the original agreement

The Final Steps Toward Resolution

Chapter 8

Y ou've had the chance to collect and review all the information you need to come to a fair division of your assets. You've decided, more or less, where the children will sleep. It is now time to look at the final process of resolution.

Often you will be able to settle your case with informal resolution techniques and little court involvement. This is always the best, cheapest, and least stressful way to go. You might need help along the way, however. Perhaps it will prove simply impossible to accomplish an amicable resolution. If this is the case, you will need to have a basic knowledge of the court's procedures, which we cover in this chapter.

Moving forward

Typically, you and your attorney, along with your spouse and his or her attorney, can identify all important issues that must be resolved. Those issues must include the care and support of any children, spousal support in some cases, the division of assets, and payment of debt. Once you have identified the relevant issues, you should work with your attorney, if you've retained one, to formulate a proposal for resolution.

The most common method of resolution is simple telephone negotiation. From the first time the two attorneys speak, they should be eyeing an eventual resolution. Of course, in the very early stages, nothing of a binding nature should be offered; however, it's often the case that one attorney will make an informal overture to test the waters—to try to find out what it is your spouse is looking for on each of the pertinent issues. Although there may be practical restraints that prevent the discussion of specific proposals—such as a pending appraisal of a business— the most amicable and successful resolutions often begin very shortly after the initial filing of divorce papers.

A good attorney will ask you to draw up a list of your needs and wants to help guide the negotiation process. Consider this an opportunity to draw up your "wish list," but don't be so unreasonable that your lawyer will lose credibility when approaching the opposing attorney. Decide what is most important to you and create a sub-list of what you consider to be "dealbreakers." It may be that you feel very strongly about staying in the marital home, at least for some specified period of time, because you operate a home business there. But do not stop at creation of the wish list—also formulate a plan for how you will afford to live in the house and how much support or assistance you will need from your spouse, if any, in order to do so. The clearer and more definitive your plan, the better your chances

 Watch Out!

If you wait until all discovery is complete before formulating or discussing a plan for resolution, you and your spouse may have found many small things to argue about and may have lost focus on your ultimate goals. This of course can only hamper your efforts.

Moneysaver

As with all phases of the divorce process, the more work you take upon your-self, the less you will spend in legal fees. You have a better understanding of your needs than your attorney does. Take the initiative in clearly stating your goals for settlement and write them down for your lawyer to use in negotiations.

of achieving your goals. It is much easier to settle an issue for which there is a clear-cut realistic answer. For example, it will be difficult to convince your spouse that you should remain in the house if you have no way of paying at least part of the mortgage. Likewise, if your plan does not include adequate provisions for your spouse, chances are you will not settle.

Polishing and presenting your proposal

Once the discovery process has concluded (see Chapter 7), the time is ripe to try to iron out a final settlement document. While most law-related television shows have at least one episode that depicts a face-to-face angry confrontation between the spouses and their attorneys, the reality is that these are extremely rare. However, if you have a good working relationship with your spouse and if the lawyers involved are not aggressive types, this may be a good time to conduct an informal meeting between you and your spouse, in the presence of your attorneys. The lawyers should conduct the meeting, although each of you should provide input. There should be an agenda set before the meeting that lays out the issues to be discussed and the points of agreement as well as disagreement.

At the meeting, each party must be prepared for give and take or the session will be fruitless. If both sides come to the bargaining table with open minds and a spirit of resolution, you may be able to settle most or all of the significant issues in your divorce. This is the reason for setting an agenda prior to the meeting that outlines the points of agreement as well as

Moneysaver

If both parties to the divorce can meet face-to-face, issues can be settled in less time and with less expense than if you have to pay hourly for a time-consuming game of telephone tag and letter-writing between your respective lawyers.

disagreement. Often when a couple realizes that they have agreed on many important issues, the remaining points of dispute will fall into place as they realize that it does not make sense to go to court on those few matters.

All issues in the divorce can be addressed in a settlement meeting, including the complex areas of custody and property valuations. However, if you find that the lesser issues are getting hung up because of problems negotiating these more important matters, agree to table the big items until a later meeting. Even if you can only agree on some of your divorce issues, you will be better off than if you have to litigate everything.

Negotiating your terms

Negotiating is not just a back-and-forth discussion—it's goal oriented and must be entered into with care and strategy. It is helpful to recognize that there are basic rules to the art of negotiating, and to learn to use them to your own advantage to get what you want from the negotiation process. Here are some things to keep in mind when meeting with your spouse and your spouse's attorney:

- Be firm. Do not waffle or act uncertain.

- Anticipate the other side's questions and points in advance and be prepared with responses.

- Prepare a formal list of your demands and requests beforehand so that everything is covered efficiently.

- Take notes of any important new issues that arise during the negotiations.

Bright Idea

Preparing an agenda beforehand will greatly reduce the time spent in negotiations. Once each topic is discussed and decided, cross it off the list and consider the issue closed. Rehashing topics you've already covered earlier in the
day or at an earlier meeting only wastes time and money.

- Bring copies of all necessary documents or evidence.
- Dress professionally. Doing so lends credibility to your position.
- Make eye contact with everyone present. Breaking eye contact is a sign of dishonesty or a lack of conviction.
- Stay calm. Do not resort to yelling or snapping.
- Do not be defensive.
- Listen carefully and do not interrupt.
- Avoid making decisions on the spot. If the proposal from the other side seems basically reasonable, at least take a "time out" with your lawyer and go to a private place to discuss it before making any agreements.
- Stick to the point—don't let yourself get sidetracked.
- Call for a break if the negotiations get heated. You can't get anything done if you're working in an atmosphere of open hostility. A five-minute break might be enough to let everyone cool down and get back on the negotiating track.
- Be reasonable and keep in mind that your goal is resolution.

When negotiations don't go well

Negotiations bring out difficult issues, and often bitterness and
hurt feelings that have been submerged for years come to the
surface. As a result, the initial meeting may be difficult, particularly if one side attempts to take advantage of the other's obvious emotional state. It is often helpful to anticipate the tensions

and emotions that are likely to arise for you during the session and work through them before the negotiation session, either with the help of a therapist or a close friend. At a minimum, give some serious consideration to how you will feel with your soon-to-be-ex sitting across the table, negotiating as though you were haggling over the price of a cow. Don't let your emotions prevent you from having the meeting, but do be aware of the turmoil you are likely to confront.

If your spouse is the angry or belittling type, the process may not work at all. In any event, there are tactics that might be employed to manipulate you or your lawyer. Some of these often-used manipulative tricks include:

- Attacks on your personality
- Attacks on your appearance
- Attacks on your role in the divorce
- Threats
- Less openly confrontational, but disturbing nonetheless, are such tactics as the "silent treatment"; referring to you in the third-person, rather than directly; or negative body language

Your best bet is to let these efforts pass by unnoticed. The less you respond, the sooner any such game-playing will stop.

The court takes over if your divorce has not been resolved after a certain amount of time (which varies depending on jurisdiction). The court may start to take steps to move it along, including scheduling various conferences. Often a conference (or a series of conferences) will be ordered with a court-appointed mediator, with the costs to be divided between the parties. Such sessions are often helpful to gauge whether you are being reasonable in your settlement demands. However, remember that a court-appointed mediator's job is to get cases resolved so that judges do not have to try them in a full-fledged proceeding, so expect the mediator to lean hard on both sides to compromise. You should only compromise if your lawyer advises you that you are unlikely to do better with a judge, and if you are comfortable with the compromise that is being requested. In any case, the mediator's findings and recommendations should be taken to heart in helping you reformulate your settlement proposal so that it is most likely to attain your goals.

> 66 When we met to negotiate, it was the first time I had seen my ex since he left the house to move in with his much younger girlfriend. He had the bad taste to bring her to the session, although she waited in the lobby. It really threw me off guard. My lawyer had to take me to another room to calm down. 99
>
> —Liz M., divorced for one year, after a successfully negotiated agreement

It is important for you to find out whether a judge will eventually see the mediator's report if you are unsuccessful in resolving your case at this level. If so, you should assume that the judge will not deviate any great degree from the mediator's recommendations, and you should consider carefully whether to accept the mediation's decision rather than proceeding to trial. Keep in mind also that a judge will generally hold unreasonable conduct at the mediation against either party who acts unreasonably, and therefore, if your spouse generally acts like a jerk in the mediation, it is quite likely that the judge will be aware of that fact at trial.

 Watch Out!

Do not file motions against your spouse for violation of a court order or agreement unless you yourself have followed the order or agreement with exactitude. Otherwise, your spouse may well defend the claims against him by pointing out your own violations, in which case the judge is likely to simply give both parties an expensive tongue lashing.

Pretrial hearings

Before the actual trial of your case takes place, you may find yourself in court on other hearings that are shorter and often scheduled on short notice. These are typically special-purpose hearings, which take place after one attorney files papers with the court (generally referred to as "motions"), relative to certain issues in the case. For instance, if your spouse has stopped paying child support, your attorney may have to file a motion to compel the immediate payment of proper support, or if your spouse has consistently ignored court orders for the payment of support, the motion may be framed as a motion for contempt. There may also be a hearing if one party has failed to respond to discovery requests (see Chapter 7) and is thereby hindering your ability to prepare your case for trial, or that an agreed-upon visitation schedule is not being followed (see Chapter 10), or that an agreement for one of the parties to vacate the family home has not been followed.

In any event, these pretrial hearings are generally scheduled on fairly short notice and take less than an hour to resolve once you are before the court. On rare occasions, you may not need to be present; your lawyer alone will handle the proceeding. (When you are present, take note of your surroundings as they will be much the same when you come to the more significant stage of your divorce case: the trial. Some people find it reassuring to have been in a courtroom, even if only as a spectator, before having to participate in a trial themselves.) In any event, while it is useful to be able to go to court prior to trial if your spouse is in violation of some agreed-upon or court-ordered

 Bright Idea

If you are dealing with a spouse who shows a consistent disregard of what the court has ordered—showing up late for visitation, paying support a few days late every month, etc.—keep a log book of these violations and turn it over to your lawyer to use when you go to court on a pretrial proceeding.

requirement, these pretrial hearings are yet another factor in causing delay and legal expense.

Going to trial

Going to trial is always a last resort, and fortunately, very few divorces actually end up with a full-fledged trial. Sometimes, however, there is simply no alternative due to the unreasonableness of one side, or even rarer, of both sides.

No matter how you analyze it, no one wins when a divorce goes all the way to trial. It is an extremely emotional and expensive procedure. It is also highly unlikely that the court will give either spouse everything that spouse wants. Generally speaking, in divorce litigation, neither party is satisfied with the result. In fact, many judges consider it a testament to their rulings if both sides walk away unhappy, the theory being that if neither side is completely happy, then justice must have been served. An odd way of looking at it, perhaps, but not altogether untrue in this context.

What are you getting into?

Understand that while there are laws that govern divorce actions, support calculations, and division of marital assets, a court hearing on a divorce matter sits as an "equity court," meaning that the judge has a great deal more latitude in arriving at a decision than if he or she were presiding over a matter that was in a "court of law." Generally speaking, a court of law deals with matters that are clearly defined by case law or statute. An equity court operates on different principles. While it is bound by general rules and legal statutes, there is much more leeway for the judge who is resolving an equity case. As a result, the judge will be guided in large part by what seems to be fair and equitable to all parties. For example, there is no definitive law that tells the court how to compensate someone who has been married for 12 years, has three children, and owns a house worth $165,000. The judge, based upon experience, opinions, biases, background, and other factors, will make that determination on his or her own, and the court will order you to obey that determination.

As we've already said, a trial can be a very expensive process. It involves the presentation of all relevant evidence, including all the information gathered during the discovery process, testimony taken from all parties involved, and testimony of any expert or lay witnesses who have information pertaining to the case. The simple fact that your case has ended up in a trial attests to the likelihood that it has been aggressively contested, and as a result the time it will take your lawyer to prepare for trial will most likely be measured in days rather than hours. In addition, the trial itself will probably last more than a day, and in very complicated cases, it may last more than a week. In other words, expect your legal fees to skyrocket. And if your case requires that you present expert testimony, you will have the expert witness's fees to pay as well.

As a general rule, courts discourage divorce trials and will only conduct one when no other resolution seems possible. Every opportunity will be given to you at each step of the way to resolve your issues cooperatively with your spouse. If your case actually goes to trial, it is probable that you and your spouse have made multiple unsuccessful attempts to settle. The judge is likely to hold you both equally responsible for the breakdown in settlement negotiations.

If the parties have been able to reach an agreement on some, but not all, issues pertaining to the divorce, a trial or hearing can be held on only those issues that remain to be decided. So, if the husband and wife reached a firm agreement on child custody and visitation, or financial support, but could not agree on division of the assets, no judge will be anxious to unnecessarily litigate the agreed-upon issues, and will probably just hold a hearing on the remaining unresolved issues. However, often one side will abandon the previously agreed-upon position once it is clear that trial is imminent, in which case you will find a judge deciding matters of great importance to you.

Testimony

For most people, the least desirable part of going to trial is the need to appear in person in court and to actually take the witness stand to testify. In addition, you will have to sit through your spouse's testimony, which may be unpleasant to hear. Each side will be cross-examined by the other's attorney. This is often a very confusing and emotional experience, and your spouse's attorney is not necessarily going to be friendly in his or her questioning. Also distressing is that, depending on the issues in your case, neighbors, friends, children, co-workers, and employers may be called upon to testify. It is not unusual for relatives to get involved as well. Most people agree that the worst part of the trial is having to re-live during testimony all of the facts and circumstances that brought about the divorce in the first place. Nonetheless, if you get a subpoena from the court (see Example 1) you'll have no choice but to appear.

At the trial, both sides will be given an opportunity to present all evidence in support of their claims, as well as refute the other's evidence. This experience is likely to be very different from anything you imagine.

If your courtroom experience is limited to watching popular television shows, be prepared for a diametrically different experience that will include frustration and probably boredom. You may feel that the judge

> **❝** A judge is a law student who marks his own examination papers. **❞**
>
> —H. L. Mencken, writer and critic

is not adequately understanding your issues, or that he or she is not giving your lawyer enough time to explain or argue certain points. Unfortunately, the judge is the master of the courtroom, and his or her own personality and judicial temperament will dictate how the proceedings unfold. You may think the judge is a complete jerk—and you may be right. We *told* you to try and settle this thing amicably! Too late now.

Example 1: Sample Copy of
Subpoena to Witnesses

JANE DOE

    Plaintiff

v. Case No._____

JOHN DOE

    Defendant

SUBPOENA TO ATTEND AND TESTIFY

YOU ARE HEREBY COMMANDED TO ATTEND AND GIVE TESTIMONY IN THE ABOVE MATTER on the ___ day of _____, 2005, at 9:00 A.M. You are further commanded to bring with you the following things or documents: _____.

    Failure to appear pursuant to this Subpoena will subject you to penalties, civil damages, and punishment for contempt of court.

Dated: _____

Signed: _____

Name of Party or Attorney

Sealed by the Court: _____

[usually signed and sealed by a clerk of court]

After all the evidence is presented, the judge will make a decision to which both parties will be bound. There is an opportunity to appeal the decision, but as a general rule you cannot appeal if the judge disagreed with your assessments of the facts. Only if the judge misapplied the law can the case be overturned. That doesn't happen often, and most appeals fail. But they do compound the overall expense of the legal proceedings.

Keep in mind also that either side can file an appeal, so even if you are completely happy with the result in the case, if your ex appeals, you will be forced to respond to the appeal and will incur your own costs in connection with that appeal. However, it is not unusual for parties who were unable to resolve their differences prior to trial to be able to do so once they hear what the judge's decision is. Even after the court has entered an order, the parties are free to agree to a different arrangement, provided that the agreement is in writing and then submitted to the court for approval. Except in the rarest of circumstances, a judge will approve any settlement, even one that differs from his rulings in the case.

Credibility is key

Most trials involve "he said, she said" testimony. Just as may have occurred in your marriage, each spouse may have a completely different recollection of the same event or issue. Because the judge wasn't there to witness whatever may have transpired, he or she must assess the testimony, in large part, based on credibility. As in any court proceeding, the credibility of the witnesses becomes a very important, if not the determinative, factor in the ultimate resolution of the case.

When there is a dispute as to the facts, the judge must evaluate who is telling the truth. Both sides will be judged, not with regard to fault, but with regard to honesty and credibility. As a result, how you present yourself to the court is of the utmost importance in a trial. Is your story believable? Is it clear and easy to understand? Are your conclusions and demands fairly obvious or do you need to do a lot of explaining? What do other witnesses think of you and your situation? What do the facts and circumstances suggest? Never underestimate the role that credibility plays in the outcome of a case. Each party's credibility is almost as important to the outcome of the case as the law that governs the case.

Susan's tips for a successful day in court

1. Dress appropriately in a manner consistent with your employment and level of earnings. If you are a churchgoer, dress as you would for church. Otherwise, dress as you would for an important business appointment. Don't be afraid to check with your lawyer on wardrobe choice. You want to project an image of being a stable person who respects the court by dressing appropriately, but this is not a fashion show. Leave expensive or flashy jewelry at home, and keep your make-up to a minimum.

2. Show up on time. Better yet, show up a little early.

3. Do not exhibit anger or vindictiveness toward your spouse or your spouse's lawyer.

4. Keep your emotions in check. Under no circumstances should you display anger, even if your spouse tells a blatant falsehood. Because tears are sometimes unavoidable, keep a tissue or hankie in your pocket and use it discreetly. If you feel you are going to break down, ask your lawyer to request a short break during the court proceedings. Most judges will fully understand and will accommodate the request.

5. Do not make obvious dramatic facial expressions while anyone is speaking in court. Practice stoicism prior to your hearing. It often helps to keep a pad of paper and pen nearby while your spouse is testifying, or his or her lawyer is speaking, so that you can make notes of anything that you believe is untrue or misleading.

6. Do not tug on your lawyer's sleeve. If your lawyer is speaking, or is listening to the other lawyer or a witness speak,

he will need to concentrate on what is being said. Again, write notes and place them near your lawyer to be read when he has the opportunity.

7. Answer questions succinctly. Going into too much detail often makes a witness appear dishonest. On the other hand, do not make your lawyer pull teeth to get information out of you. Witnesses who are too circumspect may come across as withholding information. Answer questions honestly and openly. Remember that you are under oath whenever testifying in a courtroom, and take that oath seriously.

8. Use humor very sparingly and only in the most benign of circumstances. An occasional self-deprecating remark is not a bad idea if it fits the context, but otherwise, this is not a comedy club, and regardless of any propensity you may have to be a comedian, do not audition in the courtroom.

9. Don't try to be charming or cute. It will only come across as obnoxious.

10. If your ex's lawyer bullies you, do not cower, but do not respond in kind either. Respond simply and honestly.

11. Once you have answered a question, assuming you answered it honestly, do not change your answer no matter how many times (or by whom) you are asked the same question. A common tactic of opposing counsel is to ask the same question over and over until you finally give the answer he is looking for.

12. Do not assume a "poor me" impression.

13. Never pander to the judge. While you should look directly at the judge occasionally during your testimony, do not "play" to him or her.

14. Be cautious, but do not be overly nervous. Again, your only job is to testify openly and honestly. You need to think clearly to answer questions correctly.

15. Do not memorize answers. There is nothing less credible than a rehearsed response. Judges have seen and heard many witnesses before you and will be able to pick up on rehearsed performances. Nonetheless, you are strongly encouraged to have at least one extensive "prep" session with your lawyer, during which you should discuss the substance of what will be asked during the proceeding, but do not allow your lawyer to put words in your mouth.

16. Listen carefully to everything that is said, by anyone.

17. If you do not understand a question, regardless of who asks it, request that it be repeated or clarified.

18. Take a moment or two to think before you answer a question. Do not permit yourself to be rushed.

19. Feel free to tell the opposing lawyer that you need to elaborate on a "yes" or "no" response. Many lawyers will demand that you answer a question in a "yes or no" manner. If you make it clear that you need to elaborate in order to make your answer truthful and complete, any judge will permit you leeway in your response.

20. Speak clearly and if you are soft-spoken, make sure you speak into the microphone.

21. Look the lawyer or judge directly in the eye as you answer. This connotes a sense of strength and belief in what you're saying.

22. Create no surprises for your lawyer. You should have fully disclosed all the facts of your case beforehand. Your lawyer cannot perform damage control if you've kept something from him.

23. Use exact words. If your spouse called you every name in the book, tell the court exactly what was said. It comes off as more powerful than "He called me names."

24. Don't answer a question with another question. This comes off as flippant.

25. Never refuse to answer a question. Your lawyer will object if the question is inappropriate, and the judge will rule on the objection. If you are told to answer, then answer to the best of your ability.

Settling out of court

You may have heard the expression "settling on the courthouse steps." Every lawyer knows that there is no better time to get a difficult case resolved than when their clients are "on the courthouse steps," either literally or figuratively. While most courtroom lawyers are highly experienced and actually enjoy what they do, for the layperson, there is nothing quite as dreaded as a day in court. If you feel this way as your court date approaches, take comfort in the fact that your spouse almost surely feels the same way. For that reason, each of you may be willing to compromise on issues that were previously sticking points. It is very common for settlement discussions to intensify in the few weeks before trial, and not at all uncommon for a final resolution to be reached during that time.

In the rarer case that goes to trial, there is still the opportunity to settle during the proceedings, and again, this frequently happens once one or both parties have testified and realize how difficult the questions were that were being asked by the lawyers. One or both spouses may realize that the judge did not seem as sympathetic as had been expected. Never fear that you won't have an opportunity to settle during trial: All judges are anxious for the parties to resolve the case on their own, and if there is any "movement" in settlement negotiations, the court will almost always grant a recess for an hour or even half a day to permit the lawyers to continue to try to hammer out an agreement outside of the courtroom.

The settlement agreement

Whatever your particular scenario is, if the case is settled, the resolution will eventually be reduced to written form, what is

Bright Idea

There is no rule that legal agreements must be written in a manner that only another lawyer can understand. In fact, courts favor documents that are clearly written and easy to understand. Make it clear to your lawyer from the start that you want a "plain English" document.

known as a settlement agreement, a marital settlement agreement, or occasionally a property settlement agreement. (A point of etiquette: If your lawyer uses the outdated term "property settlement agreement" for a document that includes provisions pertaining to the custody and visitation of your children, ask him to remove the word "property" from the title. It will have no bearing on the meaning and enforcement of the document, and it is neither correct nor appropriate to refer to children as property.)

Whatever it's called, the settlement agreement will govern the terms of your relationship with your ex forevermore. So long as the agreement is reached voluntarily, without coercion, duress, or fraud, it will serve as the final resolution of your case. Generally, except in instances where duress or fraud can be shown, the agreement will be binding on the parties. The only exception to this is if minor children are not properly provided for, in which case the court will step in and modify the terms to ensure their proper support. Otherwise, a party who later attempts to upset a signed settlement agreement faces a very high burden indeed to convince the court that it should be overturned.

It is very important that your settlement agreement specifically includes all of the terms and understandings that were agreed upon by you and your spouse, with your lawyers, and that it is as specific as possible. READ your settlement agreement before you sign it. Do not simply assume that your lawyer has covered it all and that if she has read it and approved it, you can safely sign it. You are the one who is ultimately going to have to live by the terms of that agreement, and you must take as much time as needed to review and understand it. Time, of course, sometimes brings changes that no one anticipated. However, your written agreement can anticipate some likely events and as a result, save you from later disputes. Items that can and should be addressed include upward adjustments in child support to account for cost of living increases (although if not included in the agreement, the courts will impose adjustments upon petition by a party, even where an agreement provides otherwise); costs of children's education and who will pay for it, whether it is college, technical school, or private secondary school; effect of a decision to sell the marital home if one person remained in it post-divorce; effect of remarriage of either spouse on any provision in the agreement; summer and holiday visitation schedules; and disability of either spouse.

The more detail, the better

All too often post-divorce conflicts arise that could easily have been avoided if these types of issues had been addressed in the original settlement agreement. For example, if you agree that your house is going to be sold three years from now, you may not wish to pick a broker or set a listing price right now—the housing market may change or that broker may not be in business when you're ready to sell. However, rather than merely agreeing that the house will be sold and the proceeds be divided, you can at least agree that the listing price will be set in accordance with a market analysis done by a specific local broker. And you can establish general rules governing the ultimate selling price—you can specify that it will be no less than, for example, 95 percent of the listing price. These types of specific agreements help avoid later conflicts.

The power of your final resolution

Both parties are bound by the final settlement agreement, or by the court's judgment if there was a trial. If the matter was resolved by agreement, the lawyers will present the agreement to

Example 2: Decree or Judgment of Divorce

JANE DOE

    Plaintiff

v. Case No._____

JOHN DOE

    Defendant

DECREE [or Judgment] OF DIVORCE

This matter having come before the Court on Plaintiff's Complaint for Divorce, and Defendant having filed an Answer thereto, and after presentation of evidence and testimony to support the granting of a divorce on the following grounds: _____,

    It is hereby ORDERED AND DECREED that Plaintiff and Defendant be and hereby are divorced from the bonds of matrimony this ___ day of _____, 2005; and it is further [if applicable] ORDERED, that the parties' Settlement Agreement entered into on the ___ day of _____, 2005, be and hereby is incorporated, but not merged, into this Decree of Divorce, and all the provisions contained therein shall hereby be given the effect of an Order of this Court.

Signed: _____
JUDGE

a judge for approval, who will essentially rubber-stamp it and then "incorporate" it as part of your divorce decree (see Example 2). What this means is that the agreement then becomes, in essence, an order of court. Any failure to comply with the terms of the agreement becomes not only a breach of contract but also a violation of the court's order, subjecting the violating party to sanctions for contempt of court. As such, a written settlement agreement, signed by both parties and incorporated by the court in its decree, has a great deal of force.

Changing times

Times and circumstances do change, and of course you will not be able to anticipate all future events. As a result, there may come a time when you feel you cannot comply with the terms of your agreement or that the terms are no longer fair and equitable. In these instances, your best first step may be for you to discuss the issue with your ex-spouse, either directly or through your attorneys. For example, maybe you have been paying child support or alimony but recently lost your job and feel that the payments should be reduced. Through discussions with your ex-spouse you might be able to resolve the issue by way of a compromise. Your ex may agree to a temporary decrease in payments while you are out of work, and expect catch-up payments once you find employment. Cooperation of this kind is always the best solution.

If despite good faith efforts the two of you cannot come to a consensus to modify the terms of your divorce agreement, you may have to seek a formal modification of the agreement by the court. If that's the case, a significant burden will be placed on you to prove the terms of your divorce should be modified. And filing a motion for modification is not enough to change your settlement. It is important to remember that until and unless the court modifies the agreement, the terms remain in effect and you are absolutely bound by them. So, as with all other phases of the divorce process, it is preferable to come to a privately negotiated

Bright Idea

If you anticipate retiring or working less in coming years, make sure your spousal support obligation that is set out in the agreement provides for modification if you earn less. Otherwise it will be enforced as written. (Note that child support is always modifiable to comport to changed circumstances.)

modified agreement, which can then be presented to the court for approval so as to establish a new court order. This is generally an inexpensive and simple procedure, usually done by way of something called a *consent order*, or an order that is agreed upon by all parties. As with the original divorce agreement, the court will not pass judgment on the terms of your modification, but rather, based upon your representation of fairness, will assume that the modification is fair and that both parties agree to be bound by the terms.

It isn't quite over yet

In this part of the book we have been concerned with providing information on the divorce process itself—but that is really only part of the story. Everyone's divorce is different because everyone approaches divorce from a unique set of circumstances. Some marriages are childless, and when a divorce looms on the horizon the primary concern is simply to equitably divide up assets and liabilities. Other divorcing couples have children, and the issues they must address are extremely important and very different from deciding how to divvy up the retirement accounts. In Part IV we turn to a careful consideration of the issues that underlie divorce and that must be resolved, from custody to the division of property. We turn then to a detailed discussion of the single most important issue that any divorcing parents can possibly address—minimizing the effect of divorce on the children. Finally, we take up the concept of alimony in its several forms.

Just the facts

- A divorce is a negotiation.

- If you and your spouse fail to negotiate an agreement, the court will do it for you.

- Trials are an expensive and emotional way to resolve your divorce, but sometimes they're the only way to get things done.

- Your final settlement agreement has the legal weight of a court order.

- If your circumstances change dramatically after the divorce becomes final you can petition for changes in the settlement through the court, but you will have to meet a very high threshold to get any changes made.

PART IV

Big Issues You Can't Escape

GET THE SCOOP ON...
Physical and legal custody ▪ Evaluating financial
assets ▪ Division of property and debt

Family Values

Chapter 9

U nfortunately, the legalities and practicalities of *getting* divorced sometimes overshadow the most important part of the process: keeping everyone in the family mentally healthy throughout. And of course the most important part of that is to ensure that any children of the marriage feel safe, loved, and wanted throughout the divorce process, and beyond.

The courts and sociologists have a meaningful phrase that has been so often used it has almost lost its importance: *the best interests of the children*. Long before the advent of no-fault laws and other modern trends in divorce, our society recognized that the single most important consideration in any divorce situation should be that the *best interests of the children* are protected.

Unfortunately, the divorcing couple (otherwise known as "Mom" and "Dad"), the lawyers, and the courts all too often lose sight of that laudable goal, and in any event, as the divorce process moves forward—especially in an acrimonious parting—each parent may well have completely different ideas of what their children's "best interests" are.

When advising clients about how to protect their children's best interests, I (Susan) always make a point to tell them one simple truth, and then I constantly repeat it during the divorce process: *Your children's best interests are best served if their parents, not the lawyers or courts, make mutual decisions about what is best for them and how to accomplish those goals.* No one knows your children, their unique personality characteristics, and their needs as well as you and your co-parent do. Now stop and re-read this paragraph again. If you and your co-parent (the person you are in the process of divorcing) are amicable enough to do so, take this book and have him or her read this paragraph. If you're not amicable enough, photocopy this page and send it by mail.

Custody and visitation

Before you and your spouse physically separate, you need a plan for where the children are going to live, both during the separation phase and thereafter. This is all part of the process of making sure your children's best interests are met: They must be made to feel that their lives aren't being turned inside out and upside down.

If there is a family home and one of you is going to remain living in it, at least for the duration of the divorce process, then the children should maintain that residence as their primary home—at least in the early stages of the separation, until they have had time to adjust to the fact that their parents are living separately. When one spouse moves out, it is critical that the family home remain as intact as possible: Do not walk out and carry paintings off the walls, leaving large gaps to serve as daily reminders to the children that their lives have been altered; do not remove large pieces of furniture, for the same reason.

There are a number of other issues relating to the two homes that are very important later in the process. For instance, the move by one parent into a brand new apartment or house,

Watch Out!

If the parents cannot agree on a custody arrangement, the court will intervene on behalf of the children. So it's in your entire family's best interest to work out a plan on your own. You don't want a virtual stranger deciding your and your children's schedules.

with spanking-new furniture and toys, can create problems when the children are intoxicated by the newness of everything and prefer that home to their family home, where the toys and furniture are comfortable, but no longer new.

Keep in mind, again, that if you and your co-parent can act reasonably and come to a meeting of the minds about where your children will spend their time and with whom, the courts will generally defer to you and will allow you to create your own custody situation. And, as with every aspect of the divorce, the more you can work with your spouse and co-parent on these issues, the less money you will be paying lawyers to fight about these issues on your behalf.

Custody is a legal term, and does not really fit the relationship between a parent and child. Your relationship with your child hopefully involves a great deal more than the issues of where that child is living and who is making decisions on his or her behalf. But again, the courts can only address tangible issues: where the child will live, how often she will see Mom and Dad, which school he will go to, etc. It is up to you and your co-parent to fill in the gaps—the nurturing, the support, the love that must be present to enable your child to go through this process with as little hurt as possible.

Custody variations

There are two types of custody: *physical custody* and *legal custody*. Physical custody is a fairly easy term to understand: It refers to where the child will live. Thus, you may hear the terms "shared physical custody" (meaning that the child spends time—maybe equal, maybe not—residing with each parent); or "sole physical custody" (meaning the child lives almost exclusively with one parent).

The term "legal custody" refers to the issue of who will make major decisions for the child concerning his health, education, and welfare, separate and apart from where the child will live. Again, you will hear the terms "joint legal custody" (meaning both parents must communicate and agree about issues pertaining to the child's health, education, and welfare); or "sole legal custody" (meaning that one parent will have unilateral discretion to make such decisions.

Even in situations where one parent has sole physical custody of the children, it is common for divorce decrees to provide that both parents will share "legal custody," thereby providing the noncustodial parent with the ability to contribute to important decisions—whether the child will have religious training, whether he should receive certain nonessential medical tests or treatment, where she will go to summer camp, etc.

> 66 Most parents, when married, will together bend over backwards to accommodate the children. After a divorce, that level of cooperation often disappears. It shouldn't, and it doesn't have to. The interests of the children should remain paramount. 99
>
> —Michael Dolan, Psy.D., marriage and family counselor

As a practical matter, however, even in situations of shared legal custody, it is important to recognize that a custodial parent will make decisions for the children on a daily basis, and it simply may be impractical to consult with the co-parent on every issue. In amicable situations, we highly recommend that the co-parents meet, together with the children if possible, on a weekly or at least bi-weekly basis, solely to discuss issues pertaining to the children's well-being. Do not use these meetings as a platform for arguing about support payments that were late, or whether you should get the treasured collectible figurines when you finally divide your personal property. Use these sessions solely to advance the cause of the *best interests of your children*. Should Zack join the Boy Scouts? Does Taylor show musical talent and should we sign her up for piano lessons? Do we need to get Michael a math tutor? Is Julia's nail-biting a normal pre-adolescent habit, or is it a sign of emotional distress?

Beware the 50/50 tax trap!

The IRS gives tax credits to any parent who has physical custody of a child *more than* 50 percent of the time. In other words, if you and your co-parent split custody 50/50 (which seems most palatable from many viewpoints), you both lose a potential tax credit. So for tax purposes only, in any given year one of you needs to be able to claim that the child spent at least 51 percent of the time at your house. The next year, and every year thereafter until the child reaches 18, you can feel free to negotiate which parent gets the credit. But one of you should.

The optimal situation

If you truly dislike your former spouse (we prefer the term *co-parent*, as you've probably noticed), then grit your teeth, and remember that every minute you spend with him or her discussing these issues is a minute less you will spend with your lawyer, who is billing you for all of those minutes spent discussing Michael's math test results. You may well find that you and your ex can find common ground on the issue of the children's needs that cannot be found anywhere else. If you are loving and genuinely caring parents, and most are, this process may well help you to overcome some of the animosity that surrounds the other issues in your divorce, particularly when you come to realize that none of the other issues is as important as the children's well-being, and that any fighting you do over the ancillary issues is going to adversely affect them.

Bright Idea

Society once reckoned that moms made better parents than dads, and women got custody. Today, judges will try to award principal custody to the parent best able to meet the needs of the children and act in their best interests, regardless of gender. But some judges may be behind the times. The Children's Rights Council can help; see Appendix B for contact information.

While we firmly believe that a shared custody arrangement is the optimal situation, we also recognize that it may not be physically possible. In such cases, it is important to work out a healthy and flexible *visitation* schedule. (We dislike both the terms "custody" and "visitation." Both are terms that are associated with prisons, and the irony of that is worth noting. Using the term "visitation" implies that the noncustodial parent is "visiting" with the children, which is so far from what parenting should be all about that it is a true misnomer. For lack of better terms, however, and in recognition that they are accepted terms in the divorce context, we use them.)

First and foremost, visitation should be as liberal and flexible as possible. The ideal is for the children to see the parent with whom they are not principally living at least several times per week. At the same time, however, children need structure, and it is generally helpful to them to have some sort of schedule so that they know they will be seeing the co-parent on certain days. Depending upon the specific needs of the family members, a visitation schedule can vary from week to week, or it can be etched in stone.

When the judge decides

If a court is making the final decision on a visitation schedule, it will be very specific and must be adhered to by the letter of the court order. It is typical for a court to award the noncustodial parent at least one evening of visitation during the week, and substantial weekend time, which may alternate by the week, or

Watch Out!

Attempting to withhold visitation from a noncustodial spouse, or from the child's grandparents, is a huge mistake. Never attempt to punish your ex or his family by preventing them from seeing the children. The court has given you custody, not supreme power over your ex's parenting rights. Such actions will inevitably hurt your children. Don't do it.

the weekend time may be split up each week. Judges simply do not have the time, resources, or inclination to work out complex schedules of visitation, and therefore you will find that a court award of visitation will generally be bare bones. If you and your co-parent are hostile to each other, you can expect that there will be regular battles over whether the visitation schedule has been adhered to. Such battles invariably lead to stress, tremendous expense if the lawyers become involved, and eventually, frustration.

Note that a court order can always be annulled if both parents eventually can agree on a custody plan.

Economic interests

A difficult area that you and your spouse will need to resolve is the division of your assets and liabilities. After all, disagreement over money issues is one of the most common reasons for the end of a marriage in the first place. As divorce looms, you'll have to think of all sorts of financial hot topics as you consider how to divide your home, property, assets, investments, expenses, and debts.

You may find it hard to be dispassionate about this. After all, financial decisions you once made together with an eye toward future goals are now just dollar figures on a certificate with a symbolic line drawn through the middle of the page. And now that you are splitting up, you're facing questions you never used to worry about—perhaps the most troubling one being: How will you make ends meet after the divorce?

Titles and entitlements

When two people get married, they bring into the marriage a certain number of personal belongings. During the marriage, the couple accumulates more and more belongings as they build their household. Chances are your assets are not all titled the same way—your vehicles may be separately titled, your home is probably jointly titled, and you may well have bank accounts both in your own name and held jointly with your spouse. The title on the property is of little importance: All property, no matter how it is titled, must be accounted for in a divorce—although not all property is equally liable to be split.

Each state is different

Where you live can have a large impact on how a court decides to split your assets. At present, nine states are so-called *community-property* states: Arizona, California, Idaho, Louisiana, Nevada, New Mexico, Texas, Washington, and Wisconsin. They approach the division of assets according to a specific set of rules: Any property owned by the husband and wife prior to the marriage is their personal property, exempt from division. And anything gained during the marriage is shared property and must be divided equally between the two spouses—a 50/50 split, for the most part, right down the line.

The divorce laws in all other states call for *equitable distribution* of marital assets. If you think about the words "equitable distribution," you can understand what the phrase means. The concept is that all marital property (meaning, at a minimum, everything accumulated by either party during the course of the marriage) is subject to division based on the *equities* of the situation. Typical factors that are considered are the length of the marriage, the earning power of each spouse, whether one spouse supported the other through college or graduate school, any disability of a spouse that would preclude employment after the divorce, and whether there are small children at home who mitigate against one spouse's returning to work. In this context, the higher-earning partner is likely to have to part with a greater share of the total marital assets than the lower wage-earner, especially if the one with the higher income has more education and a strong career history that will permit him or her to continue to earn more over the years. In equitable-distribution states, therefore, the automatic presumption that marital assets should be split 50-50, as is the case in community property states, does not exist.

The real difference between the two types of distributions is that there is no automatic formula dictating an equal split in an equitable distribution state, whereas there is in a community-property state. (None of this may apply if you have a valid and enforceable prenuptial agreement. More on that in Chapter 15.) Although states differ on the specific laws governing the division of assets and liabilities, generally, if the asset or liability was acquired while you were married, it must, in some manner, be divided at divorce. It generally does not matter whose name is on the title to the property. Unfortunately, the same holds true for debt—if your spouse ran up a $5,000 credit card bill during your marriage, upon your divorce you still share responsibility with your spouse for some portion of the obligation. Here, the presumption (however wrong it may be) is that any money your spouse spent was for services or items that benefited the marriage, particularly in the case of credit card debt.

If you do not want to be "tagged" with your spouse's debt, you need to be prepared to make a strong case that he or she incurred the debt in such a manner that it clearly should not be considered marital debt. Proof that your wife got cash advances on your jointly held Visa and then blew thousands at the slot machines may—but will not necessarily—be sufficient to overcome the presumption that she incurred marital debt. Evidence that your husband frequented houses of ill repute and then had the bad manners to put the charges on your joint credit card is likely to be accepted as nonmarital debt. On the other hand, the fact that your wife has a shoe habit to equal that of Imelda

Marcos and the charge account bills to prove it is almost surely not going to convince the court that it is not marital debt—believe it or not, those shoe bills are almost certainly going to be considered marital in nature. Never mind the fact that you can't fit into her size 7s.

Ours? Yours? Or mine?

What *exactly* happens to property that belonged to you or your spouse prior to your marriage? Does it get divided as part of your divorce? As we've noted, different states have different answers. Some states divide all property, no matter when it was acquired. But many states exclude premarital property from division, provided that the property was not *co-mingled* during the marriage. For example, you may own a house prior to your marriage. Upon marriage, your spouse moved in, but the house remained solely titled in your name. In many states, upon divorce, the value of the house will not become part of the "marital pie," subject to division. However, any *increase* in its value that occurred during the marriage may be subject to your spouse's claim for a share, as well as any increase in the *equity* in the house, due to the paydown of the mortgage, using joint funds. In addition, your spouse may be entitled to reimbursement for any improvements made to the house during your marriage. And, if that house was sold during the marriage, and the proceeds used to purchase another home that was titled jointly, you have almost certainly lost any claim to the premarital value of the home you owned alone. As a general rule, co-mingled assets are subject to division. This is true regardless of when the asset was originally acquired. The same principle applies to bank accounts—if you bring money into a marriage and place it in a joint bank account it is generally considered to be co-mingled, whereas if you kept the money separate and apart throughout the marriage it is not. But it's extremely tricky to differentiate between what is and what is not exempt when talking about liquid assets like bank accounts. Unless you have

Watch Out!

Try to hide assets from the court, and get caught, and you may find yourself facing a rather serious "omitted asset" penalty. Or, worse yet, perjury charges, depending on the nature of your omission.

a specific agreement on record, like a prenuptial agreement, that specifies that this money is exempt, you may find it very difficult to keep the money from being divided.

In most states, direct gifts and assets obtained by inheritance are exempt from the division of property rule, but here too, if you co-mingle an inheritance or gift, it is no longer exempt. For example, if, while you are married, you inherit $10,000 and use that money as a down payment on a home that you and your wife buy together, you have co-mingled the inheritance with the jointly held asset (the house). Where significant sums of money or assets are acquired prior to the marriage (as is most often seen in second marriages or late-in-life marriages), a prenuptial agreement may be the best way to protect those assets from future division if the marriage fails.

Bringing in the experts

A panoply of financial fears may fill your mind when you think about the end of your marriage. As a general rule, you should not rely solely on your attorney to resolve these financial concerns. Your attorney probably has no specialized financial training, and his financial acumen may be limited to what he has learned "on the job." Your lawyer's job is to act as your advocate, but he or she may well need expert assistance from a financial specialist. The attorney may recommend that an expert be retained for purposes of valuation of the marital estate (especially in cases where one spouse has a business interest that forms a significant part of the total pie). While your attorney probably knows a number of financial specialists whom she has used as experts in divorce cases, you should have a great deal of input in the selection of that expert, or you should do the hiring yourself. In a divorce that has significant money considerations, the financial professional is likely to be as important to your case as the lawyer you choose. You wouldn't let someone else choose your lawyer, nor should you permit your lawyer to act alone in choosing the financial expert. Interview or at least consult with a financial specialist, such as a certified financial planner (CFP), certified public accountant (CPA), or certified divorce financial analyst (CDFA), and find one you are able to communicate with and who seems to have the time and interest in understanding the specifics of your situation. Even if your lawyer has suggestions as to who should act in this role, make sure you meet with the person who will be doing the job.

Appendix B lists organizations that can help guide you toward finding the best financial professionals. Speaking as a financial professional, I (Russell) have a strong personal bias. It's important to seek a financial expert who will work with you strictly on a "fee-only" basis. That is, you want a money expert who'll charge you either a flat fee or an hourly rate. Stay away from financial "experts" who tell you that they charge nothing for their services. They charge you "nothing" because they get commissions from vendors. In the middle of a divorce, the last thing you need is someone steering you toward pricey insurance deals, annuities, and lousy investments. Commissioned financial advisors only look cheap on paper—but in the end, you could wind up paying for advice that isn't at all beneficial.

The court is going to make every effort to be fair—if you exercise basic caution you needn't fear that you'll be left penniless after the divorce (unless, of course, you were penniless during the marriage). In order to reach a fair monetary settlement, you must provide the court with a complete picture of the financial aspects of your marriage. If you omit something of great value, your spouse is "off the hook," and it will take expensive and time-consuming measures to go back to court for an amendment, and often no revisions to the court award are possible.

Watch Out!

Never guess at the value of any asset worth over a thousand dollars. Get specific information on the exact values of all of your assets.

The division problem: A case study

So, how do you go about dividing up your assets? Many couples start by listing their assets with the intention of dividing the assets between them based on what makes sense (who primarily drives the car), and on preference (who really wants Aunt Mabel's antique armoire). Let's look at the list drawn up by a couple we'll call Hal and Laurie.

Hal and Laurie's List of Assets

- House, market value approximately $180,000
- 2005 Toyota Camry, Blue Book value of $27,000
- 2003 Honda Accord, Blue Book value of $12,000
- Home office equipment, $3,000
- Home furnishings, $30,000
- Art collection, $30,000
- Gold coin collection, $10,000
- Wedding crystal set, $2,000
- Jewelry, including wedding and engagement rings, $8,000

Hal was the instrumental party in initiating the divorce and felt somewhat guilty about it. In Hal and Laurie's preliminary agreement, she took the house, the Toyota, the office equipment, the art collection, and the wedding crystal. Hal got everything else. They had their lawyers write it up in a draft agreement. In the beginning, this arrangement was fine, but as Hal saw how well Laurie was taking the split, he started to resent that he had "given her everything." Then Hal did some figuring. When he added up the dollar value of the assets Laurie got, he saw that her "half" of their assets was worth considerably more

Moneysaver

It is important to discuss your plans to divide assets not only with your attorney, but also with an accountant, because tax laws may influence your decisions regarding financial issues in your divorce. Don't wait until after the divorce to call the accountant. He may well have good advice on how best to reap tax benefits or minimize tax consequences.

than his. He stewed over that for a week and half, and then he voiced his objection to his lawyer, who in turn set forth his position in a letter to Laurie's lawyer. Laurie's lawyer responded by asserting that his client also felt cheated. And the two lawyers then turned on the billing clocks. While Hal came out with a little more of the pie than he had originally received, both he and Laurie lost money in the process to the lawyers, who justifiably charged them more in fees for the additional time that was required as a result of Hal's impetuousness in the early stages of the separation.

The point here is that while the monetary value of assets must be taken into consideration, it is vital to recognize that the division of property should not take place when one or both of you are in a state of emotional chaos, guilt, anger, or simply fatigued by the separation itself. Never will it be so important to be dispassionate and rational as when deciding who gets what. While your financial advisor will also start with a list of assets, he or she will be looking at the *values*, not the *types* of assets on that list. And while you might think that the financial advisor's list will look a lot like the one Laurie and Hal put together, you will likely be mistaken. Their list was woefully incomplete. Before you start thinking that you could certainly do better than they did, however, here's a little test for you to take: Close this book now and make a list of the assets you think will need to be divided during your divorce. Take your time about it and be as complete as you can, then come back and check your list against the one that follows to see what you've left out.

Most Often Forgotten Assets

- Life insurance
- Health insurance
- Retirement plans
- Mutual funds
- Stocks and bonds
- Company stock options
- Rental property
- Frequent flier miles
- National Guard and reserve pay
- Military benefits
- Tax return refunds pending
- Benefits other than salary from primary wage-earner's job, such as subsidized cafeteria meals, discounts on product purchases, etc.

Now, when most of us think of the word "asset," we generally think only of our belongings: the house, the car, the furniture. Or we think of things like the savings account, that mutual fund, the money in the checking account. For our hypothetical couple, these were the obvious things to itemize. But there are other valuable, intangible assets, like your spouse's future earning power, that you also need to consider. And the primary wage earner—whether that's you or your spouse—often receives benefits in addition to a paycheck that you may need to consider when dividing up the household assets. Such benefits may include a pension plan, health and life insurance, disability insurance, stock options, vacation pay, and sick pay. These are items that most couples forget to include when they draw up a list of divisible assets.

When considering each spouse's rightful share, the court always takes into consideration the nonwage earner's contributions to the breadwinner's career, but this too is an item that

Watch Out!

Consult your financial and legal experts when making any decisions regarding
selling or transferring assets while your divorce is pending. In a rush to finalize their divorce deal, some couples overlook important tax ramifications that
will only benefit Uncle Sam and may unfairly penalize one spouse.

couples frequently overlook. This can become a major sticking
point in divorce negotiations: The principal wage earner may
resent having to give half of his or her income. The nonwage
earner may fear that his or her contributions—keeping the
house, raising the kids, or just being a willing and presentable
spouse while Mr. or Ms. Wage Earner climbed the corporate
ladder—will go unrecognized and unvalued. But the law generally recognizes these contributions as real and valuable, and as
items that are deserving of recognition in the financial settlement of your divorce. You should therefore consider those
factors in your own efforts to draw up a settlement, and do not
allow yourself to be dissuaded by a spouse who pooh-poohs
their value.

Determining the value of assets

Once you've identified which of your assets are subject to division, the next step is to determine their value. For bank
accounts, mutual funds, stocks, and bonds, the answer may
seem obvious: The dollar amount is clearly printed on a statement. But it isn't nearly that simple. A mutual fund bought in
1985 for $10,000 may now be worth $30,000. However, that
extra $20,000, or much of it, may be subject to capital gains tax
(usually 15 percent). Some mutual funds also carry what is
called a back-end load, meaning you may lose another percentage point or two when you sell. If you're considering the sale of
a mutual fund purchased within the last year, you may be
slapped with a penalty of as much as 5 percent. Figuring the
true value of your investments, as you see, can be tricky.

Bright Idea

If as part of the divorce settlement you wind up with a share of your spouse's 401(k) plan, you are generally well-advised to immediately roll the money over into an individual retirement account. By so doing, you may avoid taxes and maintain tax deferral. This is sticky business and should be discussed with your financial advisor.

Note that financial assets such as stocks and bonds held in a retirement account, such as an IRA or a 401(k), especially if you are in your 50s, are generally not worth as much as a stock, bond, or mutual fund held in a nonretirement account. That's because income taxes will be due on the entire amount once the funds are withdrawn, and funds generally must start being withdrawn at age 70½. An exception is the Roth-IRA: $30,000 in a Roth-IRA is worth not only much more than $30,000 in a brokerage account or regular IRA, it is worth more than $30,000 cash! That's because the money in the Roth-IRA, if left intact, will continue to grow completely tax-free. No taxes will ever need to be paid on it, provided the funds remain in the account until age 59½. And the money can sit in the account for as long as the owner would like.

Your other assets will also have to be assessed, and this can be even trickier. This should be handled through the services of a qualified appraiser, whose assessment of the value of your property can be used in the final settlement agreement.

Let's look at some of the major assets more closely.

Your house

For many couples, the largest single asset they own is their house. The simplest way to divide this asset is to sell the property and divide the proceeds. However, the divorcing couple often doesn't wish to sell—one or the other wants to retain ownership. One way to handle this is to trade the value of the house for another asset. For example, if your house is worth $100,000 (with no mortgage) and you and your spouse also own investment accounts worth $100,000, one can keep the house and the other can keep the bank accounts. There is another alternative—one of you might consider buying out your spouse's share. To do this, you may need to refinance the property.

There are some situations where one partner is permitted to remain in the house even though he or she can't trade for or buy out the other's share. This usually occurs when the divorcing couple has children and the custodial parent wants them to stay in the home that they've always known (or the court dictates this). In such cases, it is not uncommon that the sale and division of the house is postponed—until, say, the children graduate from high school. At that time the house can be sold, and the proceeds of the sale will be divided. If the prospect of waiting that long to divide your assets fills you with dread, then you have every incentive to try to work out an alternative with your spouse, your lawyers, and your financial planners.

If one spouse remains in the house, provisions will have to be made for the payment of the mortgage, property taxes, insurance, repairs, and other household expenses. And be aware that title to the property does not always coincide with potential liability for the mortgage. If, for example, your spouse agrees to buy out your share of the house, you will transfer your ownership interest in the property. But the transfer of ownership will not relieve you of your mortgage obligation. If your name remains on the mortgage you remain legally responsible for its payment, regardless of any agreement you may have reached with your spouse. If your spouse fails to pay the mortgage, the mortgage company will look to you for full payment—and if you fail to

 Moneysaver

Keep in mind that used furniture and other related objects are worth only a fraction of what you paid for them. You are almost always going to be in a better position if you divide such property rather than sell it.

Moneysaver

If you own an expensive home and it has appreciated in value since you bought it, you might want to sell it and split the proceeds before you get divorced. That's because the Taxpayer Relief Act of 1997 usually offers an exclusion of up to $500,000 in realized capital gains for married taxpayers. The amount is half as much for single filers.

make payment, you could get sued. To avoid this, you may want your spouse to refinance the property in order to pay off the joint mortgage and assume a mortgage solely in his or her own name. With refinancing, you assign your ownership interest in the property to your spouse by way of a *quit claim deed*. With this, you legally quit all claims of ownership on the property.

But what if your spouse can't afford to refinance and so can't remove your name from the mortgage? Then you may want your spouse to sign what is known as a *hold harmless and indemnification agreement*. This agreement, which can form a part of your settlement or separation agreement, obligates your spouse to make all payments and states that he or she will reimburse you for any damages that you incur as a result of his or her non-payment. In other words, if your spouse misses a mortgage payment and you get sued or are forced to make the payment, your spouse would be obligated by the indemnification agreement to compensate you for your damages.

While this sounds like a good solution to the problem, beware: It is often unenforceable. After all, it stands to reason that if your spouse truly cannot afford to make the mortgage payments, chances are he or she will also be unable to reimburse you for your damages. Therefore, you'll want to include some additional safeguards in your agreement. You might, for example, require the automatic sale of the house if your spouse misses a mortgage payment. Or you might stipulate that you can take over ownership of the house if your spouse is unable to make the payments. Be aware that you can never take a "credit" for monies paid out in this manner against your child support obligation, unless you have a clearly spelled-out and signed agreement with your ex that you can do so, or unless the court so orders. Generally, a child support obligation cannot be modified except upon such explicit agreement or order, and the fact that you paid out money for another item will not be accepted as an excuse for failing to make—or reducing—child support.

Household property

These assets are usually divided according to practical need as opposed to their specific dollar value. For example, if the children are staying with you and your spouse is moving out, you'll obviously want to keep the children's bedroom furniture and other belongings. On the whole, there are really no rules for dividing this type of property. You can, of course, have everything appraised and then divide it all up according to value, but considering the relatively low value of used furniture and personal property, the expense of an appraisal generally does not make sense.

Automobiles are a good example of property divided according to use. You will generally keep the car that you drive and your spouse will do likewise. However, the values of the cars may differ. If you each keep the car that you drive, but there is a great disparity in their values, you can request that the difference be made up in the form of cash or other property. Likewise, consider whether your spouse is driving a car that is five years newer than yours. Perhaps you should negotiate a slight adjustment in the split of assets to take into consideration that you will be incurring new debt in the form of a car payment in the near future.

 Watch Out!

If the court is asked to evaluate a business and it believes that the records and returns indicate a potential tax fraud or impropriety, it may refer the matter to the Internal Revenue Service for further investigation.

Watch Out!

If you and your spouse cannot come to an agreement about how to divide assets that are not easily valued, the two of you may find yourself paying as much in attorney and related legal fees as the assets are probably worth.

Pensions

Pensions are generally valued by the court as part of jointly owned property, so they are usually judged as "splittable." In splitting a pension plan, you usually have two options: a buyout or a deferred division. In a buyout, the spouse who holds the pension may buy out the present value of the other spouse's share. In the deferred division option, each spouse gets a share of the payment when the plan is paid out according to its normal terms. If you and your spouse cannot agree on how to handle dividing a pension, the court will decide.

Social Security

You may think that you will automatically get half of your spouse's earned Social Security benefits. But this is only true if you are 62 or over, were married to your spouse for at least 10 years before the divorce was finalized, never remarried, and have not accrued Social Security benefits of your own worth at least 50 percent of your spouse's. If your spouse dies after the divorce, you are entitled to receive full death benefits only if you are over the age of 60 (if you are disabled, the minimum age is 50) and you meet the criteria listed above.

Business interest

It is often difficult to value an ownership interest in a business because, in addition to the tangible assets, you must consider goodwill, customer lists, and loyalty—not to mention the company's anticipated revenues. You'll need an expert—known as a forensic accountant—to determine the present value of the business.

One final note: In many small, family-owned businesses, it often happens that only one spouse has controlled all the records. This makes it difficult for the other spouse to establish an accurate sense of the value of the company, and it might be necessary to resort to one or more of the discovery techniques discussed in Chapter 7. If you must appear in court to settle this issue, this is also a time when you may need to call on the services of an expert witness.

Other assets

You may own other assets that are not easily valued; for example, a stamp or coin collection, jewelry, artwork, or other assets of significant value. In these instances, too, you will need to obtain an appraisal in order to fairly divide property. Make sure that your appraiser is someone specifically trained in valuing the specific type of asset; do not use a general appraiser for a highly specialized collection.

Some assets are more easily valued than others. If, for instance, you have frequent flier mileage or season tickets for a team that has gone to the playoffs for the last three years, you might divide them up by use and need. If you like football, you may wish to take the tickets; if your spouse enjoys travel, he or she takes the mileage.

Dividing liabilities

If you have outstanding credit card debt, loans, or other obligations that were incurred while married, these, too, will need to be divided equitably. But, as noted in our discussion of the household mortgage, your divorce agreement won't necessarily relieve you of the responsibility for a debt. For example, you may have a credit card that's solely in your name, but the debt on the card may have been incurred to pay for household goods during the marriage. Divorce law may say that your spouse is responsible for a share of this debt. However, the credit card company generally cannot try to collect the debt from your spouse, because his name isn't on the account. How, in such a case, can you ensure that your spouse pays his fair share? If you and your spouse have sufficient assets, you may simply decide to pay off all marital debt at the time of the divorce. Alternatively, your spouse may agree to "buy out" his portion of the debt.

If you have a joint credit card, you will be liable for payment even if you and your spouse agree that he will be solely responsible for the entire debt as long as your name appears on the account. You can try the hold harmless and indemnification agreement we mentioned in our discussion of mortgages, but as we've seen, this is not always an enforceable solution. And, in any event, the credit card company is not bound by the indemnification agreement between you and your ex.

Just the facts

- Resolving your custody issues is the single most important task facing you and your spouse as you prepare for divorce.

- Shared physical custody requires physical proximity of the divorcing parents and a high willingness to cooperate for the sake of the children.

- The children's interests in custody negotiations are strongly protected by the court, but are always best dealt with by caring parents.

- Different states have different laws regarding the distribution of your assets. Brief yourself.

- Whatever state you reside in, the debts and financial obligations of your marriage are shared even after you divorce, until they have been fully resolved.

Chapter 10

GET THE SCOOP ON...
Working out custody arrangements ▪ Staying
flexible ▪ Child support issues

The Children's Hour

Divorce can be traumatic, especially for children. Even in the most amicable of situations, the kids will feel unstable and worried, at least for a time. They will need your help to get through the process and to grow up as happy, well-adjusted people. The most helpful thing you can do is to ensure that they still feel like they are part of a solid family, albeit a family that occupies two homes. Whether they split their time equally with their parents or whether you work out some other kind of schedule, the children should feel safe, comfortable, and loved in both homes.

Custody arrangements

Generally speaking, bitter custody battles arise for two reasons: You or your ex may want full custody because you truly believe that the other is a lousy parent. Or it may be that one of you reckons that arguing for full custody is a good negotiation ploy. *"You want to see your children? Fine, then you support them and pay for their education. And, oh yeah, throw me the keys to the Lexus, too."* If money is your motivation in asking for full custody, shame on you. Shame on your attorney if he or she assists you in using this tactic. In using your children as pawns, you've just created a lose-lose situation for everyone involved.

If you end up in a custody battle with your ex, expect to be evaluated and re-evaluated during the process. You may be subjected to court-ordered psychological evaluations and possibly joint counseling with the co-parent. You may be asked questions about everything from your sex life to how much beer you drink. You may have a home visit from a court-appointed social worker to see how your household functions. Your lawyer will charge you for hours and hours of document preparation, meetings with you, meetings with your psychologist, and court appearances. You may end up having to pay through the nose for expert witnesses. And the expenses will go on and on, and up and up. We're talking tens of thousands of dollars here, as much as that Lexus, maybe more. And you know what? Unless your ex is truly a horrible parent—really, really, horrible with a history of something like drug usage or pedophilia—the court is very unlikely to give you sole custody. In today's times, the court is most likely to award shared custody of your children.

Worse than the money you'll be throwing to lawyers, that custody battle will scar your children. They will be under constant and tremendous pressure. They will be worried about both of their parents, and they will be worried about themselves. No matter how hard either of you tries, you cannot completely insulate them from the effects of a custody dispute. They will get sucked into the maelstrom of anger and hate, of psychologists and lawyers, and they may suffer emotional wounds that will

---

 Moneysaver

The best way to save money on a custody dispute is not to have one. Avoid the need for costly evaluations by working with your ex to form a workable custody arrangement.

Watch Out!

Before you do or say anything that may alienate your children from your ex, remember that it is the children who will be hurt most by your actions.

never heal. Fortunately, most courts today will refuse to involve the children directly in the process. Rather, there is a dependence by the courts on the expert input of social workers, psychologists, and other professionals as to which parent can best serve the interests and needs of the children.

Your children deserve both parents. That's the way it was meant to be. They need to know it is okay to love both parents. They need time with both parents. And they deserve two parents who, although they may no longer love each other, at least treat each other with respect, if only for their children's benefit. A caveat: We are not talking about a situation in which one parent is abusive, neglectful, or patently unfit. But ask someone else to objectively evaluate your ex if you think he or she falls into one of those categories. Just because Dad cared more about his job than his family does not automatically make him unfit, and is almost surely not the basis for an all-out custody war.

Try mediation first

To avoid custody trials as well as nasty court battles over the division of assets, we strongly suggest that you first try to talk out some reasonable compromises with your spouse. If you fail, you still have a couple of avenues open to you before you march before a judge. One would be to try to find a mediator, a neutral party or parties who can make recommendations regarding both custody and money issues. To make mediation work, you and your spouse must agree beforehand to be guided by the decisions of your mutually chosen mediator(s). This process works best when both people are generally reasonable and objective thinkers. Don't waste your time or money on mediation if you're dealing with someone who has never been able to think rationally.

Here are some people who might make good mediators:

- A professional divorce mediator. Contact the local courthouse for names and numbers.

- Occasionally, collaborative attorneys (more on this in Chapters 5 and 6), although it is rare for attorneys to be willing to participate in this process—not because they are sharks, but because they are governed by certain rules of ethics concerning their obligations to divorcing parties.

- For matters concerning the children, you might want a licensed social worker, a psychologist who practices family relations, a member of the clergy, or perhaps a close friend who knows both of you and your children well, but is objective and neutral.

- For financial matters, such as the proper amount of child support, you might contact a certified financial planner (CFP), a certified divorce financial analyst (CDFA), or a certified public accountant (CPA).

Daily scheduling

Where will the children spend their days? Where will they sleep? These are the biggest custody questions. If it turns out that one spouse is awarded sole physical custody of the children, you will have to develop a visitation plan to ensure that the co-parent has adequate opportunities to be involved in the lives of the children. Many factors—the children's ages, school schedules, activity schedules and interests, as well as the parent's work schedules and living arrangements—must be considered in establishing a reasonable plan.

Visitation is not only an opportunity for the noncustodial parent to spend time with his or her children, and for the children to spend time with that parent, it is also time for the parent with primary physical custody to relax and to get away from the pressures of being a single parent. Whatever schedule you work out should allow for overnight and weekend visitation with

Bright Idea

Each of the children's homes might be given a name other than "Mommy's house" and "Daddy's house." The houses are, after all, home to parents *and* children. We allowed our children to choose the names for our houses, and they came up with "The Cedarwood House" and "The Doe Trail House," reflecting the two street names they are on. It works.

the children to allow for an extended time together. In fact, "visitation" is really an outdated (but still often used) term. Most custodial arrangements today provide for "primary physical custody" to be with one parent, and "partial physical custody" to be with the other. This properly connotes the concept of the children staying with the other parent overnight or longer. "Visitation," on the other hand, is the act of "visiting with" the children and is not really accurate, except in very limited circumstances where a parent truly is only allowed to "visit" with the children, usually in a neutral place or the home of the other parent. This is generally only seen in situations where there is a genuine concern about the children's safety if that parent is allowed to take the children alone.

Our two children spend roughly 50 percent of the time with Dad and 50 percent with Mom. We have no firm schedule. If Susan's trial schedule is intense one week, the kids might spend most of it at Russell's house. If Russell's schedule is tight, the children might spend most of the week at Susan's house. If either of us has travel plans, we let the other parent know well in advance, so that there will be no scheduling glitches. For us, that works. We have dinner together with the children every Tuesday night, and we map out where the kids will spend the rest of the next couple of weeks. We live within blocks of each other, and minutes from both kids' schools. We are also very amicably divorced. We realize that our plan isn't going to work for everyone, but there are certain features of it that we encourage for everyone. In particular, if the two of you can stand to

Moneysaver

The best and cheapest form of day care or babysitting is with a parent. If the two of you can cooperate, you will find that the amount of time your child has to spend in paid day care or with babysitters may be greatly minimized.

spend a limited amount of time together, we strongly believe that the children benefit tremendously from a once-a-week scheduled dinner, during which the conversation is limited to the children, what's happening at school, upcoming plans, etc.

Holidays

In addition to daily or weekly visitation, typically you will want to address the issues of holidays and vacations. If you celebrate Christmas, you and your ex-spouse may both wish to spend that holiday with the children, but they obviously can only be in one place at one time. *Do not*, under any circumstances, put pressure on your children to make the decision about where to spend these important holidays. And no matter how unhappy you may be that the kids aren't with you this year on Thanksgiving, there is no need to share that fact with them. Never underestimate how guilty children can be made to feel by circumstances that are beyond their own control. You don't want them sitting at the Thanksgiving feast—wherever it may be—feeling sad and dejected on your behalf. Commiserate with friends, your parents, anyone else, but never with your children.

It is common for divorced parents to decide to alternate the holidays, and be aware that courts will almost always order that arrangement if the parents cannot agree. For example, if you have the children this year on Thanksgiving, your ex-spouse will have them next year. Or you may decide to divide the days. For example, you have the children on Thanksgiving until 2:00 P.M. and your ex-spouse has them the rest of the day. (Keep in mind that this particular arrangement can be a burden on the children, and may just serve to accentuate that they are leading split lives. Would you really want to have to eat two Thanksgiving feasts in one day? Consider instead splitting up that long weekend—Thursday, the real holiday, with one parent; and then Friday with the other, if this is feasible.)

Courts invariably will order that Mother's Day, logically, will be spent with Mom, and Father's Day with Dad. Ditto for the parents' birthdays—the children should obviously be with the parent who is having a birthday. As for the children's birthdays, we again strongly encourage all parents who are in close enough physical proximity to one another to put aside their differences for that important day, so that both can be with the child, at least at his birthday party, if there is one.

If your children are of school age, you may need to address visitation or day care during school breaks, such as winter and spring recess. If you and your ex-spouse both work, these holidays are often a scheduling problem, but if the noncustodial parent can arrange for time off during these periods, it may serve as a very good time for extended visitation. If the noncustodial parent is unable to schedule time off around the children's vacations, the parent with primary physical custody will most often be responsible for them. Additionally, if both you and your co-parent plan to take a summer vacation, you should schedule summer visitation to coordinate your respective plans. You may agree on a fixed time; for example, the first two weeks of August, or consult one another each year about your respective vacation plans.

 Bright Idea

Visitation schedules should always keep in mind the best interests of your children. If your children are of school age, it might be best to tailor your visitations so they do not interfere with your children's schoolwork or participation in sports or other after-school activities.

Custody complexities

Even if you work out the "perfect" custody arrangement, things have a way of changing. You or your co-parent, or both of you, will likely form other relationships, perhaps involving other children. One of you may be forced to move for economic reasons. As they get older, the children will have different needs for parental involvement. For these reasons, custody arrangements must remain somewhat flexible.

Moving and visitation

Regardless of your divorce and whatever custody arrangements you've come up with, we hope that you and your co-parent can at least remain neighbors. As we've said, we live several blocks from each other, and our children walk or bicycle between their two homes almost every day. It's a good arrangement that permits us to each see our children almost daily. On a more pragmatic note, it is highly convenient when one child suddenly remembers at bedtime that he needs his soccer uniform the next day—and it happens to be at the other parent's house.

Some parents decide to move after a divorce. If the move is more than a few miles away, it naturally will present some special challenges. The children can only be in one school, and so can't hop between cities on a daily basis. So if you live in different cities or states, it effectually relegates the children's time with their noncustodial parent to weekends, holidays, and vacations. This may mean that you'll need to compromise a little more than you'd like—you may have to allow that noncustodial parent some additional time during those breaks from school or work. But that compromise is important. Just because one parent has moved, it should not diminish his or her role as parent. Nor does it reduce the children's need to maintain a good relationship with the noncustodial parent. The two of you will simply have to address the distance factor as best you can.

When one parent lives far away, transportation of the children back and forth between homes will be an issue. When there is a significant expense, such as train or plane fare, or additional time and effort involved, such as a four-hour drive, you and your co-parent will have to decide who should bear the burden of these added costs and this extra effort. In deciding who should bear the costs, you might take into consideration the reasons *behind* the move. For example, if you and your children live in the cold Northeast and after your divorce your ex-spouse decides to move to the warm Southwest simply to soak up the rays and play tennis, you would probably not be inclined, nor generally expected, to share in the costs of transporting the children. But if the move is involuntary—say your spouse has been transferred to an office in another state and must go or lose his or her job, it may be reasonable to treat the transportation costs as a shared expense.

If you have physical custody of your children and your divorce has been less than harmonious, the court may order that you cannot move more than a certain distance (typically 100 miles) from your current home unless good cause is shown. If you want to leave the area, you will need to petition the court for permission to do so. Expect that permission will only be granted for very good reason, such as economic need (no jobs in your current location, and a solid job offer somewhere else, for instance). This is done to ensure continued

> 66 The rules and regulations for the children should be the same in both the mother's and the father's home. And it is not enough to merely have them laid out in conversation— they should be written down. There should be no inconsistencies. 99
>
> —Michael Dolan, Psy.D., marriage and family counselor

visitation of the children with both parents. In the case of a job transfer, you would have to certify that your employer *requires* you to move and you will lose your job and be unable to support yourself if you do not comply. Your ex-spouse may object. But generally, if you are forced to move for economic reasons, the court will permit you to do so. Of course, as part of your move, the court will most likely order a visitation schedule that permits your co-parent as much time as possible with the children.

Visitation disputes

Hopefully, you'll be able to schedule where the children spend their days without any involvement from the court. Sometimes, however, couples cannot accomplish this. Visitation disputes that involve the court tend to occur most frequently in situations where one spouse considers the other to be unfit or incapable of proper and safe visitation with the children, when the noncustodial parent demands more time with the children than the custodial parent believes to be reasonable, or when one parent consistently violates the custody arrangement.

If you believe your spouse should not be entitled to visitation because he or she is unfit and therefore the visitation would be detrimental to the safety and welfare of the children, the court will have to decide the issue in a manner much like that employed in a custody dispute. You will need to first convince the court that you have good cause for concern. For example, if throughout your marriage your spouse watched the children every night for two hours until you got home from work, you will probably not be able to convince the court that he or she should not have liberal and reasonable visitation—after all, you have entrusted the care of the children to your spouse in the past. If, however, your spouse is an alcoholic and drinks while caring for the children, the court will be more likely to consider your objection and may request more extensive testimony and evidence. The court will also require expert testimony on these issues from psychologists or medical personnel, and will evaluate the facts and circumstances in much the same way it would if it were asked to decide custody. As with custody disputes, the expense will be daunting. You should never employ litigation tactics unless you have real concern and evidence of the other parent's unfitness as a parent. In addition, consider whether there are solutions to the problem short of denying any visitation to the other parent. Perhaps you want a court order preventing the other parent from driving a vehicle with the children in it (if she is known to have a drinking and driving problem), or perhaps you want the added precaution of having another responsible adult present—perhaps a trusted grandparent—while the visitation is taking place. These are less severe ways of restricting visitation, while still permitting it to occur; these will be more favorably viewed by the court than a request to outright prevent any visitation from occurring.

As with all other divorce issues involving children, the court is really only interested in what is best for the kids. Unless there are very significant reasons to suggest that visitation should be limited, the court tends to be generous in allowing the noncustodial parent time with the children. It will typically allow visitation during weekends or alternate weekends, on holidays, and even time during the school week if that is not disruptive to the children's schedules. The court tries to establish an alternating schedule whenever possible. It may alternate weekends, holidays, and summer months. What it cannot do is tailor a partial physical custody plan to suit the specific details of your schedule. This being the general rule, try to agree on a plan that best suits your specific needs and schedules without the aid of the court.

But what happens when your ex either refuses or fails to appear for scheduled visitation? Since visitation is considered a right and not an obligation, you cannot force someone to visit his or her children. Visitation disputes can occur when your ex-spouse is chronically late or fails to show up at all. When this happens, you may find yourself constantly arguing over the issue, and you will find it difficult if not impossible to plan anything around the scheduled visitation times because of your ex's unreliability.

To alleviate this problem and to protect the children's best interests, the court may decide to restrict or rescind the right of visitation when the noncustodial parent habitually fails to adhere to a visitation schedule or in some way abuses it. This does not mean that the court will take an action if, on occasion, your ex-spouse arrives or returns the children 30 minutes late. However, if he or she constantly comes late, or cancels, or involves the children in activities that are against their best interests, you may apply to the court requesting that it narrow the scope of visitation.

A visitation dispute may also arise as a result of financial issues. For example, you may have sole custody of the children and your ex may visit on a regular basis but may not pay timely child support. Keep in mind that visitation is viewed as an issue that is independent of financial concerns. Do not retaliate for late or missing support payments by withholding visitation—that only puts *you* in violation of the court's order. Instead, petition the court for assistance in collecting the child support.

Unless there is a very good reason to order otherwise, visitation is normally allowed to be unsupervised. In other words, during his or her allotted time for visitation, your ex and the children are free to go and do whatever they wish. This is almost never a problem. However, in extreme situations, you may feel that your ex-spouse should be restricted in the location or manner of visitation. For example, you may have an infant and your ex-spouse may not really be capable of caring for the baby alone. You may want another adult, such as your co-parent's mother or father, to be present. Or your ex-spouse may be battling a drug or alcohol problem, in which case you may wish to limit the location of the visitation and insist on some supervision. If your circumstances dictate such restrictions, present your concerns to the court.

 Watch Out!

It should not be children's responsibility to make, change, or cancel visitation plans. That is the responsibility of the parents, and the parents alone.

Child support

While visitation is considered a right, child support is an obligation. We would hope that all parents would see the financial support of their children as an obligation, without the need for a court or co-parent to point that out. Keep in mind also that whatever the grounds for your divorce, or how much you hate your former spouse, child support is for the benefit of the kids, not the parent. Do not use child support as a weapon against your ex. You will only hurt your children, and they will come to associate you with being the person who has deprived them of things they need, due to failure to pay support.

As with custody arrangements, child support issues are best dealt with by the co-parents themselves, or, failing that, with the help of a mediator. If the courts must get involved, however, here is what you can expect.

Both parents, regardless of the circumstances, have a responsibility to provide financial support for their children until the children are *emancipated*. Most courts define emancipated as anywhere from the time the child turns 18 and graduates high school (or 21, in some states) until the time the child finishes college or enters the military. The custodial parent, in essence, pays support by paying for the household expenses. For example, if you have primary physical custody, some portion of the food that you buy and the rent or mortgage that you pay represents support for your children. Courts generally have formulas for determining how much of an average household's bills are attributable to the children in the household, and will use these formulas in calculating child support to be paid by the noncustodial parent. The noncustodial parent fulfills his or her end of the financial obligation by making regular child support payments to the custodial parent. As a general rule, the custodial parent is free to spend the child support in any manner necessary for the benefit of the children. It is assumed that the money will be used appropriately. To ensure that the children are adequately supported, and to minimize inconsistencies in the amount of child support awarded from one situation to the next, every state has its own child support guidelines, which are basically mathematical computations of an average family's expenses, based on household income, divided by the number of people in the household. These formulas are extensively relied upon by the courts, especially in situations where there is no common ground between the parents.

For example, many states start with a simple formula: For one child, the noncustodial parent is required to pay 20 percent of his net income as support. For two children, the figure would increase to 25 percent; for three children, 30 percent; for four children, 35 percent; and so forth. However, these formulas are guidelines only, and it is up to your lawyer to show any reasons for deviating from them. Perhaps your ex receives a windfall bonus each year which will not be taken into consideration if the court simply reviews paycheck stubs. Or perhaps one of your children has a disability requiring medical attention and expense, thereby justifying an upward deviation from the guideline figures. But generally, as you earn more money, you pay more support. The better you do, the more money your children should receive. The opposite is not true, however. Upward deviations in the earning power of the parent with primary custody will not lower the paying parent's child support obligation. The general idea is that improvement in the custodial parent's station in life will flow naturally to the child (such as a bigger house or better vacations), but the paying parent nonetheless has an obligation to support the kids to the best of his or her ability. Of course, as with most matters in a divorce, the parties are free to negotiate some other arrangement, and if the well-to-do custodial parent is willing to waive or reduce the paying parent's obligation, that is completely acceptable.

And as many judges have stated, if you cannot afford to support your children, you should not have had them. The fact that the state-imposed guidelines may leave you very little income to support yourself is *not* the concern of the court.

Unless presented with very good reason to do otherwise, the court will ensure that child support is paid in accordance with the guidelines.

One question that frequently presents itself is whether child support to children of an earlier marriage can be decreased when the parent moves on to another relationship, and has more children. The resounding answer is "no," at least in most states. The principle here is again that one should only have as many children as one can afford to support. If you are unable to maintain your child support to your first family when the new children come along, you will find no sympathy from the courts. Again, the idea here is that your first children should not suffer because you have moved on in your life to new relationships, complete with more children. It will be up to you to figure out how to support them all, and the courts will not expect the children from the earlier marriage to sustain a reduction in their lifestyle.

Conversely, however, if you marry into better circumstances, you may well find that your new, elevated standard of living will justify either an increase or decrease in child support, depending on who is the parent with primary custody. A woman with primary physical custody who enters into a second marriage with someone vastly more wealthy may find that her first husband's child support obligation is reduced because of her new circumstances (which permit her to shoulder more of the children's expenses). Or a parent who does not have primary physical custody, who pays child support to the other parent, may get remarried to someone who is very comfortable, with a fully paid-for home and other accoutrements of the good life. He may find himself with an increased child support bill to his first wife, not because his second wife is being expected to pay for those children, but simply because his expenses for his own support have been reduced, thereby leaving more money available for the children of the first marriage.

Child support is intended to cover expenses of children associated with household overhead, necessities such as clothing and food and, to some extent, entertainment and other extracurricular activities. In other words, the "basics" are covered by child support. In addition, the court will generally enter an order that anticipates certain medical costs (both health insurance and expenses that are not covered by insurance), and prorates them between the parents. Day-care expenses, depending on the state, will generally be allocated between the parents as well. As a general rule, the child support guidelines will determine how much support you should pay or receive.

Regardless of your opinion of the level of support it stipulates for you, the court will adhere to the guideline recommendations. But the guidelines are based on typical circumstances and cover a typical family, with typical expenses, so if you can prove that you have exceptional circumstances and that the guidelines should not apply, present that information to the court. Be prepared to make a strong case for why these guidelines should not apply to you. Keep in mind that the guidelines were developed over many years, based on many litigated and nonlitigated cases, and you will have to convince the court that there is something unique about your familial situation. In instances in which the court does not believe that the guidelines should apply, it will base its support calculations on actual spending habits and needs, the standard of living enjoyed by the children and their parents while the marriage was intact, and the current financial status of both parents.

 Moneysaver

The child support guidelines may not be applied to parents who have extremely large incomes, as the percentages would result in extraordinarily high payments, beyond what might be considered necessary and reasonable to cover the expenses of the children. Instead, the courts may look to actual expenses in the context of that particular family's lifestyle.

Bright Idea

No matter how young your children are at the time of your divorce, you may wish to address the issue of college education in your divorce settlement agreement so as to avoid a potential argument many years from now.

Other expenses

The term "child support" is generally intended to cover such items as basic food, clothing, routine medical care, and usual day-to-day expenses. However, as any parent knows, there are a multitude of other costs associated with raising a child: piano lessons, summer camp, athletic dues, proms (and the dresses that go with them!), transportation, etc. Be aware that the courts loathe having to delve into the nitty-gritty of each family's needs and expenses to address these issues. Rather than itemizing each expense and then allocating it to one parent or the other, the courts will generally employ a simply formula—usually based on each parent's income—to determine who pays how much of these extraneous expenses. Because the child support formulas set by the states do not take into consideration the "extras" like summer camp and piano lessons (the theory being that these are privileges enjoyed by some segments of the population, but unavailable to others), you should ask your lawyer to make sure that any support order specifically addresses these extras if you believe they apply to your child's situation. If your children have attended summer camp each year during the marriage, it is not unreasonable for your lawyer to ask the court for an order that includes a specific percentage of that expense to be paid by the other parent, separate and apart from the child support award.

As an equitable principle, both parents typically share to the best of their ability in the costs of raising children. However, there is no formal chart or guideline that dictates the terms of sharing expenses other than child support. You and your ex will need to develop your own plan, depending on your specific facts and circumstances, to ensure that these extraordinary types of expenses are paid. For example, the costs of private school and college are not covered by child support payments. Instead, these are considered extraordinary expenses and are often divided as a ratio of your earnings. But since public schools are available for secondary education, there is no requirement to pay for private school costs. You and your ex will have to mutually agree to send your child to private school and establish your own plan for dividing the costs. If one parent won't agree, the other parent will have an uphill battle trying to convince the court that this is an essential expense that should be shared. (However, if the balky spouse has children from another relationship who *do* attend a private school, the court will be much more likely to order that the children of this marriage also be afforded that privilege.) Moreover, no state currently requires that parents contribute to the cost of children's college education. It is essential for this issue to be addressed in a signed settlement agreement between the parents if you want to have a legally binding and enforceable obligation to assist with college expenses. Keep in mind also that college financial aid offices will expect both parents to contribute to tuition costs, regardless of who has physical or legal custody.

Although you may not know whether you or your ex-spouse will in fact be able to contribute toward a future college education, you may wish to at least resolve the issue in principle. Like other expenses involving children, a general rule of thumb is to divide the expense as a ratio of your earnings to total earnings. Further, if you and your ex are determined to help your child attend college, you may wish to consider establishing a method to save together in order to cover the expenses. Again, however, the courts will generally stay out of these decisions, and it will be up to you and your co-parent to agree upon an acceptable formula and means of saving for these future costs.

Modifying child support payments

More than any other term of your divorce agreement, the amount of child support, over time, requires modification. This is especially true in the case of very young children. As children grow older, the amount of support will generally increase. Inflation alone will require an increase in child support. As a result, you may wish to consider a regular increase in child support consistent with the rate of inflation or other economic indicators; for example, the consumer price index. Or, you may consider a periodic review of child support in consideration of the actual expenses of the children, your income, and your ex-spouse's income. Whatever the case, you may wish to recalculate the guidelines on a periodic basis in order to keep pace. Generally speaking, most courts have an office of domestic relations that will assist people who are seeking to have their child support orders modified. You may find that you do not even need to employ your lawyer's services in the future when you want to have your child support order reviewed, as these offices generally have simple forms that need to be filled out and submitted, after which a relatively routine conference will be scheduled with both parents present, and a decision made solely based on computerized calculations.

Enforcement

If your ex does not pay his or her child support obligations, you have several methods of recourse. For instance, Child Support Enforcement Agencies (CSEA) are established in every state and are usually a part of the State Department of Social Services. These agencies can help enforce child support, help collect back payments, and help locate an absent parent. Your lawyer can put you in touch with the appropriate agency in your state, and you can use that agency's resources to pursue your case. Again, you may not need a lawyer for this process. Failure to pay child support very quickly becomes a criminal matter, which the authorities will address for you. You may need to bring it to their attention if it is an overloaded court system, but once you do, you will probably find that the enforcement action proceeds almost without your involvement.

In order to ensure the payment of child support, it is often the case that you can have your ex-spouse's wages garnished and the money sent to you from his or her paycheck. Many states, as a matter of course, require that child support be directly deducted from paychecks and remitted by the employer directly to the state bureau of collection, which then remits payment to the custodial parent. If child support is not paid, most states have laws that automatically enter a contempt order against your ex-spouse for his or her failure to pay. They also have a wide variety of child support collection mechanisms at your disposal. For instance, Minnesota recently passed a law that suspends the driver's license of any person who has not paid child support for the last three months. It is not uncommon anymore to see the names of so-called "deadbeat" parents posted on county Websites. And many jurisdictions have "sweeps" a couple of times per year, where deadbeats are arrested at their homes or places of employment and taken immediately before a court for a hearing. At such hearings, the nonpaying parent has the choice of either paying up or going to jail. You may occasionally see announcements of "child support amnesty periods," in which a delinquent parent can bring his or her arrearages up to date, and if paid in full within a certain amount of time, no court fines or penalties will be incurred. Clearly, all jurisdictions are taking the child support obligation very, very seriously.

Unlike other applications to the court, your ex-spouse does not really have any good faith defense for not paying support. Even if he or she has become unemployed, the court does not consider this fact to relieve him or her of the basic obligation to support the children. The court may modify the amount of *future* child support payments, but it will only on rare occasion modify money that is past due. The obligation is always on the paying parent to seek a modification of a court order of support if his or her circumstances have changed adversely. If you are in that situation, be proactive. Do not simply stop paying support and then hope you will be able to convince the court later that you were justified in doing so. Instead, seek assistance through the domestic relations office of the court in your area for a temporary reduction in your support obligation, so that you do not find yourself on the wrong side of the law.

If, on the other hand, you are the parent to whom support is paid and you discover after the divorce that the amount ordered is too low, you may file a motion seeking to increase your support payments. But, like all other modification requests, the burden will be on you to prove that there have been changes in your circumstances significant enough to warrant changing the amount of support. Changes in the child's situation (for example, a new medical condition or need for tutoring) may warrant a modification. A loss of your own job may also warrant modification, but only temporarily.

It should be clear by now that the court will place your children's needs well ahead of your own. The court will not seriously entertain arguments claiming that, after the payment of guidelines-calculated support, you do not have enough money to meet expenses. Therefore, if you find that you truly cannot pay support (for example, if you lose your job), you must petition the court for a reduction in child support based on your new financial hardship. Keep in mind that you still have to pay your present level of support until a new court order is established. Do not be deterred by the prospect of having to pay a lawyer for this service. As we noted previously, there are highly experienced offices in most court systems that will walk you

Bright Idea

If you notify the Internal Revenue Service that your ex-spouse is in arrears on child support, and provide proof of that fact, any refund that is due to your ex will be withheld until proof of payment is made.

through the process of paying and receiving child support, or seeking modification or enforcement of an existing support order.

In the end, it is important to understand that neither parent has the right to desert his or her responsibilities with regard to the children, and the courts and social service agencies have become more and more strict in enforcing children's rights. The legal system recognizes that children have needs and rights independent of the preferences of their parents—needs for financial support, for a secure home, and for ongoing contact with both parents throughout their lives. The simple fact that the parents are divorcing does not change these basic rights of children.

Just the facts

- Joint and equal custody is almost always the best arrangement for the children.

- Where there isn't equal custody, the parent with partial physical custody has a right to spend time with the children.

- Both parents, regardless of the circumstances, have a financial responsibility to support their children.

- Most states have laws that will automatically commence an enforcement process against an ex-spouse who fails to pay child support.

GET THE SCOOP ON...
The different types of alimony ■ Taxes and
alimony ■ Keeping your eye on the future

What Will I Live On?

Divorce, as you'll quickly learn if you haven't already, isn't cheap. Especially if you're the spouse with the smaller income, or no income at all, you may find yourself in a state of panic over finances. Rest assured, however, that no one expects you to go it alone. Custom and law dictate that the bigger breadwinner in the marriage should assist the smaller breadwinner, at least for a certain time.

What is alimony?

Let's start this discussion by first getting some terms straight. *Alimony* is the word generally used to describe the amount of money one spouse pays to the other, by court order or by agreement, for support and maintenance. You may hear the terms "maintenance," "spousal support," "rehabilitative alimony," "permanent alimony," "temporary alimony," alimony "pendente lite" (a Latin term meaning "while something is pending"), or some other terms to describe such payments. There are a few fine distinctions among the terms, and not all of them are used in all jurisdictions.

For the sake of convenience and easy reading, we refer here only to alimony and spousal support. The two words are almost interchangeable, except that the term "spousal support" generally refers to payments made while you are still married, but separated. Alimony is a term that refers to payments made generally after the divorce is final. Either way, the payments are designed to help the spouse who is less financially secure pay bills after the divorce. It is typically based on one party's financial needs and the other party's ability to meet those needs. For example, in instances where one spouse was employed and during the marriage the other stayed home with the children, upon divorce it may be impossible for the homemaker to pay the bills without some contribution from the employed spouse. Perhaps one spouse has not worked for a lengthy period of time and lacks the requisite skills to enter the job market. Or it may simply be that one spouse earns significantly less than the other and without spousal support, will not be able to continue to live in the manner to which they both became accustomed during their marriage. In any of these cases, alimony may be warranted.

As with all other aspects of your divorce, the ideal situation is for you and your spouse to agree upon a just and equitable result, perhaps with the assistance of your attorneys, who can advise you—often within a few dollars—of what the court is likely to award in alimony or spousal support. But the issue of alimony, even more than custody or child support, is something parties simply cannot agree upon, and if that is your situation, the court will hold a hearing or trial on the issue and resolve the matter for you. Alimony tends to be a "hot button" in divorce proceedings, and otherwise-reasonable individuals often see red when the word is even used. As the following information should demonstrate, the concept of alimony should not be inflammatory, and even the paying spouse may find an advantage in structuring the divorce settlement in such a way that some amount of alimony is paid, at least for a limited time. Know that the concept of alimony is *not* intended to guarantee that you or your spouse can forever maintain the lifestyle to which you've become accustomed. Rather, its aim is to allow each of you to support yourselves, and perhaps, to get back on your feet. In reality, both you and your spouse may have to *reduce* your standard of living after your divorce, because whatever income the two of you relied on to support a single household will now have to stretch far enough to support two households. In most cases, a spouse who previously did not work outside the home will find that she must obtain employment, at least on a part-time basis. The courts will not use alimony as a permanent subsidy to a nonworking spouse, provided that spouse has the ability to work.

Who deserves the support?

Alimony is generally awarded when two spouses have significant differences in income—or in the ability to *earn* income. Let's imagine a couple where one spouse, an adjunct English professor, earned $30,000 a year, while the other spouse, a dermatologist, earned $280,000 a year. The couple has two children and lives in a luxurious home. While the couple was married—for 20 years—they enjoyed a combined household income of $310,000 per year. But once they got divorced, the income available to each of them dropped—most dramatically, of course, for the professor. On just the professorial income alone, that spouse would likely not have sufficient means to pay for the mortgage and taxes on the family home (assuming she ended up in it), never mind any of the luxuries the couple previously indulged in. There would be a need for support from the more lucratively employed spouse, above and beyond any funds that would be provided for child support.

Years ago, alimony typically was paid by the husband to the wife, for obvious reasons: Men almost uniformly earned more than women, and many women didn't work outside the home. Today, alimony is just as likely to be awarded to the husband as the wife, and courts are keeping abreast of the trends in society that show women are often the higher wage earners in a couple. Today, all that matters is the parties' respective incomes. Which one wears the dress and which one the pants will be irrelevant in either an out-of-court settlement or a court mandate.

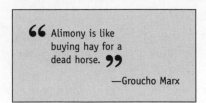

❝ Alimony is like buying hay for a dead horse. **❞**

—Groucho Marx

(We recognize that not all courts have fully entered the 21st century and that there are some judges, particularly in certain regions of the country, who are not yet ready to enter awards of alimony in favor of husbands. It is imperative that you seek your lawyer's guidance about the trend of the courts in your specific community or state. You may need to secure your financial future through a better award of the marital assets, rather than spousal support, if you are in one of the jurisdictions that lags behind the times.)

What determines alimony?

All 50 states have some kind of guidelines to determine spousal support. Compared to the rules that determine child support, however, these guidelines are very loose. If the court decides what alimony will be, the judge, rather than you or a mediator, will have a lot of discretion.

Let's look at the factors that normally go into a decision to grant alimony.

How much is needed to survive?

This is the prime question. Does the recipient have enough to live on? In the case of the adjunct English professor making $30,000 a year with custody of two children and living in a huge house on the hill, there may be a struggle to pay the bills, for sure. Unless the professor has a $10 million trust fund from her parents, she'll be broke in no time. (Of course, if that spouse *does* have a $10 million trust fund, she is very unlikely to get alimony.)

How much can the wealthier spouse afford to pay?

In our example, the dermatologist making $280,000 per year can obviously afford to fork over a check every month. This person isn't exactly living on the edge of poverty, even though he may well claim to be. If, however, the dermatologist were to suffer a disability and not be able to work, the picture would change and the professor might no longer see that check in the mail every month.

How long was the marriage?

Here's another big factor. Some courts in America figure that alimony should last about half the length of the marriage—five years for a couple married 10 years, 10 years for a couple married 20 years, and so on. The longer the marriage, the more the couple's economics were mingled, or the more one partner's career may have been put on the back burner. Be aware, however, that courts are loathe to award spousal support or alimony for extended periods of time, and the trend today is to alter the distribution of marital assets, so that the lesser-earning spouse gets more of the marital pie, rather than to award indefinite alimony. It is not at all uncommon to see alimony awards that continue for only one to five years after the final dissolution of the marriage, regardless of the length of the marriage. The concept apparently endorsed by the courts is that alimony tends to encourage the lesser-earning party to remain dependent on the other—a condition that obviously should not continue in a post-divorce situation. The thinking is that when the receiving spouse understands that she will only be getting those monthly checks for the next 12 months or so, she will be that much more motivated to go out and secure employment.

How high on the hog did you live as a couple?

While it's true that some people survive—and may survive fairly well—on $30,000 a year, the dermatologist married to the professor for 20 years who argues that $30,000 is plenty will be laughed out of court. The couple was living on $310,000 a year.

No judge will expect the professor to take a huge reduction in living standards. On the other hand, if it's clear the couple was jointly living far beyond their means, the court will simply slash their "necessary living expenses," often forcing the sale of the home and other assets, to bring them both into the zone of reality.

Who is at "fault"?

Every state in America now has "no-fault" divorce. In some states, however, a spouse's immoral behavior may be used as an argument for or against alimony. In most states, the judge has considerable discretion, and may be swayed by the moral turpitude of one spouse, particularly where the behavior left the other spouse feeling abandoned and emotionally devastated. A skillful attorney can make a showing that the spouse who suffered indignities due to the other's behavior may well be in need of serious emotional assistance before he or she will be ready to attack the job market, and therefore will need more and longer spousal support. Be aware, however, that the issue of fault—unless it is truly egregious—is rarely considered in alimony battles anymore.

Alimony now, alimony later

Alimony may be affected by the division of your assets and liabilities. For example, if you and your spouse have significant assets and you receive a significant share of those assets, you may require less alimony. Courts far prefer an unequal distribution of marital assets to an award of long-term alimony, and for good reason. There is every reason in the world to favor a clean break of the parties (with the exception of child support, of course). If it is possible to split the marital assets in such a way that the lesser-earning spouse will not need to receive a monthly "paycheck" from her ex, so much the better. For example, if your total "marital estate" (more on that term later) is worth $280,000, of which there is $110,000 in so-called "liquid assets" such as bank accounts and short-term investments, the court may well award the lower-paid spouse most of the $110,000 in those accounts, plus an additional sum in nonliquid assets (such as real estate, antiques, jewelry, retirement accounts), so that that spouse can draw upon the $110,000 in lieu of receiving alimony. Of course, if that spouse has to deplete the liquid assets over the next few years to support herself, and the other spouse is simply awarded nonliquid assets that he does not need to draw against because he earns a good living, then the ultimate result would be unequal treatment for the lesser-earning spouse who draws against her assets during the first few years post-divorce, and then has very little left. With that in mind, the courts will generally award her something more than 50 percent of the total marital estate, so that she will still have something a few years hence. Again, all of this is assuming that the court decides that this situation is preferable to awarding alimony.

Sometimes, a lopsided division of assets works better than alimony, or is best combined with alimony. In many cases, for example, where one spouse expects to re-marry, that spouse will often want to break economic ties with the former spouse and would rather not give or receive alimony. In such cases, the two of you may agree that instead of dividing your assets on a 50-50 basis, you will receive substantially more of the assets, say, 75 percent. The extra 25 percent is intended to provide you with the extra money you need to get on your feet after the divorce that would otherwise be addressed by alimony, but it is paid "up front."

The role of debt in this equation should not be overlooked. If the parties have racked up considerable debt during their marriage, the court may order that most or all of that debt be paid by the higher wage-earner, but in turn, will reduce that party's obligation to pay alimony to the other.

When dividing assets as a form of alimony, it is important, naturally, to consider the value of the assets being divided, and the tax ramifications of such a division. But it may be just as important to consider the *liquidity* of those assets. In other

Moneysaver

Ordinarily, you have to actually be legally divorced to deduct alimony payments from your income taxes. In some cases, however, spousal support can qualify as alimony and become deductible under a separation agreement. You will need to be living in separate homes. Talk to your attorney about this.

words, if you're planning on selling any of the assets in the near future, which you may have to do to pay the bills, you'll want assets that can be readily sold. The family house, for example, is not very liquid. After all, you need a place to live. And even if you're willing to move, selling a house isn't always easy. Ditto if there's a family business.

Long-term CDs, stocks (which may go up or down in price dramatically between now and the time you want to cash out), stock mutual funds (which can also be volatile, and may in addition have a penalty for early withdrawal), and jewelry are all more liquid than real estate, but not entirely liquid. The most liquid assets include cash, short-term CDs, money-market funds, and most bonds and bond mutual funds.

When does alimony start?

You and your spouse can agree to begin alimony or support payments at any time. If you have separated prior to your divorce, you may need to begin the payments before your divorce actually becomes final. In this instance, you and your spouse can determine the necessary amount and frequency of support payments, either by voluntary agreement or through court order. You may also wish to address the ultimate duration of the payments. For example, you may be separated for one year prior to your divorce and agree only that support will be paid for this one-year period. In any event, the paying spouse should consult with a financial professional or lawyer who is well versed in these issues, to ensure that the necessary legalities have been followed to permit him or her to deduct the payment on tax returns.

Bright Idea

If, at the time of your divorce, you and your spouse reach an agreement on the specific term of alimony payments, specify in writing the date that payments commence. You may assume that they started on the date of your final divorce; your spouse may have begun "counting down" from the date of separation. A written stipulation will save you from future conflict.

Voluntary payments made without a court order or legally binding separation agreement are generally *not* deductible. As we'll discuss later, the IRS takes a very keen interest in how money passes hands during and after a divorce. Depending on how you structure your settlement, you may wind up paying more taxes or less. If you can keep your divorce relatively amicable and out of court, an accountant or financial planner can guide you through the process so that Uncle Sam winds up with less money in his pockets, and your family unit—both of you, your children, your pets, and maybe your grandchildren—wind up with more. Even the most bitter of ex-spouses can usually agree that the taxman should get the smallest piece possible.

How long will alimony last?

In rare cases, alimony may be granted for a lifetime. In most, it will be granted for a period of between one and five years. It depends on all of the same factors that determine the amount of monthly alimony, and the judge's view of how long the subsidy will be necessary, or is warranted, given the couple's history. Did he put her through law school? Did she raise two children and drop her career in the process? Is she 30 years old, with a degree in computer engineering, or 60, with a degree in art history?

Unlike child support, there is a presumption that alimony should be nonmodifiable. Your lawyers will want to negotiate this aspect of any agreement, and it is not uncommon for the receiving spouse to want alimony that is nonmodifiable (meaning that the obligation doesn't change even if the paying spouse loses his or her job), and unconditional for a certain number of years (meaning that even if the paying spouse becomes disabled, alimony must continue), and that it will not cease even upon death (meaning that the estate of the payor would become liable). Conversely, the paying spouse may want to negotiate that the alimony *is* modifiable in the event of reduced earnings or disability, and that it will cease upon the death of either party.

Unless otherwise agreed between the parties, alimony typically ends upon the death of the paying spouse, and always ends upon the death of the receiving spouse. It generally also ends upon remarriage of the recipient. Many settlement agreements specify also that alimony will terminate if the recipient sets up housekeeping with an unrelated partner. That's because the court sees that cohabitation as likely producing additional income to support the household, thus decreasing the recipient's need for financial support. And, in the case of the paying spouse, he or she generally balks at the idea of supporting a new boyfriend or girlfriend or spouse.

The recipient may also want to obtain life and/or disability insurance policies to secure the amount of money that is expected to be received in alimony. If the court order or agreement provides that alimony terminates upon the death of the payor, as is the usual case, the party receiving the alimony may purchase term life insurance on the paying party's life to ensure that the full amount of money is received, even if death occurs. Because the recipient has an insurable interest in the person who is the subject of the policy, the recipient will be able to buy

 Bright Idea

Unless otherwise specified, alimony is generally subject to modification by the court only if there is a change of circumstances. Because of this, it's often a good idea, if you're on the receiving end, to negotiate as much money up front as possible. But don't be unreasonable in your demands.

the policy herself, although the paying party (who will be insured) will have to cooperate in medical exams and the application process. Therefore, any court order or settlement agreement which includes alimony should specifically address the paying party's obligation to cooperate in the insurance process.

Alimony is never intended to permit the recipient to abdicate financial responsibility forever. In the case of the adjunct professor, five years after the divorce, she will be expected to be able to support herself, assuming health and/or age are not significant issues.

Taxes and other considerations

The tax consequences of alimony must be taken into account on both sides. We will discuss this in some depth in Chapter 17, but a few preliminary remarks are in order here. Your division of assets and liabilities—provided it is done within a year of your divorce decree—is generally done tax-free. But alimony payments—payments made in accordance with a legally binding separation agreement or court decree—must be included as taxable income on the recipient's federal tax return. The payment of alimony is tax deductible to the giver. This is different from child support, which is neither taxable to the recipient nor tax deductible for the payor. Why? Alimony is basically a substitution for "income" to the person receiving it, and as such, he or she should have to report it to the IRS and include it in taxable income, which of course also means that the person paying it should get to deduct it. But child support shouldn't be considered as income to anyone, simply something that needs to be paid to support the children.

All things considered, it is very important to understand the tax implications when making any alimony agreements, before the agreement is signed. You should always discuss the tax consequences of alimony with your attorney *and* accountant, and specifically address how your payment or receipt influences your tax obligations.

Watch Out!

Because you will have to pay taxes on your alimony you may need a higher award than you might think. And if you are *paying* alimony, it's probably costing you less than you think. It may be very useful to do a full analysis of your finances and how they are tax-affected when considering the amount of alimony.

Enforcement issues

If your alimony payments are not arriving, or are consistently significantly late, you will most likely have to petition the court for relief by way of a motion or other similar application. As with child support, most jurisdictions now have domestic relations offices that will assist you in processing your request for enforcement. At this time you will present the facts of the matter and provide evidence of your ex-spouse's violation. Often, this is very simple: You simply present the court order (your divorce decree) as part of your motion papers and allege that your spouse is not making the requisite payments. However, your spouse will be given the opportunity to respond and either disagree or explain why he or she did not comply with the terms of alimony.

In your spouse's response to you or your lawyer, before he or she addresses the court on the topic, you will most likely receive sob stories about banks forgetting to process deposits, increased car insurance payments, or the unreliable U.S. mail. Courts are generally not receptive to these arguments, but at the same time, tend not to be as harsh on the deadbeat as they are with failure to make child support payments. In contrast to the situation where child support has not been paid, in the case of missed alimony payments, you will probably need to enlist your lawyer's assistance to make sure that the court is sufficiently impressed with your need to receive those payments, and the reasons and basis for the amount originally awarded. All too often, a nonpaying spouse will try to use the enforcement proceeding as a means to have his or her alimony obligation reduced. This should not be allowed to happen, but it may well take a skillful lawyer to make sure it does not.

If the court believes the violation to be willful, it will most likely direct punishment. In cases of willful violation, you may be entitled to have your ex-spouse's wages garnished and the payment sent directly to you from his or her paycheck—this is one way to avoid future violations. Even if the court does not believe the violation to be willful—for example, your ex-spouse may have recently lost his or her job and at least for the present truly does not have the money—he or she may still be found to be in violation of the court order. In these types of cases, the court frequently rules that you are entitled to any arrears due to you, but may, at your ex-spouse's request, modify the terms of future payments to accommodate the change in employment circumstances. And keep in mind that although the court may punish your ex-spouse for failure to comply with the terms of its order of alimony, collection of the money due you may be difficult, if not impossible, if your spouse truly does not have the funds. It is not unusual for arrearages to be ordered to be paid over a period of months—meaning that the $5,000 you are owed in back alimony may end up being paid out over the next 50 months at the rate of $100 per month, which may seem insignificant when received. However, the payments on arrearages are generally ordered to be paid out along with each future payment as it becomes due, and if the paying spouse violates that order, the arrearages typically become payable in a lump sum once again.

 Moneysaver

Legal fees incurred or paid for a divorce are personal in nature and are not generally deductible. However, legal fees incurred or paid for the production or collection of taxable income may be deductible, says the IRS. In other words, you may deduct legal fees if your lawyer is helping you to collect alimony, because alimony is taxable income.

Watch Out!

It is almost never a good idea to make or receive alimony payments in cash: You'll have no record of your payment in the event that you or your spouse make a claim of nonpayment, or in the event of an IRS audit. A cashed check is many times the best form of proof that you have made your payments on time.

In alimony issues, as in any other, remember that unless you tell the court there is a problem, it cannot take action. For example, you may have been ordered to pay alimony and may do so on a timely basis for a while. But later on, if you find you simply cannot meet your obligation—let's say you've been laid off—you *must* inform the court of your change in circumstances. Until the court order is modified, your obligation to pay continues according to the original terms of the divorce, despite the fact that you can no longer make the payments. You cannot assume that the court will modify your obligation retroactively.

So let's say that you're paying alimony and you've missed six months of payments. Your ex-spouse may petition the court for relief—specifically seeking payment of that six months of alimony. You should not assume that the court will deny your ex-spouse's application merely because you were unemployed. In other words, if you want the court to consider your period of unemployment as a reason for not making timely payments, you should be proactive and petition for relief yourself, before your spouse takes you to court. Do not be deterred by the prospect of attorneys' fees. Again, you should avail yourself of the self-help methods that most jurisdictions have implemented in domestic relations offices, which are adjunct to the courthouse. Remember, when it comes to alimony, if you want to modify the terms of the original court order, the burden is on you to affirmatively seek the modification.

When the money stops

Alimony payments may end for a variety of reasons, including your former spouse's inability to pay. Even though you may continue to require support, a court may be hard pressed to order your ex to pay if he or she, in good faith, cannot afford to do so. For example, if your ex-spouse retires or becomes disabled, alimony will most likely cease, unless your settlement agreement or court order says otherwise. These possibilities should always be discussed by you and your attorney when considering alimony and your future lifestyle.

In addition, alimony, like child support or other forms of ongoing support payments, is subject to the review of the court if a significant change of circumstance occurs. Much like any other modification of your divorce agreement, if you can prove to the court that due to a significant change of circumstance such that the present payments are no longer fair, the terms of alimony payments may be changed or modified. You or your ex may make such a request by filing a motion with the court. At that time you will be expected to prove the validity of your request. For example, you will have to prove that your petition to lower or terminate your alimony payments is not due to miserliness on your part, but rather to a change in your circumstances that makes it impossible for you to continue providing support at the levels originally ordered. The fact of a new husband or wife, and perhaps a new house and a baby on the way, will not suffice to convince the court of your need to stop supporting your ex.

Looking toward a new day

As you look forward to your new and newly single life, you will begin to recognize that the legal institution of divorce can only address some of your concerns. You've worked out a custody plan and sorted out a financial division, but there are still a great many important issues left to be addressed. In fact, what you are likely to be discovering is that it is now time to stop looking backward at the marriage that used to be, and to start looking forward—to the life that you are now about to begin. It won't always be easy, but it *can* be an adventure if you take care to avoid some common pitfalls and develop a good, positive attitude.

In upcoming chapters you'll learn some of the classic situations that can make the time during and just after a divorce difficult to get through. But don't become discouraged. Yes, it can be tough to figure out just how to start your new life, but others have managed it successfully and so can you. In the next few chapters you will learn about the changes that everyone faces post-divorce, and how best to handle them. You'll learn to recognize the difficult emotions that can get in your way of moving on with your life, and you'll get the lowdown on where to turn for support and advice in coping with them. Finally, you'll learn some proven tricks for coping with stress, so that you can come through the divorce process stronger, smarter, and better than ever.

Just the facts

- Alimony, or spousal support, is designed to help the party with less economic clout to pay the bills.

- Alimony is typically based on the financial needs of one spouse and ability of the other to help meet those needs.

- Some states have developed formulas to assist you and the court in determining a proper and fair amount of alimony.

- It is extremely important to consider the tax consequences of alimony when structuring a divorce settlement.

- Failure to pay alimony or spousal support may land you back in court, subject to penalties for violation of a court order. Such penalties can include payment of your ex's attorneys fees, court costs, and fines.

The Aftermath: Coping Well

PART V

Surviving the Ordeal

Chapter 12

When you first face the prospect of divorce, you may feel as if you've entered an alternate universe. Much of what you once believed in is gone. You're likely to feel hurt, angry, frustrated, or sad. Some people take to their beds for months, almost literally. Some just can't stop crying. Some carry on stoically—or seem to carry on stoically—as though nothing has happened. It is important to understand that no matter how amicable or welcome the divorce is, you and the rest of the family are nonetheless experiencing a loss, and all losses require coping devices. While each person's reaction may be different, one common denominator when confronting divorce is the need to learn to cope with your reaction. Somehow you must find your way through the quagmire and, hopefully, help your family get through it too. That's what this section of the book is here for—to help you discover ways to not only survive your divorce, but also to come out of it stronger than ever.

> 66 I feel as if I've had three lives...before marriage, during, and after. Recovering from the second was tough. I felt as if I'd failed deeply but discovered gems along the way...supportive friends, unexpected joys. This third life is incredible. I feel so lucky. 99
>
> —Cindy, divorced at 39

When you think about the end of your marriage, especially if it was once a good marriage, and especially if it was a long marriage, you may feel very isolated. How can anyone truly know what you're feeling? Add to that those well-meaning people who tell you that time will heal your wounds, and it's all a bit hard to take. Right at this moment is the time to face up to two truths. One: You are not alone—not only have many others faced the same torment you find yourself in, but you will also find that many people are willing to help. Two: This wound *does* heal. It's a process and takes time, but it turns into a journey of discovery, even "rebirth," for many.

Change and continuity

In your new spouse-less life, it may feel as if everything is now different and will always be so. This is probably one of the most distressing things about facing a life-change this big; you've spent decades building and becoming comfortable with your life, only to have it all transform in what feels like an instant. But you may be surprised to learn that whole portions of your existence do *not* change. Each life is a series of interconnected scenarios, some solidly linked and others standing neatly on their own. Many of those scenarios are constants—they are essentially *you*—and you can turn to them for support when the going gets rough. Your marriage isn't all that you are about. You are many things, and some of your positive constants may include:

- You still have your talents, skills, and personal strengths.
- You still have your friends and family.

- Your children still love you and need you.

- You still have your faith, your religious beliefs, your spiritual grounding.

- You still have your life's work—whether that means your career, your responsibilities in the home, or your connections to the community.

Take a moment right now to make a list of your own positive constants and post it prominently, somewhere where you'll be able to see it when you need a boost.

We're not trying to kid you—of course your life will change. It already has, and it will certainly continue to do so. But it's best to start out by remembering what you have, not by dwelling upon what you may have lost. It will help you stay aware of the fact that there are still healthy things going on in your life, and you'll be able to gain some perspective on the pieces that *will* change.

> 66 Look at what will endure, the things you've personally worked on. 99
>
> —Dr. Paula Bortnichak, family therapist

Who am I now?

It can be very disconcerting to find yourself single, especially if you were married for a long time. Suddenly you're no longer part of a couple. In marriage you were a "we," but now you are an "I." That's an extremely difficult adjustment for some people to make, depending on how fully they merged with their former partner.

During your marriage ceremony, the minister, rabbi, or other officiant may have spoken about how "the two become one." Now that your marriage is over you may feel like half a person—after all, during your marriage you may have done most everything with your partner. You went to the movies together, entertained friends as a couple, and so forth. Perhaps that's the hardest thing to adjust to—you're no longer so-and-so's husband or Mrs. so-and-so.

If you start feeling like less than a whole person, think of the starfish, which grows a new arm whenever it loses one. Keep that image in mind and remember that what's missing will eventually be replaced by something new and perhaps totally unexpected. You will feel whole again. So now is the time to remind yourself of all the things you are. Most important of all, though, is to remember that you are an "I."

If this is difficult to do right now, here's a trick that might help. Take some time to make another list, writing down all of the roles you play in life. Are you a parent, sibling, friend, painter, engineer, sports fan, student, volunteer, organizer, supporter? Every time you make another entry on the list, you are acknowledging the many aspects of your individuality, some of the interconnected scenarios we discussed earlier.

Finding new routines

Another thing you might find tricky to get used to now that you are no longer part of a couple is how it alters your day-to-day activities. Think about the daily routine you followed during your marriage. You probably woke up together, got ready for your day, perhaps went to work. Maybe your husband always made the coffee and it was ready for you when you came downstairs. At the end of the day, you returned home to start dinner for both of you, and grew to expect the sound of your spouse's key in the door. Maybe you did things together in the evenings, like reading or watching TV. You slept together. Over time, this routine became comfortable to you and became part of the background of your life. Now, with your partner gone, your daily routine is entirely different.

But the change doesn't *have* to be negative. Now that you are on your own, you may find that the alteration in your daily routine is a relief, a liberation. You suddenly have the freedom to explore and find what works best for you. The possibilities are limitless. Take a nightly bath. Read in bed. Eat in bed while

Watch Out!

While your routine will likely change, if you have kids, keep their routine as normal as possible. They've had enough upheaval. A dependable home routine gives them stability.

watching the evening news, if that's what suits you. Try in-line skating or knitting or gourmet cooking. Go for a walk around your neighborhood. Make a point of having dinner with a friend you may not had time for while you were married. Watch a television show you've always wanted to see. Join a gym. And think about how wonderful it can be to have total control over your daily routine.

You might find that weekends are particularly hard—many newly divorced people do. This is probably the time you used to spend together, having fun or working on the house or running errands. Worse still, if your ex has visitation with the children over the weekend, you may feel truly alone. Your tendency might be to look at weekends as an endless chasm, but if you indulge this attitude you'll only be emphasizing your feelings of aloneness. Take a cue from how your weekdays are often easier to get through. During the week you have work and a stricter schedule to keep you busy. Use that fact: Instead of just hanging around the house, fill your weekends with activities—the kinds that you like to do. Maybe your former partner wasn't into museums or sporting events. Or maybe he was never willing to let you sleep late. If your co-parent has the children for the weekend, try to take some pleasure time for yourself, since you won't have to do the usual ferrying of children to soccer games and birthday parties. Think of the weekend as a time of opportunity, a blank slate, and go ahead and indulge yourself. Here are some ways you might choose to expand your weekend horizons:

■ **Take a class.** Check with your local adult education center or YMCA/YWCA. The options are endless—from dance classes to cooking classes to professional certifications.

It will give you something to do, and along the way you may discover a whole new talent. At the very least you will meet a few new people who are interested in something you enjoy too.

- **Attend sporting events.** They could be pro ball games or the Little League match-ups at the park—it really doesn't matter which, as long as they are events that you enjoy.

- **Volunteer your time.** Help out at a local hospital's children's wing or serve meals at a local shelter. Helping others can rejuvenate you and reinforce those feelings of self-worth that might need a boost. Also, helping others less fortunate will help put your own situation into better perspective.

- **Take a walk—in the mall, on the beach, or explore neighborhoods in your town.** It's good for your body and your psyche, will get you out and about, and you'll begin to establish a new, single-you identity for the rest of the world.

- **Visit a day spa for a massage, a manicure, a facial, or whatever form of pampering appeals to you.** If money is tight, buy a fragrant candle and some good bubble bath and creams, and indulge yourself at home.

- **Start a big project.** Paint a room, put up wallpaper, install a ceiling fan. You may find it helpful to change the appearance of a room or two, especially your bedroom, if you are staying in the house that was once your marital home.

- **Take up a new hobby.** It's never too late to learn to play tennis, do ceramics, or play a musical instrument. And it can be lots of fun.

- **Read.** Load up on the latest best-sellers at the library and get lost in the adventures.

- **Go for a drive, destination unknown.** Explore...drive down a few roads you've never checked out before.

Bright Idea

Check the community bulletin board column in your local paper. You'll find a wealth of local events listed according to category: lectures, plays, comedy, movies. Circle the events that you may be interested in. It might open up a world of possibilities that you never knew existed.

- **Cultivate a new look.** For many, a new haircut often feels like a new beginning.

- **Plan events for your family.** Picnics, parties, reunions, dinners—all will help your family to bond in an enjoyable way, and you'll be taking advantage of one of those positive constants that define you outside of your marriage.

- **Eat out.** Make a list of new area restaurants you'd like to try, and go to one each weekend. Be adventurous—now is the time to replace those old favorites with a few new hangouts.

- **Get together with friends.** Cook a great meal for friends— or don't cook at all!

- **Visit others.** Take some time to get re-acquainted with old friends you haven't seen in a while.

- **Reconnect with people by e-mail or letters.** Your new status is reason enough to write, but wait until you feel you can do it objectively and without complaining. You want to let people know the news, and you would like their support, but you don't want to become the object of their pity.

Whatever you decide to do, the important thing to realize is that now your plans come first and there is no reason to shelve them for someone else. This can be a very positive realization, and you'll soon learn to relish this new freedom to indulge your own interests.

Role adjustments

If your ex always assumed the majority of the child-rearing, you are probably realizing that you now must find ways to provide

Moneysaver

When it comes to minor home repairs, you might be tempted to hire professional help to take over your ex's old chores. But you may be able to learn to perform these jobs on your own. Check with your local library for a listing of adult-ed courses. Some large home fix-it stores offer free how-to courses.

the kids with a lot more care than you once did. Similarly, if your spouse always handled the finances, you're going to need to learn how to balance the checkbook, pay the bills, and handle the insurance. And if your spouse was the social secretary, now it's you who'll have to keep on top of birth dates and holiday preparations.

When a marriage dissolves it might seem as if your workload has suddenly doubled—and at first it can be frustrating to have to learn a myriad of new skills. But think of it as a challenge. A friend of ours spent six hours trying to assemble a desk that she knew her ex-husband could have put together in one. But she was going to get that desk assembled, and she succeeded—not only in the assembly, but doing so with a feeling of immense satisfaction. Many divorced people find a particular contentment in being able to handle the jobs that used to belong to their ex. They learn that they can do all kinds of things they never thought they could—handle the money, whip up a decent meal, change a blown fuse, or sing a lullaby. Think of this as a lesson in self-sufficiency and a way of adding on to that list of life roles you created.

Social life? What social life?

As you may have noticed already, some of the people in your life are not going to take the news of your divorce very well. It might make them uncomfortable. Your married friends may hesitate to invite you to dinner if they're used to having you as part of a couple. They may measure their words when they speak to you. When called on it, they may say—and it might be genuine—that they didn't want to make you uncomfortable. If you and your spouse were particularly couple-oriented, your old friends may simply not know how to deal with the newly single you.

And it's not just that you're no longer part of a couple. If your divorce was particularly unfriendly, people may wonder if you're still angry or moody or upset. Will you be bashing your ex in front of everyone? Will you bring everybody down? What if they genuinely liked your ex as well as you? If they're not sure how you're handling your divorce, they may just be trying to give you time and space to get your emotions sorted out.

You might be surprised at how people interpret your situation. For instance, if it's common knowledge that your spouse cheated on you, your friends may suddenly find themselves uncomfortable going to the movies with you if infidelity is a small part of the storyline—even if it doesn't bother you in the slightest. Divorce is still a difficult issue for most people to handle, and they may express their problems with the issue by simply avoiding you. And, of course, there are the people you might lose to "the other side." Friends you made through your spouse may stop calling.

It may be difficult to keep from taking all this personally. Try to maintain a common-sense attitude by acknowledging that some people in your old social circle are simply going to go, no matter what you do. But remember, too, that other people will stay. And the good news is that you'll know that the people who stand by you are true friends.

In fact, it's not unusual for a recently divorced person to grow even closer to some friends and family during this time. As your loved ones provide you with their support, send you cards and funny e-mails, and tell you to call them, no matter what time—well, they're showing you just how much they really love and appreciate you. This is very important. You may have taken them for granted when you were all wrapped up in the day-to-day demands of your marriage, but you can value it now. Consider this newfound appreciation of your friends and family as another fringe benefit to your divorce.

Sex and intimacy

Even if you and your partner's sex life hit a slump toward the end of your marriage, it's a little distressing to realize that suddenly even the *option* of regular sex is not there anymore. For many people this is a real blow to their self-esteem. They start to worry about all sorts of things:

- Will anyone else find me attractive?

- Maybe my partner didn't find me satisfactory in bed—will anyone else?

- What will it be like when I'm with someone else?

- The last time I had to take my clothes off in front of a stranger was 20+ years ago—how is that going to feel now that I'm older??

Let's get one thing clear right away: Don't go there—yet! It's a smart idea to put the whole issue of a new relationship out of your mind during the early days of your divorce. It's true that you'll never sleep with your spouse again, and you may miss the romantic moments you used to enjoy together, but it's counterproductive to worry about future relationships while you're still working your way out of the old one. There will be plenty of time for that once the divorce is behind you.

Of course, there is more to the issue of sex than just the love-making part. Your partner's physical presence is gone, and that's often the hardest thing to get used to.

> ❝ Touch is important for survival itself. We're meant to be touched. It's part of our inherent genetic development. ❞
>
> —Elliot Greene, the American Massage Therapy Association

It's proven fact that simple human touch can make an enormous difference in our sense of emotional comfort and even our body's physiology. Touch can tone down the area of our brain that controls the "fight-or-flight" response. It can increase our level of endorphins, the feel-good hormones, while lowering stress hormone levels, all leading to a greater feeling of well-being.

If the touch comes from someone you already have a positive connection with, chances are your bonds with that person will only become stronger and more positive. So if you miss the simple awareness of having someone near, try getting into the habit of hugging friends and family more. But don't confuse this desire for touch with wanting your spouse back—what you're probably lonely for is simple physical intimacy. That will eventually come to you again.

Recognizing and handling stress

As we've mentioned, divorce ranks second—right behind the death of a loved one—as a stressor. For many people, the end of their marriage means that their greatest fears have been realized. They feel betrayed, abandoned, guilty, hurt, rejected, thrown away. You may feel those emotions even if it was a truly mutual decision to split up. Many people are worried about their future and afraid of the prospects of starting over. Some people have to deal with difficult revelations about their spouse. And even if all these negatives are absent, the simple fact that your life is changing so extensively is bound to cause you to feel some stress.

If children are involved, the pressures can go to an entirely different level. You may experience guilt over causing upheaval in their lives, or worry about maintaining continuity and security for them. They may need you more at a time when you feel at your most powerless, and you might feel stress over expenses. The presence of children also introduces differences in stress factors for men and women facing divorce. Although it is traditionally assumed that women have a tougher time with divorce, this is not always so. Since women still most often become custodial parents, men often not only lose the role of husband, but their roles as fathers change dramatically. In addition, men generally are more reluctant to seek and accept help, compounding their difficulties with divorce.

The important thing is not to let stress run—or ruin—your life. And it can indeed cause serious problems. You've read the articles and seen the TV programs—you know what stress does to your physical health. It can cause high blood pressure or heart palpitations. It can lower your immune system, making you more susceptible to colds, flu, viruses, heart disease, even cancer. Your body *does* suffer under extreme or prolonged periods of stress, so it's best to get a handle on it before it destroys your health.

Left unchecked, stress can also escalate into serious emotional disorders, most commonly depression, anxiety, or a mixture of both that can last several months. If your symptoms are severe and have a negative impact on your ability to handle your life's responsibilities, you may want to see a therapist. But usually if you take proper steps the feelings *will* diminish. After a separation or divorce, it's easy to fall into the habit of neglecting your own health and well-being. After all, you have more than enough on your plate—how can you worry about your health too? But ignoring your physical and emotional state is not something you want to allow to continue for long. Although the breakup of your marriage may have hurt you, you don't have to hurt yourself.

Here are some things you can do to stay healthy and keep your stress levels in check:

- **Eat something healthy.** In the earliest and most intense periods of the divorce process, you may gag when any food comes near your mouth. Or you may take the opposite approach, eating anything in sight; and what's in sight most often happens to be junk food. However, in order to maintain optimum health, make sure your food choices include protein, vegetables, fruit—plenty of nutrients. Drink plenty of water to keep from getting dehydrated, and take your vitamins!

- **Exercise.** You've read and heard enough to know that exercise is good for you. It helps keep your energy up, it produces endorphins (the body's feel-good hormone), and at the very least it distracts you from your troubles for a while. It will also help you with your body image, and the sooner you start, the better off you will be when it is time to re-enter the dating scene.

■ **Meditate.** Yoga or other meditation techniques will help teach you to relax. Buy or rent a yoga or meditation video and see what it does for you. Other calming activities: taking a warm bath, reading a great novel, watching a favorite movie again.

■ **Get a massage.** Most doctors and chiropractors are happy to recommend a qualified massage therapist, and your insurance may even cover it if your doctor recommends it as an antidote to stress.

■ **Get your feelings out.** Start a journal in which you can record all of your thoughts. Simply putting your words on paper can provide release of the pressures that cause you stress and help you figure out some of the sticky situations that seem so prevalent in your life now. If you still have a lot of anger toward your ex, write him or her a letter—but don't mail it. Save it, share it with your lawyer or therapist, but don't send it to your ex. This is a therapeutic process to assist you, not something to escalate the tensions.

Take care of yourself and keep your health in check. Do it for yourself. Do it for your children, and do it for your family.

Managing your career

Somewhere in the middle of all this upheaval, you still have to continue to take care of your responsibilities—whether that means running your household, taking care of the kids, holding down a 10-hours-a-day office job, or all three. You need to think clearly enough during your working hours (wherever they may be) that you can stay functional and strong. Newly divorced people who have to work outside the home run into a special set of problems because they are out in public view during a difficult time. It would be unrealistic to advise you to keep the divorce entirely out of your workplace, but you can protect your best interests by establishing a few ground rules for yourself:

- **Don't cry.** The office is not the place for emotional outbursts. If it has to happen, take it to a private area such as a restroom. Or go sit in your car in the parking lot and vent there.

- **Tell your manager about the situation and make it clear that your work will not be affected.** Even if it means working twice as hard, you must make every effort to keep up your usual standards of excellence.

- **Keep it out of the workplace.** Don't allow your divorce schedule to interfere with your work schedule, and don't work on any divorce-related issues from the office. Give your lawyer your home or cell phone number and speak with him or her after work hours or during your lunch break (in a private place). Don't discuss your divorce in the office. Acknowledge it, accept consolations, and move on. Your colleagues do not need to be kept up-to-date on your legal proceedings. And by all means, don't converse or argue with your ex while you're at work. These conversations need to take place in the privacy of your own home.

- **If thoughts about the divorce sneak into your mind, distract yourself.** Lose yourself in the job-related task at hand. If you have the flexibility, take a short, brisk walk to clear your head.

The people in your office are going to be very curious about your situation. Perhaps you've told them directly, they've overheard something at the water cooler, or they've noticed you're not wearing your wedding ring anymore. In some senses, people's response to divorce is similar to the way they respond to a death. Many become uncomfortable. You may have a sense that people are "walking on eggshells" around you, or you may receive a stream of consoling comments from your colleagues. Invariably, there will be those people who want to share their

Watch Out!

While you may have a good support system in your friends at the office, you may also become a target for your competitors. Don't bring your divorce into the office—you don't want anyone taking advantage of your distress to hurt your career or chances for advancement.

own "war stories" with you, on office time. Some people will respond by expressing support, but others may avoid you. As with your friends, some of them may just be uneasy about their own feelings about divorce, while others may be sincerely concerned but want to avoid upsetting you.

Whatever else is going on, it is very important that you take action to make sure you're able to function well at the office. If you're a total wreck, consider taking some time off so that you can straighten yourself out without having to deal with your colleagues or with the problems on your desk. Take a few vacation days if you feel the need to regroup. Do what you must to make yourself stronger, then go back to the office ready to plow into your work. Not only will you be showing your co-workers that you have inner strength, but you'll also be doing something constructive that takes your mind off your troubles.

Happy holidays?

Don't be surprised if you have a particularly rough time during the holidays and on landmark days like your wedding anniversary. All divorced people struggle during such memory-loaded times as birthdays, anniversaries, Valentine's Day, Thanksgiving, Christmas, and Passover. These were important days during your time together. You had traditions, routines, and activities that you shared and enjoyed. It wouldn't be unusual for you to have somewhat of a backslide into a little depression or sadness, especially at the first such holiday without your spouse.

So how *do* you get through, say, the first major holiday after your divorce? In a word, distraction. Fill your days with as much merriment as you can, spending a lot of time with your family and friends. Once again, look for those positive constants—the portions of the holiday that don't change, even without your spouse there. Take the initiative to get together with others, whether you invite them to your place, or let it be known that you wouldn't mind an invitation to theirs. You may enjoy writing and receiving holiday cards, getting the perfect gifts for the kids, enjoying that delicious but fattening holiday meal, and going to religious services. If you don't have close friends or family nearby, consider volunteering, perhaps at a soup kitchen, battered women's shelter, or animal shelter.

Above all, concentrate on the real reason for the season, not on the ways you *used* to celebrate it. Put the focus on what you're celebrating, and remember that you had many holidays before your ex came along in the first place. With a little effort on your part, you can make this first "solo" holiday a good one, and you'll lay the groundwork for many happy ones in the future as well.

Just the facts

- Not everything in your life will change with divorce. You have positive constants in your life that will continue to nourish you, and may even grow in wonderful, surprising ways.

- Your own basic sense of identity will change. You are no longer part of a "we." You are now an "I." If you look, though, you will see that "I" includes many worthwhile, enjoyable roles.

- Your routine will feel different. Finding new ways to fill your free time will have the added benefit of allowing you to indulge in activities you've always wanted to explore.

- Relish your time alone. It will take some getting used to, but eventually you will find that such time is healthy and good for you.

- Holidays are a great time to get involved with other people and meaningful activities.

GET THE SCOOP ON...
The emotional aftermath ▪ Support groups ▪
Church, synagogue, and spiritual resources ▪ Tips
for staying functional

Chapter 13

We All Need Help Sometimes

Even an amicable divorce such as ours is an extremely trying time. That's especially true when there are children involved. But regardless of whether you have children or whether your divorce is amicable, you are likely to experience a wide range of emotions. Denial, anger, depression, guilt, fear, loneliness, hatred—these can all be part of the divorcing person's life. Expect at least some of them and accept them as natural reactions.

In part, time itself will help you to recover from the massive change that seems to have overtaken your life. But there are also tools that can help greatly. In this chapter you'll learn a little bit about these tools and how to best use them so that you can move onward and upward in your life.

Dealing with your emotions

Recovery from the upheaval of divorce is, in many ways, a sort of death—of your love, of the life you led together, and the one you envisioned for the future. At a minimum, it is a loss. Although your healing may progress differently, chances are you will hit each of the stages Elisabeth Kübler-Ross discussed in her book *On Death and Dying*. Let's take a look at several of them. Which stage are you in now?

- **Denial:** "This isn't happening," "She's just in a bad mood," "She doesn't mean what she's saying."

- **Anger:** "How can he do this to me after all I've done for him?" "I hope he gets hit by a truck," "Who does he think he is, ruining my life?"

- **Depression:** "I feel so alone," "I have no future now," "I don't even want to face the day without him."

- **Acceptance:** "We haven't been happy in a long time," "We'll both be happier apart," "Now I have a chance for the future I've always wanted."

These and countless other emotions will filter through your life before the divorce process is over. If you understand these feelings you will have a better chance to work through them and come out not only renewed, but also a more resilient person. Let's take a closer look at some of these emotions and how you can work through them.

Denial

When you first realize your marriage is over, it all may seem like a bad dream. You're on the brink of a cliff and you just know you'll wake up before you slip over the edge; after all, this is much too important to go any other way. This is also a pure case of denial. Think of it as the starting point in your healing process—it's the universal first step to moving on to a new life.

Your symptoms of denial may not be obvious. There are, after all, many different ways denial can manifest itself. Maybe you're keeping your divorce a secret from your friends, perhaps even from your family. Maybe you haven't taken off your wedding ring. Perhaps you still think of yourself as "Mrs." Or maybe both of you are in denial and haven't even stopped sleeping in

Watch Out!

Denial is one of the most common responses to divorce. If this stage just seems to drag on and on, it may be time to seek professional counseling. Ditto for any other emotional stage you seem to be stuck in.

the same bed, even though you've already taken steps to start the legal proceedings. None of these are healthy practices. They keep you emotionally numb, if not in a perpetual state of anger or sadness, and they prevent you from accepting the realities of your life and moving on. Here are some tips on getting yourself through the denial phase:

- Let it out. Talk about your feelings with your support system (see later in this chapter). This will cement the reality and help you deal with your life as it is right now.

- Remove all images of your married life—wedding pictures, rings, gifts. Unless there's a realistic chance of reconciliation, there's no point in letting reminders of your marriage constantly draw you into the past. One exception: Do not remove family photos that include all of you if there are children at home, at least not for now. (Don't throw away photos and other mementoes of your marriage in a bout of anger or depression. Box them up and put them away until you're in a better frame of mind to deal with them. You may decide that you want to keep them or that your children should have them in the future.)

- Get out into the world. Don't isolate yourself. Yes, a horrible thing has happened to you and yes, the world is still there. See it. Experience it. Let other people and nature nurture you through this.

Anger

Anger is a normal part of divorce. In the initial phases, living with anger can be difficult, even overwhelming. You may experience feelings of exasperation, even rage, that are entirely new to you. It's important to recognize that this emotion is not only directed at your spouse, but also at the entire situation. After all, your life has changed in some fundamental ways and it will take some major adjustments to become comfortable with it.

Making decisions while acting out of anger could also negatively affect your divorce proceedings. Taking revenge, for example, could backfire and make the situation worse. And if you have children, you are jeopardizing their well-being as well as your own.

So what do you do when anger rears its ugly head? Channel that negative energy elsewhere and turn it into a positive force. Talk to someone, take a class, pray, go for a vigorous walk, participate in group events, volunteer to help someone who is in worse shape than you, or join a support group. The energy it takes to maintain anger—and it is considerable—can be better directed toward positive activities. Work to improve yourself or to help others. There are many worthwhile causes, and just a small effort to help pull someone else out of a rut can go a long way toward getting you out of yours.

Depression

You may feel empty, cry incessantly, or become frustrated with simple tasks. It's hard to enjoy the things you used to like to do. You may experience physical symptoms such as significant weight loss or gain, or a disruption in your sleeping patterns (sleeping too much or not sleeping enough). Maybe you're feeling fatigued, finding it hard to concentrate, or having a tough time seeing the point in even *trying* anymore.

The experts say that most depression linked to major life-changing events, such as divorce, is time-limited, meaning it normally fades within a short period of time. In the most acute stages, the symptoms of depression can be completely debilitating, but again, they should fade. It's important to keep in mind, however, that what you think of as just the blues could actually be the signs of a real medical problem.

Watch Out!

Over the past few years, herbal remedies for depression have become quite popular, but before you self-medicate with any herbal remedy, make sure you check with your doctor. And never mix an herbal depression remedy with a prescription anti-depressant.

If you have symptoms of depression that seriously affect your well-being or your ability to cope—for instance, if you find it impossible to get out of bed or cannot function at work—talk to your doctor. He or she may be able to tell you whether you are "clinically depressed." If you are, psychotherapy or medication may help. Often, a combination of the two can be very effective. However, take personal responsibility for periodically reassessing your need for medications or therapy—only you will know when you no longer need either or both. Of course, always speak with your doctor before discontinuing any medication.

Guilt

It's amazing how many different ways we can find to feel guilty during a divorce. If you initiated the split, you may feel guilty over the pain you are causing your spouse. If you are on the receiving end of the news, you may fixate on a past argument or mistreatment that you think might have contributed to your spouse's decision to divorce. You may be tempted to dwell on all the things you should or shouldn't have done (and it's only now that it becomes glaringly obvious how many of those there are), but this is counter-productive. You can't change the past.

Why do we blame ourselves? Maybe it's an attempt to push away another emotion. Perhaps it's too frightening to acknowledge the depth of your partner's deviousness. Maybe it's too overwhelming to admit how unhappy you were in your marriage, and you may be angry with yourself for putting up with it for so long. No matter what the cause, guilt is an emotion that can only lead you into negative feelings. And that is not the direction in which you want to head.

With a little objectivity, you can see that a marriage is made up of *two* fallible human beings. The mistakes you've made in your life together—the miscommunications, the impatience, the nagging—are not unforgivable and neither one of you is totally at fault. And if you look at those errors as an opportunity to learn, you are presented with one more chance to turn this painful process into a positive experience.

Fear

Several kinds of fear can arise during this emotionally charged time of divorce:

- You may feel palpable fear based on a real physical possibility (such as running out of money).

- You may feel apprehension about your ability to handle the challenges of day-to-day life on your own.

- You may feel a a persistent, vague alarm that bubbles up unbidden from some deep, primal place in your psyche.

Each fear can seem overwhelming, and yet with a little insight and some effort, each one is beatable.

If you were abused during your marriage, you may fear for your safety, or you may have a genuine fear of your spouse's retribution if you are the one who initiated the divorce process. Fears such as these should be passed on immediately to your lawyer and the police department.

Or maybe you're afraid of being unable to cope with the more practical matters of life. What if the car breaks down? What if your 13-year-old daughter has questions about sex? What if the township informs you they will be taking 20 feet of your front yard to widen your street? Hold on to the thought that, if such things happen, you're not entirely helpless—you can learn how to solve the problem, or call on a trusted friend or relative to help.

Possibly your biggest practical fear is facing the unknown—your post-divorce future. Will you be alone forever? Will anyone ever love you again? You may have a fear of failure, of winding

Watch Out!

Don't ignore threats of physical harm. Change your locks at home, don't walk alone in public, get a dog, or ask the court for a restraining order if necessary.

up homeless or jobless, or of losing your kids. Nearly everybody faces these fears of the unknown at the start of a divorce. Get a handle on these irrational thoughts by talking them out with friends, family—and yourself. You can be your biggest ally. Your future has a great chance of being wonderful.

The most practical way to cope with fears of the future is to start now to envision what you'd like your new future to hold. Think about what you'd like your career to be, imagine a cozy home of your own—and start thinking about how to turn those things into reality. Plan a vacation, if nothing more than a weekend getaway with a friend. Think about new talents or skills you'd like to develop. All these thoughts can get you thinking constructively about the future, and you just might find that your fear has been replaced with a sense of excitement about all the new experiences waiting for you around the corner.

The third kind of fear we are prone to is more subtle. When going through a divorce, small anxieties may accumulate and seem to assume a life of their own. One common cause of these fears is missing the sense of protection your spouse gave you in any of several ways: as a companion in social situations, as a confidante in times of emotional turmoil, as a protector. Any of these thoughts can leave you feeling more vulnerable, and it's important to remember that even if you see yourself as more exposed now, that doesn't necessarily mean you *are*. Fears that arise out of loss are peculiar. Although each one may be legitimate, they can easily build on each other, creating an anxiety that soon turns into a constant companion.

There are practical steps you can take to assuage these kinds of fear, such as making sure your home is secure or taking a course in self-defense. The most helpful tool, though, will be

Bright Idea

Mantras, phrases repeated to oneself to facilitate meditation, are helpful to some people. A phrase such as "I have an incredible life ahead" can keep you in a positive frame of mind. Find one that clicks for you and get in the habit of saying it to yourself regularly.

your awareness that you may be finding a way to place all of your emotions in one bag. Divorce can be bewildering in so many ways, and sometimes our natural sense of survival will funnel the pile of worries into just one emotion so that we can, hopefully, deal with it more easily. Those things you fear may not actually be as scary as they seem. Perhaps they're simply a handy way to express the many negative emotions stirred up by your divorce. If you suspect you may be doing this, take a closer look whenever a fear crops up. Is it really something to be afraid of, or is your unconscious working overtime to pack all of your worries into one easily recognizable emotion?

Find a specific coping mechanism to use when fear comes up. If you feel frightened at home at night, turn on the lights and TV, or perhaps call a friend to chat. If you start to worry about finances, focus on one specific way to bring in more money or reduce expenses, such as taking a part-time job or scaling back on your Christmas buying. Sometimes taking a small affirmative step will empower you and help to eradicate a fear—at least temporarily.

Self-esteem

Chances are that whatever level of confidence you carried through your marriage will be taken down a notch upon its breakup. A sense of rejection or failure is almost a certainty to some extent during divorce, and even the most secure among us will lose some poise when going through this roller coaster of emotion.

So how do you boost a deflated self-esteem? You start accentuating the positive. There are all sorts of ways—one is to sit down and make a list of all of the good qualities you see in yourself. Don't be shy, and don't be modest. (No one else will ever see the list unless you want them to.) Your entries can be general and weighty (I keep my promises, I'm kind to my family, the kids love me) and they can be more specific (I'm a really good tennis player, I completed my taxes on time last year, the dog loves me).

Now make another list: Think about the triumphs in your life, the things you're most proud of accomplishing. And think of what the people who love you say to remind you of your worth. They obviously see the value within you. If you're not ready to really believe in yourself just yet, keep in mind that they certainly do.

Make a positive change or two. Get a new hairstyle. Lose five pounds. Go to bed 30 minutes earlier and then get up and head to the office early. Small positive changes can work wonders in rebuilding your self-esteem.

And don't forget about mantras. Consider adding one to your daily routine. Waking up every morning and having your first thought be "I am a wonderful person" may seem like an insignificant gesture, but it can go a long way in helping you feel good about yourself.

Loneliness

You're not used to the house being so quiet. You're not used to sleeping alone. You miss having someone to hug. You miss hearing your partner's voice. If you remember that we marry for this sense of human connection, it's logical that losing that bond with a partner can leave us feeling lonely.

Make the effort to battle loneliness. Spend more time with your family and friends. Fill up your days with the company of others. Being with other people is a good distraction. And keep in mind that being alone doesn't have to mean being lonely. The other people in your life, whether they are relatives or friends, spend time with you because they enjoy your company. Learn to appreciate what they already do—you!

Above all, don't let simple loneliness drive you immediately into a new relationship. Doing this may be unhealthy, perhaps dangerous, and almost certainly futile. You need to heal and find peace within yourself before you can be part of a new, healthy union—otherwise, you risk repeating whatever mistakes existed in your old relationship. Taking one "broken" piece from an old machine and putting it in a new machine does not help that machine work well. And when the machine involves you, you want to do whatever you can to have it run smoothly and blissfully.

Acceptance

Yes, you're there. It may have seemed as if you would never arrive at this place, but all of those negative emotions are simmering down and awareness is dawning that perhaps your divorce is not such a bad thing after all. Maybe you can acknowledge that your marriage was not what you wanted it to be all along, or just that your future looks a lot brighter than your past. Savor and nurture these thoughts because they are the building blocks of the rest of your life.

Accepting emotional support

The first and most helpful thing you can do while going through the divorce process is to surround yourself with a strong support system. Your family and friends are going to be there for you if you'll give them a chance. This is no time to be a hero. They'll give you a shoulder to cry on or a sympathetic ear to listen as you unload your thoughts, fears, and frustrations. Some of them will be helpful because they've been where you are now, and some will simply provide comfort. They all will be willing to understand that you're going through a big change, and chances are they will not judge you because of it. Divorce has become a common part of everyday life in our culture, and your friends and loved ones know this is quite possibly the roughest time of your life. Consider them your first level of support. Respect their willingness to be there for you and turn to them when you need their help.

Support given by your friends and family can come in many different forms, from providing you with the chance to talk things out, to helping with the kids, to picking up groceries when you're tied up with other things. Those of your friends who have already gone through a divorce can be a valuable resource—even if you may not want advice from them, remember that they've been where you are, and they made it through.

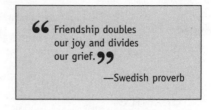

66 Friendship doubles our joy and divides our grief. 99

—Swedish proverb

What about support groups?

Sometimes it helps to talk to relative strangers who have "been there"—or maybe are going through the experience right now, just like you. Even if you have lots of friends and family, sometimes you may not get the support you need, or you might not wish to burden them with your woes.

It might sound maudlin to think about sitting in a group, airing your angers, fears, and frustrations. After all, they're strangers! But look at it this way: You might recognize a bit of your own situation in theirs, and you might learn what worked for that person. At the very least, it's a place to go to vent, and chances are the people there will understand. And sometimes, a room with a group of strangers will be the perfect place for you to air your feelings without having to worry about how they will react.

Support groups are built on the dynamics of the members, so it's in your best interest to find one that includes people who are either similar or sympathetic to you. Support groups often list their meetings in the announcements section of local

Bright Idea

Many recently divorced people report that talking about their feelings with others allows them to put their feelings in proportion. When you have the chance to voice your emotions and fears you may hear how unfounded some of them are, and you will be able to ease them from your mind more quickly.

newspapers. Here are some things to consider as you shop for a good support group:

- Find a special-interest group. It may be a divorce support group for women, for people in their 20s, or for a particular religious faith. Having a common interest serves to cement the members of the group, to start them off on common ground so that they can relate to each other better.

- Look for a workable size. A support group with five to eight members assures that everyone will get a chance to talk.

- If you can, find out about the group's dynamics ahead of time. Perhaps you can sit in on a group before you join. Does one person dominate the conversation? Does everyone speak? How is the feedback? Is the conversation kept on track by a facilitator?

- Is the location convenient for you? What about the meeting schedule? The objective here is to help, not make things more difficult, so you want to join a group that you're likely to attend on a regular basis.

- Has the group been around for a while? This will provide a clue on whether it will continue for the amount of time you need it.

One of the best things about support groups is that while you're getting help for yourself, you're helping others. It may come as a pleasant surprise to find that you can get a great boost by saying the right thing to someone who's having trouble.

There are also a few cautions to keep in mind:

- Support groups are most helpful if the dialogue stays to the point rather than veering off into extraneous areas of members' lives. If you're not getting anything out of the group or you feel uncomfortable, find a new group that will help you.

- Be aware that some people attend meetings with an ulterior motive. A salesperson, for example, may show up at meetings to cultivate new sales prospects.

- Don't date within your group. Other members of a support group are in the transition stage, just as you are. Trying to date too early will only compound the upheaval you're trying to work through.

- Think twice before attending a group that includes people you know—you will lose the benefit of talking things out with objective members who have no preconceived notions of you.

Spiritual resources

Many churches, synagogues, and other spiritual organizations run their own support groups. If you are a person of faith, you may want to connect with a group that emphasizes the role of religion or spirituality in your healing. You could gain a sense of direction, increased insight into coping with hardship, and a feeling of fellowship with others who have the same beliefs you

 Bright Idea

You can now find divorce support groups throughout the world online. Visit www.divorcecare.com, www.divorcehq.com/spprtgroups.html, or www.divorce support.meetup.com to find one near you.

do. Although your intention may be to use religion or spirituality as a tool to help you cope with your divorce, you may find
that this connection becomes one of the benefits derived from
your divorce; many recently divorced people find their faith
grows stronger during this time.

Beyond support groups, your church, synagogue, or other
spiritual affiliation can provide another valuable asset: a new
entry into social life. You may find study groups, singles clubs,
charity groups, and other opportunities to connect with people in
the outside world. Becoming a volunteer, counselor, study group
member, or leader will not only provide social activities and allow
you to meet new people, but also provide you with another way to
become comfortable with your new life as a single.

Church leaders can also be a good resource. Many divorced
people find that talking to their priest, minister, rabbi, or mul-
lah is a great source of support. These spiritual leaders have
counseled people countless times and they've seen hundreds
with the same struggles as yours. They're there to listen and to
give you counsel. In addition, the leader of your spiritual group
may share with you helpful literature, books, tapes, even suggestions for spiritual retreats. They might put you together with
a peer within the church, a knowledgeable "buddy" who's been
through this process before and can attest to the healing power
of faith.

Staying functional

You may be lucky enough to sail through your divorce without
too much adjustment in your routine or your temperament, but
most divorced people feel profound changes. A big key to maintaining equilibrium is getting through the day, taking care of all
the little things that have to be done. If you find yourself putting
your cell phone in the refrigerator, or driving to work when
you're actually on your way to pick up your children, or simply

missing appointments or paying bills late, take heart. This foggy time can be frustrating. But it is *very* normal—and we have some coping tips to help:

- Make lists, even if they're for the everyday things you normally would do. You'd be surprised at how easy it is—with a distracted mind and no sense of time—to forget to do the simplest of things. A list organizes your day for you, and you get a little burst of satisfaction whenever you can cross something off as accomplished.

- Use your calendar. Leave nothing to memory, even if you know you always have your chiropractor appointment at noon on Mondays, Wednesdays, and Fridays. Write it down so you don't forget. Use color coding. Remember to record your kids' activities as well. At this time in your life, you'll need easy-access information, spelled out clearly for you.

- Pay bills as soon as you get them, or note them on your calendar to take care of well before the due date.

- Open your mail right away. Don't let it pile up.

- File important papers right away so that nothing gets lost.

- Keep a spiral notebook by the phone and use it to record any phone messages, phone numbers, or appointments. The information will be handy, and you won't have to look for missing slips of paper.

- Make shopping lists. A simple list will prevent frustrating returns to the store for bread. Even if you've always had the shopping routine pretty well under control, if your mind is not completely focused a list may save you trouble and keep you efficient.

In the end, this foggy period will pass. Until that day comes, all you can do is take steps to keep yourself on top of things so

that you don't feel trapped in the middle of a tornado with all
of your tasks and obligations swirling around you.

Just the facts

- The post-divorce period can be filled with emotion, but
  there are ways to cope and even thrive.

- A good support system will help you immensely—use it!

- Spiritual groups and activities can provide much-needed
  emotional support.

- Maintain your equilibrium with a focus on managing your
  daily life with organizational tools.

Surviving Sticky Situations

PART VI

GET THE SCOOP ON...
Identifying sources of conflict ▪ Domestic
violence issues ▪ What to do if you're being
stalked ▪ Dealing with family disapproval

Chapter 14

Spouse and Family Discord

While some divorces, such as ours, are based on a mutual decision to part ways, that is not always the case. When one person wants a divorce and the other doesn't, the situation is usually unpleasant. When a marriage ends over an affair or other egregious conduct, things can get *very* ugly. In marriages where violence and abusive behavior already exist, danger will abound.

Even in cases where a couple wants to divorce amicably, sometimes extended family members start to vent their negative feelings. Or maybe your family just loves your spouse and they decide to vent their anger at *you*. This chapter takes up the issues of conflict, violence, abuse, and stresses caused by the extended family—what to do to avoid them, deal with them, and move on with your life, safely and happily.

Conflict resolution

The first step in diminishing conflict, simple as it sounds, is to zero in on the exact source of the

283

conflict. Let's say, for instance, that you're angry with your spouse because he or she will not agree to a level of child support or alimony that you deem fair, forcing you to court. Is that all you're angry about? Or are you perhaps "loading on" other issues: Your spouse was always controlling your actions, for example, or monopolized access to the household finances. Twenty-five years of marital resentment may be at play in your situation. Or are you allowing your own psychological "garbage" from childhood to cloud your vision? By letting your anger overcome your good sense, you can no longer keep straight in your mind the actual issue(s) you're trying to resolve (in this case, setting the proper level of child support). Instead, you focus on other issues, which just intensifies your emotional distress and—ultimately—sets the stage for a divorce battleground.

Get to the core

If you strip away your own emotions from the facts of the conflict, you might see a way to address your spouse's point of view. Of course, you must make certain you fully understand that point of view. An essential first step in conflict resolution is to ask questions. Know exactly what your spouse is thinking and what his or her goals are before you start making your own demands.

Work for peace

All successful negotiators—and yes, divorce is a negotiation—think "win-win" rather than "I win-you lose." Your spouse isn't going to let you walk away with all the goodies. You'll need to give some. And remember that you are not only negotiating for material things, and not only the children, but you are also

Bright Idea

If communication breaks down, don't immediately start communicating through your lawyers. That's bad practice. Lawyers are trained to argue and win, not to negotiate peace. Try a relationships counselor.

Bright Idea

Listening is the core of good communication. It is the first part in the process of creating an amicable divorce. In all discussions, try to see your spouse's point of view.

negotiating self-esteem. Rip into your spouse's self-esteem, and you are asking for big trouble. Especially if you're the one holding most of the cards, don't strut your stuff, unless you want your spouse to turn the divorce into a vendetta. And, if you are happy to be getting out of the marriage, don't flaunt that fact. Your spouse may be truly hurting, and even if she is not, there is no reason to make her feel abandoned. If you have a new relationship waiting in the wings that you are anxious to be in, don't advertise it. There is nothing harder for the spouse who doesn't want a divorce than seeing his ex merrily going about her life without a care in the world.

Domestic violence and abuse

Spousal beating is a silent epidemic: Too many cases go unreported out of shame, guilt, or fear of reprisals. You might think that only men batter women, and you may have a picture in your mind of a particular class of people. If so, you are wrong. In 5 percent of reported cases, domestic abuse is also committed by women against men, and abusers exist in every racial and economic class.

Are you being abused?

It's a mistake to think "Well, my spouse has never *hit* me, so I don't have a problem." Domestic violence reaches far beyond a punch, a slap, or a shove. Threats or intimidation are also abuse. Emotional abuse is marked by efforts to control or demean a spouse in order to keep that person in a position of dependence and inferiority. An abuser is simply doing everything possible to assert dominance over a partner. How can you tell if you're in an abusive relationship? Ask yourself—does your partner:

- Punch holes in the walls?
- Throw objects out of anger? Are they aimed at you?
- Destroy your belongings?
- Threaten you with objects (a kitchen knife, a bat, etc.)?
- Threaten to injure the children?
- Physically restrain you from leaving the home?
- Insult or ridicule you?
- Make you account for your exact whereabouts every minute that you are apart?
- Manipulate you with promises and lies?
- Isolate you from your friends and family?
- Make you ask permission to go out or to make a career move?
- Abuse your pet to frighten or intimidate you?

All of these behaviors are abusive. The number of your "yes" answers indicates the degree of abuse prevalent in your marriage. At this point, you may be pretty shaken up—some people spend many years refusing to recognize the signs of abuse. Among the many difficult revelations brought about by the beginning of your divorce process might be the realization that, after years of denial, you *were* an abused spouse. But now is the time to face facts, to stop making excuses and finally admit to yourself the facts of your relationship with your spouse. And most importantly, you must keep in mind that you are not the only one potentially affected by your spouse's abusive behavior—what about the kids?

> **66** Never hate your ene-
> mies...it will cloud your
> thinking. **99**
> —Michael Corleone, from
> the movie *Godfather III*

Domestic violence and children

Domestic violence affects children deeply. They may be directly affected if your spouse vents his or her anger toward them, intimidates them, or beats them. They may also be hurt by the *indirect* effects of abuse in the home if they observe domestic violence between the parents.

Even if they are not physically beaten, children absorb injury from the abuse they see. They may experience excessive fear, worry, confusion, and stress—the last of these most noticeable in the children's levels of stress-related health problems such as headaches, abdominal problems, ulcers, and bed-wetting. Older children are clearly at a higher risk for drug or alcohol abuse, juvenile delinquency, and violence directed toward their peers or siblings.

These are your children's formative years. What they experience is likely to have a profound effect on their own self-esteem and interpersonal skills later in life. If they witness domestic violence in the home, children—especially males—are more likely to repeat the same patterns when they get older. If you are being abused, and you think it's best to keep the marriage together "for the sake of the children," think about the abuse the children will witness if you stay. Think about the effects on your children's health, and think about what lessons they're learning from their environment and their experiences. If you can't summon up the strength to leave for your own sake, do it for your kids.

> ❝ What got me out of there for good was thinking about what lessons my son and daughter were learning. I don't want my son to be an abuser later on in life, and I don't want my daughter to get the message that she should stay in an abusive relationship. ❞
>
> —Carla, an abused spouse now happily divorced

Getting out

If you feel you are in *any* danger of retribution from your spouse, *get out of the house.* Pack up the children and any special or necessary belongings, and just leave. There are domestic abuse hotlines in every state, so call information and get the number. Many hotlines are connected to or can refer you to various shelters and safe houses that will provide you and your children with a place to stay, meals, and protection from your spouse. These shelters are usually at unlisted locations—the hotlines will not give out the address to your abusive spouse. You will be safe there.

There are a few things to keep firmly in mind when you are getting ready to leave—first and foremost, do *not* confront your spouse and make a big production about leaving. If your spouse is prone to physical abuse, this statement is interpreted as your break from control, and he or she may increase the level of violence and intimidation as a reaction. Don't announce your intentions, just leave as quickly as possible.

Some experts say you shouldn't worry about taking the time to settle your financial affairs before you go, and in situations of immediate danger, that is definitely the best advice. However, if you have time to plan, calling a lawyer before you go can be a good idea. If nothing else, you may be able to protect yourself from financial retaliation from your spouse. Most important, however, is that you make sure you're out of the house before your spouse finds out about what you've done. Nothing should be allowed to threaten your physical safety and that of your children.

Legal maneuvering

If you are in an abusive relationship, document the exact details of your spouse's mistreatment of you and the children. If it comes to court, the judge is going to require some proof of the abuse that you charge. A journal or daily log of abusive episodes will go a long way toward substantiating your claim should your spouse deny the charges. A trusted friend or relative may have witnessed acts of abuse and should be prepared to testify if necessary. Photos of bruises or damage to walls might also be helpful to make your case.

Once you're safely out of the abusive situation, you must take some time to safeguard yourself and the children, and to think to the future. If you have had to go to the emergency room with injuries due to physical abuse by your partner, or if your children have been injured by him, make sure you provide those medical records to your lawyer. The medical record is viewed as an impartial source of evidence, and the specifics of any injuries recorded will be given great weight in a courtroom. In many cases, hospitals that suspect domestic abuse will call in a family crisis counselor to talk to you. If that has happened—even if you maintained at the time that you simply collided with a door, and adamantly denied spousal abuse—there are notes to that effect in your medical records. These notes should be made available to your lawyer and, if necessary, the court. In addition, testimony from any family members or friends who have witnessed firsthand any abuse you have suffered serves as proof to the court that your claims are true.

Stalking

One variant of abusive behavior is stalking. An estimated 80 percent of stalking cases involve women stalked by ex-husbands or former boyfriends. Stalking is a frightening reality that reduces your world, making you live in constant fear. Perhaps your ex has made threats to you, or perhaps you have seen your ex lurking outside your home, intimidating you with his simple presence. Most states have their own definitions of stalking, but all agree that a stalker is someone who willfully and repeatedly follows or harasses someone else with the promise to harm that person or members of that person's family. Stalking laws have been established in all states in the aftermath of the 1990 stalking and murder of actress Rebecca Shaeffer. These laws serve to protect the victims of stalking and make it easier to punish convicted stalkers. The laws differ from state to state and are constantly evolving. To find out about stalking laws in your state, log on

to http://members.aol.com/lrfuzzl/StalkingLaws/StateLaws.
html.

In most states, you can bring a civil suit against your stalker,
and you can ask for monetary damages from that person.
Criminal charges can also be brought, resulting in a possible jail
sentence. The courts do take stalking very seriously, often issu-
ing restraining orders (which we'll discuss in a moment) that
prohibit the stalker from coming within a certain distance of
the victim and the victim's family, and they do take a hard stand
on the repeat offender. The penalties dramatically increase if
the stalker continues to pursue a victim in violation of a court
order—then the charge of stalking can carry stiffer penalties,
even including longer-term incarceration.

Steps you can take

If you feel you're being stalked but don't have enough evidence
to convince the police to arrest your stalker, you must take some
steps to protect yourself:

- Keep all doors and windows locked.

- Install motion light detectors around your home.

- Install a quality home-security system.

- Keep lights and a radio on a timing mechanism for when
  you are away from home.

- Don't walk alone, and carry a cell phone at all times. (You
  can dial "911" even from a nonoperable cell phone, and
  the call will go through.)

- Get a big, snarly dog and take him with you wherever
  you go.

Restraining orders

Stalkers, like any other abusive spouses, can be issued a restraining order requiring that they stay away. When a restraining
order is issued, it becomes effective immediately and is served
upon the stalker or abusive spouse typically by a local sheriff. In
most states, the spouse upon whom the order is served has the

right to appeal the order—usually within 30 days of being served. Why would this be allowed? Consider the circumstances of Olivia and Darren. After Olivia filed for divorce, Darren continued to see his children on their agreed-upon times. Olivia was not happy with the way the divorce settlement was shaping up, so she trumped up charges of abuse against Darren. The court, in assessing her charges, served Darren with a restraining order. Darren filed for the appeals hearing and was able to convince the judge that he not only had never abused Olivia or the children, but also that Olivia was using this tactic to punish him for having an edge on her in their divorce case. Without the opportunity to appeal, Darren would have been unfairly shut out from his children's lives.

The court takes all requests for restraining orders—and their appeals—very seriously. Every effort is made to assess the facts of the situation, and if it is found that one partner attempted to use a restraining order as a bargaining chip or punishment against another, that move could be damaging to his or her case.

A restraining order is simply a court-ordered mandate that one partner stop abusing or threatening the other partner or the children. It may specify that the partner in question stay a certain distance away from the other partner's home, place of business, relatives' homes, or the children's school. Depending on the circumstances, it can effectively remove the abusive partner from the home or provide police protection for any family member who wishes to pack up and leave the home. It can also form the basis for a temporary custody arrangement for the children.

A restraining order is not just for the abusive spouse who stands outside your home waiting for an opportunity to injure you. Look at the example of Marti. Marti's husband left her for another woman, a longtime friend of Marti's. Stung by their betrayal, Marti repeatedly called up her ex at the old friend's apartment and yelled at him, calling him and the new girlfriend a string of names. Marti's husband got a restraining order that forbade Marti from calling him at his girlfriend's home or at

Watch Out!

Unless you have police presence outside your home and around your person 24 hours a day, you can never be fully protected from an abusive or vindictive person. Use the restraining order in conjunction with the self-protection tips listed earlier in this chapter. Don't hesitate to call the police as often as you need them.

work. This incident became an issue within their divorce proceedings, quite ironically giving Marti's husband an edge in the settlement.

Extended-family discord

There are other disruptive situations that may arise in conjunction with your divorce that need careful handling. While not as immediately dangerous as spousal violence, they can have a strong impact on the well-being of you or your children. We've already established that friends and family may react in a variety of ways to the news of your impending divorce. But what happens if their reactions result in serious difficulty for you and for your children?

Dealing with disapproval

Just as there will be people who support you, there will be others who shun you. When these people are members of your own family, it may be especially hurtful. One woman tells of certain members of her family practically disowning her when she reported her plans to divorce her husband. There had been no divorce in her family for three generations, and her decision meant that her family's "streak" had been broken. Her relatives snapped back at her, unbelievably, with "How could you do this to us?"

But some forms of disapproval cut closer to the heart. Your family may have a sense of loyalty to your ex that is so strong, it seems like their love for your ex surpasses their love for you. If you kept your displeasure regarding your ex to yourself for years, your family may only see that person in the positive light that you created. Now, your uninformed family will be surprised that your spouse is not that ideal partner.

Because they are working with what may be a false idea of what your spouse was *really* like, your family may be surprised and shocked at your announcement of plans to divorce. This is not the time, however, to indulge in a crash course of spouse-bashing for their benefit. Acknowledge to yourself that your family's false positive image of your spouse is partly of your own creation. There is nothing to be gained by trying to tear your spouse down at this late date. Instead, understand the reasons for their reactions, but don't

> **66** My sister actually called my wife and said 'it's about time you're dumping him!' (meaning me). Years have passed, but I still can't get over that. Needless to say, my relationship with my sister hasn't been quite the same. **99**
>
> —Bruce, divorced three years ago

let their disapproval sway you from the course you know to be best for you. The flip side of the coin is that your family never really liked your spouse, and now they're ready to let it rip. But their anger isn't what you need right now.

Remember that just as you needed time to handle the decision to divorce, so may your family. Understanding this may help you realize that your family may not be in a position to help you right away; they have to deal with their own "stages of grief" first. This is a difficult time for everybody, and you're going to have to give people time to come to grips with the changes. Don't take it personally.

Dealing with in-laws

Your in-laws will have their own reactions too, and these are likely to be complicated by the fact of family loyalty—to your soon-to-be ex, their child. While some people are lucky enough to be able to maintain a relationship with their in-laws even after a divorce, just as often this is not possible, at least not right away.

Bright Idea

Encourage your children to stay in contact with your spouse's family on their own. Many children of divorce exchange e-mail messages with their grand-parents, keeping the bond strong and sharing stories of their lives with people who care about them.

And the loss of loved ones on your spouse's side of the family can hurt tremendously, especially if you considered yourself to be very close to your in-laws. The disappearance of this group of loved ones, confidantes, and friends can be very painful, especially if you didn't cause the end of the marriage. And complicating matters further is the fact that they are still your children's grandparents, aunts, uncles, and cousins. They may have shut you out, but they still are likely to maintain contact with your kids, and you will undoubtedly encounter them at family events involving the children for years to come.

When there are children involved, establish some ground rules for contact with your former in-laws:

- Encourage regular visits between your children and your spouse's family. Doing so removes any suspicion that you are trying to separate your children from the other side of the family.

- Invite your in-laws to such family parties as your child's birthday, graduation, other celebrations. They then have the option of deciding whether or not to attend, but at least you've made the effort to include them.

- Keep your in-laws informed of your child's accomplishments. Send out announcements of such triumphs as making the honor roll, winning a sporting championship, or being elected class president.

- Establish beforehand that your in-laws are not to discuss the divorce with the children. Under no circumstances are the in-laws to discuss the mechanics of the case or any tensions that exist between you and your spouse.

The reactions of most in-laws are likely to fall somewhere between complete rejection to total acceptance of you, post-divorce. There may be a chill in the air, but you generally can create a new relationship with your in-laws that reflects your new position in their lives. Here are some points to keep in mind:

- Make contact with your in-laws right away, as soon as the decision to separate has been made.

- Without going into detail and without trashing your ex, briefly explain the basic reasons for the end of the marriage, and tell them that it in no way reflects on how you feel about them.

- Express a wish, if applicable, for you all to remain close.

- Let them know that you will fully accommodate their wishes to see the kids.

- Do not try to sway them to your "side." Acknowledge that this is not a competition. It is a family sorting through issues.

- Do not discuss the divorce process with them. The business end of your split is not their business, and you never know what news will get back to your ex.

- Maintain a normal relationship as best as possible, continuing to send holiday cards or gifts if you so choose.

If you and your spouse do not have children, the issue of maintaining a relationship with your in-laws becomes a wholly individual issue. While the absence of a bond through your children might mean that you have no real reason to maintain a relationship, you might choose to keep these people within your circle of loved ones, if on a different level. The formation of a continuing relationship is dictated by your wishes and theirs.

Regardless of whether you have children, it is going to take some time for your new relationship with your in-laws to form. It will take a concerted effort on your part to maintain a relationship with your in-laws, and only you can decide whether that

Bright Idea

If your chldren will be spending the holidays with your co-parent (that is, your former spouse), consider having an "early" Christmas or Hanukkah at your house this year.

is something that you might desire. (There's more on your relationship with your in-laws in Chapter 16.)

Handling the holidays

As we discussed in Chapter 10, the holidays are likely to be hard for you the first year after the end of your marriage. They are also a time when most people are heavily involved with family—and now, ex-family. Not only will you have to deal with the loaded issue of the absence of your ex and the changing of your own personal holiday routines and traditions, but you will also have to find a way to fit that entire issue into your family's holiday plans. And, unless you've worked out a joint-custody arrangement, and you and your ex are friends enough to spend the holidays together with the children, you have to share them during this special family time.

Forming your arrangements can be quite a headache, so consider two ground rules for dealing with custody during the holidays. First, plan to share the holiday by splitting up the time equally. This is the best and most fair arrangement. Second, make sure everybody involved knows the schedule—the kids need to know where they'll be spending the holidays, and grandparents want to know where to call the kids.

Just the facts

- Conflict resolution techniques can reduce the amount of confrontation you face in your divorce.
- Your state, the police, and the courts can provide protection from the threat of violence, abuse, or harassment by your ex, should it ever come to that.

- If you or your children face immediate physical threat, get out of the house and work out the details later, once the situation has been secured.

- Family disapproval can be difficult but must be overcome—especially when there are children involved in the divorce.

- Children should be encouraged to maintain a relationship with your in-laws.

GET THE SCOOP ON...
Divorcing a business partner ▪ Long-distance
divorce issues ▪ Do you need a prenuptial
agreement? ▪ Lawyer troubles

Special Circumstances

Your own divorce situation may call for special handling. If, for example, you and your spouse run a business together, life at the office is going to change. If you signed an ill-considered prenuptial agreement back in the early days of your relationship when you were young and infatuated, that may now come back to haunt you. Perhaps your spouse has fled the state, and you find yourself without child support. Or maybe you've discovered that the peach of a lawyer you felt so good about hiring has turned out to be something of a lemon.

Divorces are like marriages in that no two are the same. Just about anything can happen. In this chapter we'll look at some special—but not all that rare—circumstances.

Divorcing your business partner

The Mom-and-Pop store is as American as apple pie, but when Mom and Pop divorce, the pie can turn to crumbs. Few things can devastate a business like a messy divorce of the partners. If you and your spouse own a business and you've decided to split, you're going to have to find a way to work together during, and probably after, the divorce to see that the business you've built stays intact. Unless one of you buys the other out, maintaining a working relationship after you part ways is going to take, quite likely, a big effort on both of your parts.

Get your business act together

Now, with hurt feelings and possibly some bitterness between the two of you, you may find it hard to put your emotions aside when it's time to sit down and work on the new account or draw up that proposal for a business loan—but that's precisely the kind of cooperation you're going to have to manage.

Obviously, the best post-divorce working relationships are achieved when the couple has mutually agreed to divorce and can stay on friendly terms with one another. That, however, is not always the case. To keep the effects on your business to a minimum, you're going to have to establish some new ground rules for working together.

Don't alienate the troops

First and most important, keep all divorce talk out of the office. This is not the place to discuss your child custody agreement or the division of household property. Tempers will flare, and your employees (or customers) will be left feeling uncomfortable. A hostile or tense working environment leads to lack of productivity, employee attrition, and loss of customers or clients. Your employees simply do not need to participate in this with you. Save your discussions for the lawyer's office. If you have employees, and they catch wind of the fact that the owners of the business are splitting, they are going to be on edge. Like the children, some of them may even feel the need to choose sides between you, with potentially devastating consequences for your business. Or they may be afraid of losing their jobs.

In one case we know of, husband-wife business owners divorced after the wife discovered the husband had been secretly carrying on an affair with one of their employees. The

Bright Idea

If you and your spouse own a business that has employees, inform them of the impending divorce but keep the details to yourself. Make it clear that you and your spouse will still be working together as professionals, and you expect no less of your employees. They will take their cue from the two of you.

"other woman" quit her job, and the rest of the workers—all female—were disgusted by the husband's conduct. They all sided with the wife, becoming outright hostile to the male owner. The resulting clashes ultimately hurt the functioning of the business, and the female owner had to tell the workers to cease their warfare. She explained that it was hard enough to come into the office every day during this time—she did not need the business to go under, too.

To avoid allowing your divorce to harm your shared business you must think constantly of your partner's business strengths. Your new business relationship should be kept separate from the negatives that have ended your marriage. For this partnership to work, you will somehow have to stop thinking of this person as your ex, and start thinking of him or her *only* as your partner in business.

Long-distance support battles

One of the most difficult "special circumstances" arises when the divorced parties no longer reside in the same state, but there are ongoing issues pertaining to either alimony or child support. This may come about innocently, as in situations where one party moves to another state to pursue better job opportunities, or as a result of remarriage, or because one party actually flees the state in an effort to avoid enforcement of support orders. Occasionally, a person may leave the state prior to finalization of the divorce in an effort to defeat the completion of the divorce. Whatever the circumstances, there is no question that it becomes more difficult—and more expensive—to enforce court orders pertaining to the divorce when there is more than one jurisdiction involved.

While it is neither easy nor inexpensive to enforce interstate support orders, both federal and state governments have recognized the growing problem of nonpayment of support, and certain laws have been enacted in the past decade that make it far easier than it ever was before to enforce a domestic relations order. As recently as the 1980s, many individuals found themselves completely unable to collect support from a deadbeat co-parent. Much of the problem lay with the fact that the federal government has traditionally refused to become involved in the enforcement of orders entered by state courts for domestic relations support. In recent years, however, this has started to change.

Recent changes in the law

What prompted the federal government to make changes was a study conducted in the early 1990s by the United States Department of Health and Human Services, which showed that, overall, only 67 percent of existing support orders were being complied with. Of even greater significance, from the federal government's point of view, was a report of the General Accounting Office in the early 1990s which revealed that individuals who were owed support by out-of-state payors were significantly less likely to collect the support owed to them than were individuals who had support orders against their former spouses who still resided in the same state.

In response to these and other reports, the federal government entered the forum of child support and enacted a federal statute known as the Full Faith and Credit for Child Support Orders Act (FFCCSOA). In passing this Act, Congress determined that a lack of uniformity in state laws regarding child support orders encouraged noncustodial parents to relocate to other states to avoid the jurisdiction of the courts of the home state. This contributed to the relatively low levels of child support payments in interstate cases and to inequities in child

support payment levels that are based solely on the noncustodial parent's choice of residence. Congress specifically provided
that the central purposes of FFCCSOA were to facilitate the
enforcement of child support orders among the states, to discourage interstate disputes over child support in the interest of
providing great financial security for children, and to avoid
"forum shopping" by parties seeking a more favorable state's
laws pertaining to child support. The Act specifically lays the
groundwork for states to recognize and enforce other states'
family support orders.

In addition, following the enactment of FFCCSOA, all 50
states and the District of Columbia subsequently enacted various forms of the Uniform Interstate Family Support Act, a law
that had been drafted by the American Bar Association. While
highly technical, the crux of the Uniform Act is to provide that
the "home state"—meaning the state that originally entered an
order for support, or, in the case of child support, the state
where the child resides—shall be given deference by another
state's courts. In passing this Act, the courts effectively ended a
pattern that had existed for many decades, whereby a parent
obligated to pay child support would often move to a jurisdiction that had more favorable support laws, and would then seek
to have his support order from the original state modified (low-
ered) by the new state. These laws apply to both child and
spousal support, but are most often invoked to enforce child
support obligations against a deadbeat parent.

As encouraging as it is that the federal and state governments have recognized the importance of consistent enforcement of support orders, it is nonetheless still a highly technical

---

 Bright Idea

If your ex has relocated to another state, log on to the Website of the Federal
Office of Child Support Enforcement, located at www.acf.dhhs.gov, for additional information on collecting the support that is due you.

and complicated issue for which a divorced parent will almost certainly need legal assistance. Moreover, the lawyer in your home state may need to enlist the assistance of an attorney in the state where your ex has moved to assist with the filings and specifics of domestic relations procedures in the courts of that state. Therefore, you often must make a determination in advance whether the probable outcome is encouraging enough to warrant an expenditure of what will almost surely be high legal fees. If your ex is a perpetual deadbeat who has trouble holding down a job and no assets to speak of, you may want to reconsider the wisdom of pursuing an interstate legal battle. Often, where a parent with the obligation to support is unable or unwilling to pay, the courts will enforce the child support obligation by issuance of a contempt order, which may result only in having the deadbeat thrown in jail. While that may be emotionally satisfying to the parent who is struggling to make ends meet and to support their child, jail time does not put any money in your pocket, and actually may make it even harder to collect support later, since the now-jailed individual may well lose his job in the process. In many cases, the jail time served by a deadbeat parent is done in a work release facility to avoid loss of a job or inability to pay toward a support order while incarcerated.

On the other hand, where there is sufficient evidence that the deadbeat parent has assets and income, by all means use the laws enacted in the past decade to your own advantage. A good lawyer should be able to make a strong claim for an award of your attorneys' fees as part of this process.

Bringing in the tax guys

Another very important tool for collecting past-due child support comes courtesy of the Internal Revenue Service. If a former spouse owes past-due child support and is owed an income tax refund, the IRS will withhold the refund if properly notified of the child support arrearage. This does not mean that you can simply contact the IRS and make a claim that your ex owes support. The proper notification must be sent by a governmental child support collection agency, which is usually your local domestic relations office. Contact your local courthouse for further information. You probably will not need legal counsel to pursue this avenue of collection. Many states also have procedures for withholding state income tax refunds of deadbeat parents.

If you are not yet divorced but are owed support by your soon-to-be-ex and will be filing a joint income tax return with him or her, you may file IRS Form 8379, the Injured Spouse Claim and Allocation form, to seek your portion of any tax refund owed to the nonpaying spouse. The Internal Revenue Service's Website, www.IRS.gov, has forms that can be easily downloaded and submitted. You should not need a lawyer's assistance.

Prenuptial agreements

A common misconception is that the only people who have prenuptial agreements are the very, very rich. The prenuptial agreements of people like Donald Trump always make the front page, and we often learn the details of a celebrity couple's pre-nup when their divorce hits the gossip pages. But prenuptial agreements, also known as premarital agreements, are no longer just for the jet-setting crowd. More and more "ordinary" couples are entering into pre-nups as they wait until later in life to marry and therefore have accumulated more assets than newlyweds traditionally have. And pre-nups have become almost standard operating procedure for second and third marriages, especially for those who vow not to repeat hard lessons that were learned the first time around.

If more and more couples are signing prenuptial agreements, you can be sure more and more couples are also dealing with pre-nup jitters. The presentation of a prenuptial agreement is not exactly the most romantic expression of your love.

Many people who are presented with a pre-nup and asked to sign decide that it is a deal-breaker. Every domestic relations lawyer has stories of couples who were madly in love...until the pre-nup was presented. (An equal number of lawyers have stories about couples who should have had pre-nups, but didn't, and the disastrous results that followed.)

Love (as you've discovered) isn't always forever

There may be significant pressure put upon the intended signer of a prenuptial agreement, especially if the fiancée's family is wealthy and there is fear that the new addition to the family is seeking a cut of the family fortune. But some people reluctantly sign a pre-nup out of love and loyalty to their intended, or out of fear that if they don't the marriage will be called off. And they tell themselves that this love will last forever, so the pre-nup will never be needed.

If you signed a prenuptial agreement before you were married you may now be worried about the consequences of signing that agreement. Perhaps you did not read the document fully. Perhaps you signed an extremely limiting pre-nup in the love-is-blind belief that your marriage would last forever. All may not be lost. Although consenting adults may generally contract for anything that is legal and consistent with public policy, a prenuptial agreement may be found to be invalid for a number of reasons. The most common reason for not enforcing a prenuptial agreement is a finding that it was signed under duress. "Duress" does not have to mean that a gun was pointed at your head when you signed. For legal purposes, duress can be shown in a number of ways, including:

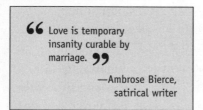

66 Love is temporary insanity curable by marriage. 99

—Ambrose Bierce, satirical writer

- Fraud or falsehood (for example, failure to disclose one party's actual net worth or assets).

- One partner was not represented by counsel while the other one was, and the unrepresented party was led to believe that the lawyer would protect the interests of both.

- Being presented with a pre-nup to sign the evening before the wedding, or so close in time to the event that duress can be construed from the circumstances.

- One partner had unequal bargaining power. This often exists in pre-nup situations, so there will have to be something special about your situation in order to use this as a reason for invalidating a pre-marital agreement. Factors may include differences in education/sophistication/ station in life or vast difference in age.

- Gross unfairness in the terms of the prenuptial agreement.

The limits of a pre-nup

There are some things that can never be contracted away in a prenuptial agreement. Most significantly, issues of child support and child custody cannot be signed away, either prior to the marriage, during the marriage, or even at any time after the marriage (unless one parent specifically relinquishes all parental rights with court approval). Issues pertaining to children are always governed by a "best interests of the child" standard, and therefore, even if two consenting adults enter into an agreement that purports to sign away support rights, the courts will refuse to enforce such an agreement on the basis that to do so would not be in the child's best interest. Moreover, and just as importantly from the court's point of view, if a parent is permitted to abandon his obligation to support a child, that child may well become a ward of the state, in need of welfare or other public assistance. The courts simply will not permit a parent to walk away from support obligations that may lead to the child becoming a burden on taxpayers.

Similarly, because custodial arrangements must always remain flexible, to allow the child's best interests to be served, an agreement entered into pre-marriage that dictates where future children will live and with whom will not be enforced.

In the early 1980s, a Uniform Premarital Agreement Act was drafted seeking to provide uniformity among states on whether such agreements are enforceable and the circumstances under which they would not be enforced. However, since its drafting in 1983, only 27 states have adopted the Act, and many of those states have varied the language of the original Uniform Act. Because there is considerable variance among the states as to whether premarital agreements will be enforced, and if so, what they may include, we strongly advise anyone contemplating a prenuptial agreement to first consult with a lawyer to determine the likelihood that it will be a binding agreement, and to specifically tailor the terms of the agreement to the state in which the couple is planning to live. Similarly, if you are in the divorce process and a prenuptial agreement was signed, you should consult a lawyer regardless of whether you wish to have the agreement upheld or invalidated. The laws pertaining to these agreements are simply too lacking in uniformity to give precise advice in this book to address the laws of each jurisdiction.

Dissension in the ranks: problems with your attorney

The advertisement said Attorney Joe would be there for you every step of the way. He'd fight hard for your rights. He'd give your case his full attention. He would apply his years of experience and wisdom to help win your case. But ever since you paid his whopping retainer fee, you haven't even been able to get Joe on the phone. Perhaps the attorney has taken on too many additional cases since being hired to handle your divorce. Perhaps he doesn't know what he's doing. Or maybe he just doesn't care. Whatever the reason, the problem must be addressed, and quickly.

Common complaints

By far, the number-one complaint about divorce lawyers—at least from their own clients—is a lack of communication. When an attorney commits this offense, the case can drag on for months and, without contact from the attorney, the client is left to wondering what's going on.

We mentioned earlier in this book that a good lawyer will keep in regular touch with you, updating you on the progress of your case. Such updates are an absolute minimum that you should rightfully demand from your attorney. Even if no action has been taken, or if your attorney has yet to receive responses and documents vital to the progress of the case, he or she should regularly inform you about where things stand. The attorney should also be able to give you a fairly accurate estimate of when court hearings will take place and when your case will be fully and finally resolved. Your attorney should respect your right to know and understand your need to keep abreast of the developments of your case.

A related and frequently heard complaint is that the attorney is never in when you call. While it is true that your attorney does have other cases and may be in court from time to time, your case is as important as any others being handled by that attorney. Do not accept the suggestion that your attorney is always available for the bigger, more important clients. If you get that impression, you need another lawyer. On the other hand, if you have a generally good rapport with your lawyer but dislike the amount of time it takes for her to respond to your

 Bright Idea

If you're not getting callbacks, let the attorney's receptionist know of your displeasure. After the second unreturned phone call, tell your lawyer's assistant that you are considering terminating the relationship. You deserve timely and efficient service, and you should take your case elsewhere if this attorney can't provide it.

calls, inquire whether there are other ways for the two of you to communicate regularly. Does she use e-mail, and if so, will she respond more consistently to your e-mailed questions? Some lawyers really are in court most of the business day and use the hours outside of normal business times to catch up on their "mail." You could also ask whether there is an associate attorney or trusted paralegal or assistant who can field your routine calls when the attorney is out of the office. Often these individuals will know more about the status of your case than the attorney will, as they are more often in the office dealing with paperwork and filings. A caveat, however: Even if you receive regular contact from individuals who work with your attorney, you deserve occasional substantive communications from the attorney himself. The other people in the office do not represent you; he does. And the success of your case will largely depend on the quality of your attorney, not those around him.

How much?!

Another common attorney complaint has to do with billing practices. While the receipt of a large bill is never a pleasure and may be cause for complaint in itself, the thing that most frustrates clients is the format and delivery of legal bills. If, say, your case is handled on a retainer basis, chances are your attorney's bookkeeper will send you a monthly account statement, listing deductions from the retainer amount. The problem is that the codes used for individual entries may be less than informative. One commonly encountered code is "memo." This code does not accurately explain the charge, which may represent hours of research, writing, editing, and strategic planning that went into making a good legal brief for presentation to the court. As the client, you have the right to insist on more detail, or better descriptions, of the items for which you are being charged. You should feel free to assert yourself in this manner—many clients do, and lawyers are used to it. To avoid the problem, ask for a sample copy of one of your lawyer's bills right up front, before you

Moneysaver

Keeping a written record of your attorney's activity is a handy way to keep track of the hours he or she spends with you. When you receive billing statements, you can check your accurate records for discrepancies in your attorney's billing totals. Insist on receiving copies of all letters or papers sent or received by him that pertain to your case.

pay the retainer. You will have more leverage with your lawyer at that time, and if your expectations are made clear from the beginning, your chances of getting a descriptive bill are better.

In addition to these common beefs, you may have more specific problems with your lawyer. You may feel that your lawyer is unprepared when you see him in court for the first time. You may sense that your ex's lawyer knows more about child support laws than your own. Or you may find out that the lawyer you hired, thinking she was a divorce specialist, really has a very general practice with only a smattering of divorce cases.

How to complain

If you have any problems with your attorney, your first step should always be to talk to him directly. Explain exactly what it is that displeases you in a diplomatic and respectful way. This is not the time to be demanding or condescending. That approach will only put your attorney on the defensive, and that is not the way to open up a good dialogue. If you have difficulty confronting him or her directly, consider sending an e-mail or note expressing your concerns. Sometimes it's easier to voice criticism in this manner, and you will be better able to express yourself if you take the time to write it down, without having to face the lawyer directly.

When you *do* go to your attorney with a complaint, be specific. Avoid resorting to generalized statements. If your problem is with billing, say so and offer examples of the bills you find unclear. If you have a problem with accessibility, provide the

dates and times you called. The more specific you can be, the
better your attorney is able to solve the problem.

Here are some other tips:

- **Be honest.** If you are displeased with some action or inac-
  tion on your lawyer's part, do not ignore the problem or
  deny the problem out of a sense of intimidation or shy-
  ness. Remember, you are paying your lawyer to serve
  your best interests. He or she has an obligation to give
  you the kind of service you expect. It is counterproductive
  to your goals to accept inferior service in deference to
  your attorney.

- **Be realistic.** Are you expecting too much from your attorney? You must remember that your attorney does have
  other cases, and you cannot expect her attention to be
  focused only on you. So make allowances for normal time
  spans, and remember that your attorney is only human. It
  is unrealistic to expect results overnight, especially if you
  have a very involved case. And always remember that your
  attorney is an attorney, not a therapist. If you are the kind
  of client who calls your lawyer every time you have an
  argument with your ex, you can expect huge legal bills
  that reflect the number of calls. Just as bad, you will slowly
  find that your lawyer is dodging your calls. She is trained
  to be your lawyer, not your therapist. Don't become a nui-
  sance client.

- **Be assertive.** A lawyer should appreciate a client who will
  state his needs, since that is the only way to maintain true
  communication. If you feel your lawyer brushes you off
  when you state your concerns, look for another lawyer. Do
  not allow him to imply that because you have less knowledge of the law, you must "just trust me." You are entitled
  to thorough explanations of why things are progressing
  the way they are and a game plan for future action. If you
  aren't getting it, even after asking, then it's time to find a
  new attorney.

Taking it higher up

If your attorney does not fix any problems you have with his office or with him, take your complaints higher up. If you're working with a junior lawyer in a big firm, talk to his or her direct supervisor or a senior partner in the firm. Your lawyer represents the whole firm, and any complaints you have with your lawyer directly reflect on the firm that employs him. Just as your lawyer depends on your satisfaction with his handling of your case for future referrals and future income, so too does the firm. If you originally went to a firm expecting to have a certain attorney handle your case but then were referred to someone else (whether within the same firm or not), feel free to go back to the original attorney with any disappointment you may have in the lawyer who was suggested to you. A simple phone call from the referring attorney to the one who is working on your case is often all it takes to get your problem resolved. And since lawyers generally find it easier to talk "lawyer to lawyer," the original attorney may be able to get an explanation of what is going on and share it with you.

If your problem with the lawyer involves misconduct, a breach of confidentiality, or neglect of your case, you should immediately contact your State Bar Association for guidance. Most bar associations maintain hotlines for this purpose and will be able to give you input on whether your expectations are reasonable and whether your lawyer has acted improperly. If so, you will need to find a new lawyer as soon as possible, but you should also consider filing a formal complaint through the State

---

 Watch Out!

Everyone handles constructive criticism differently, and lawyers are no exception. While your lawyer might accept that you've gone "upstairs" with your problems, you could also find yourself facing a vindictive attorney who is angry you went over his head. If that's the case, get a new lawyer. This is not the person you want to represent you.

Bar channels. Such complaints are essential to keeping only competent, honest lawyers in the legal profession. The bad ones should be weeded out, and one of the best ways of doing so is by using the mechanisms that have been put in place by the legal profession itself to police its own.

If you find yourself in the position of having to discharge your lawyer and obtain a new one, ask the new one for advice about payment of any legal fees still due to the former lawyer. You may be able to work out a compromise or even a complete write-off of the fees, especially if the termination of your relationship with the lawyer was due to improper handling or neglect. You should also be aware that it is completely improper for a lawyer to attempt to withhold your file from you until you have paid your bill in full. To do so may well jeopardize your legal rights, as you will need the file to find a new lawyer and to enable him or her to get up to speed on your case as quickly as possible. If your original lawyer resists giving you the file, find a new lawyer and tell him or her of the problem. Usually, the new lawyer will be able to secure the file promptly or can take court action to have it released.

How to fire your attorney

You have every right to fire your attorney if you feel he or she is not serving you well or is damaging your case. Many people, intimidated by their lawyer's authority or afraid of "making waves," are hesitant to proclaim, "You're fired." But remember—your best interests are the most important factor here, and you

 Watch Out!

When you fire your attorney, you may still be responsible for paying any fees incurred up to that point. If your lawyer is on retainer, you should remember to get the unused balance of that back.

may need to take this step for your own protection. One way to go about firing your counsel is to send a formal termination letter, making clear that no services are desired from that date forward. It doesn't need to be long or fancy:

A Sample "Pink Slip" to Your Attorney

Date: _____

Dear _____:

It is with regret that I must inform you of my plans to terminate our working relationship. I feel that it is in my best interests to seek other counsel. Please have your secretary contact me to advise when my file will be ready for me to pick up. I will require no further legal services from you after the date of this letter. Thank you.

Sincerely,

_____

You may choose to go into more detail, but a simple statement will suffice. Do *not* use this letter as an opportunity to launch a personal attack on the lawyer, no matter what your feelings are. Just state your intentions and move on. If you are uneasy about firing your attorney personally, another option is to hire a new attorney and have that person contact your former lawyer about the change. Your new lawyer will handle the details of terminating your old relationship with your former lawyer, and your former lawyer is ethically obligated to cooperate in the transition.

Just the facts

- Maintaining a business partnership with your ex will require setting ground rules to govern your new working relationship.

- If your ex flees the state, you and your lawyer will have to pursue your ex through the courts of the state to which he or she has fled.

- Prenuptial agreements can be challenged if they appear to have been entered into under duress.

- If you have serious difficulties with your lawyer, do not hesitate to replace him or her with counsel who is more capable of seeing to your needs.

Chapter 16

GET THE SCOOP ON...
Your relationship with your in-laws ▪ Getting
remarried ▪ Managing a stepfamily ▪ Attending
the wedding of your children and other
milestone events ▪ A death in the family

Considerations Beyond the Horizon

A t this juncture, we look into the future. What will life be like for you and your children, and perhaps someday your grandchildren, now that your marriage is no more? What will it be like to, say, attend the college graduation of your daughter? The wedding of your son? How will you handle matters when one of your former spouse's parents—your children's grandparent—dies?

This chapter will look not only at the etiquette of being a divorced person, but will also shed light on how to carry on what hopefully began as an amicable separation. And if it didn't start off amicably, you may find that the passage of time will heal wounds and smooth over a rocky road, leading to a more amicable—and less stressful—future.

And what of the in-laws?

You've been calling her your mother-in-law for 20 years. He's been your brother-in-law for just as long. Now that you are divorced, do they stop being your mother-in-law and brother-in-law? What kind of relationship can you expect from here on? That's largely up to you. While some in-laws may write you off, most will wait to take their cues from you.

But what do you call them?

In our case, after 22 years of marriage, we are both still very close to our respective in-laws, and will be for life. Do we still refer to them as in-laws? Sure. Why not?

Says one writer colleague of Russell's, herself married for many years and now divorced: "English is a relationship-poor language to begin with, and the frequency of divorce these days has complicated the issue. Margot, the woman I still call my sister-in-law, was never technically my sister-in-law. She is the wife of my brother-in-law, my ex-husband's brother. I am an only child, so I never had a 'real' sister-in-law. But Margot and I met when we were 18 and we've been extremely close ever since. Also, I continue to refer to her three boys as my nephews even though they are not blood relatives. They are my kids' cousins and we are all still very much a family. Divorce notwithstanding, I'll never stop using familial terms for any of these people."

> 66 Both my first husband and my second were there at my third wedding. I wouldn't have wanted it any other way! Just because we were once married and divorced doesn't mean we can't be friends. 99
>
> —Lisa, 50, no children

In-laws you never liked

They say you can pick your friends, but you can't pick your family. Divorce puts "family"—at least some family—in with the ranks of friends. Yes, you can now pick and choose. Don't like them? Let them go. But don't do so rashly. Don't let anger over the divorce cloud your vision. If you have children, exercise extreme caution about alienating your children's grandparents, aunts, and uncles. Remember, you'll still see them at your children's weddings.

> **“** No, I don't still call them my in-laws. I call them my out-laws! **”**
>
> —Terry, divorced three years

New relationships, perhaps remarriage

More than 50 percent of all those divorced remarry within five years. As the years go on, more will take the plunge. The odds of remarriage will depend on what age you are and how vigorously you pursue a second marriage. But even if you don't remarry, or don't remarry for a very long time, you will undoubtedly have relationships. If there are children on the scene, then so is your ex. If you have joint custody, then your ex is very much on the scene. Congratulations. Your divorce just widened its circle. It now involves yet more people. Can you handle it?

Introducing the new significant other

Admit it. No matter whether your divorce was friendly or ugly, no matter whether you were married for three years or thirty, you're curious to see what kind of person your ex winds up with. And your ex is curious to see what kind of person you'll be bringing home. Following society's cue, and its neuroses, women expect the ex to come home with a thinner, leggier, younger blonde. Men expect the ex to come home with a richer, more muscular, more-hair-on-top, CEO-type. Sometimes it happens that way, but often not.

 Watch Out!

If you get remarried, you may lose the right to tap into your ex's Social Security benefits. That is probably no reason to hold off on remarrying, but do check with your financial advisor. (If your ex gets remarried, it won't affect your benefits in any way.)

Whatever he or she turns out to be like, try to give the new "significant other" a chance. Every date your ex brings home may wind up as the stepparent of your children. And at that point, that person will play a big role in your children's lives—and by extension, your life. It pays to get started on the right foot. Even if she is drop-dead gorgeous and 25, and even if he was on the cover of last month's *Fortune* magazine, make an effort. Remember that the newcomer may be equally intimidated by you, simply by virtue of your status as the original spouse!

> 66 Allow six months to a year, at least, to grieve for your marriage before you enter another serious relationship. 99
>
> —Michael Dolan, Psy.D., psychologist and marriage counselor

Wedding bells, ringing again

In one recent year, 43 percent of all new marriages in America were remarriages, at least for one of the two participants. On average, it usually takes about three years. At that point, chances are that one or both of you may be ready to tie the knot once again. There's nothing wrong with offering a hearty congratulations to your ex, and maybe even a gift.

When and if either of us remarries, the other (and the new "significant other") will be a guest at the wedding, as will our "former" in-laws. Russell may even be asked to offer a toast to Susan and her new husband. Okay, that may seem strange to some of you, and we're not suggesting that everyone can or will want to go that route. By no means. But wouldn't it be nice for your children on this big day to see their parents both involved and happy?

The stepfamily

Volumes have been written on stepfamily issues, with good reason. There are so *many* issues. This being a book on divorce and not a book on stepfamilies, we cannot address every nitty-gritty issue that may arise. We will simply acknowledge that running a step-household isn't easy. The last thing you need is an angry ex making things more difficult. The last thing your ex needs is an angry you making things more difficult. Keep in mind it is in your children's best interest to facilitate the making of two happy households.

The nuts and bolts

Okay, we won't get into the nitty-gritty, but just a quick word on the nuts and bolts: Most experts agree that the best way to make a stepfamily work is to adopt a "trusted babysitter" model for the nonparent. That is, the nonparent should help enforce the rules of the parent (rules that the parent is hopefully making in consultation with the other parent). The nonparent should *not* be responsible for being the rule-maker, or the disciplinarian, or the nurturer. Those are the jobs of the two biological parents, at least for the first few years. (An obvious exception exists where one of the original parents is absent or neglectful.) The nonparent is to be accorded respect and obedience, as you would expect of your children with a "trusted babysitter."

Father's Day, Mother's Day

On special occasions, such as your ex's birthday, Christmas, Hanukkah, Father's Day, and Mother's Day, the children should have some cash to buy presents for their parents. Even if you and your ex are not on good terms, the gift is as much for the giver as the recipient, and it is important for the child to feel she is able to buy her parent a gift. So give your children a few bucks to buy Mom or Dad a gift, okay? Yes, it is *your* responsibility—not

---

 Bright Idea

Encourage your children to maintain a good relationship with their other biological parent. Encourage your new spouse to make a good connection with your ex.

the responsibility of his or her new companion. *You* are the co-parent.

Be there for very special events

We were married in Baltimore on Independence Day, 1981. Russell's parents were there, of course. And so were Susan's mother and father, with their respective new significant others, since they had been divorced years before. How sad it would have been for us had either parent boycotted the wedding because of the other. As it is, Susan's parents had a rather amicable divorce, or at least it became amicable after a little steam had blown off. If the steam in your divorce hasn't yet blown off by the time your child gets married, tough—you'll just need to put aside your animosity for the moment.

> 66 When we broke up, Kevin and I put it into our divorce agreement that we would each cough up money to give to our son to buy gifts on special occasions, like each other's birthdays. I wanted to make sure to get it in writing, or he probably would never have done it. 99
>
> —Janet, divorced 10 years

If any of your children are getting married, or having a bar mitzvah, or graduating, or celebrating any other big event in their lives, both parents should be present. If you're even thinking of boycotting such an event for any reason having to do with your ex, think long and hard. If your child wants you there, you should be there. No ifs, ands, or buts. However, if there are legitimate reasons to keep the child's other parent away—and by legitimate, we mean really nasty issues, like prior child abuse, uncontrollable drug or alcohol abuse, or total abandonment—these issues should be discussed with the child who is having the event, and the other parent should be excluded if that is the child's desire—not yours. Don't allow your feelings about your ex to dictate whether the other parent attends. The children deserve to have both parents present.

Yeah, but who's gonna pay for it?

If you're chipping in to help cover the expense of the wedding, the confirmation, the graduation, or whatever, the same rules apply as would apply to any other expense for the children. You should first agree—together—what amount, if any, you are contributing, and then you should pay proportionate to your ability to pay. If one spouse earns $50,000 a year and the other earns $100,000, assuming neither of you has a $2,000,000 trust fund, then the higher-earning spouse should chip in twice as much, more or less. Of course, if the grandparents would like to pay or contribute, great! However, a contribution by one set of grandparents should not substitute for a co-parent's contribution, unless he or she is unable to pay.

When your children have children

Our oldest is only in middle school, so we don't expect to be grandparents for some time yet. But when that day comes, and we hope it does, we'll be there to love, support, and play Go Fish with the new generation. It doesn't matter at all whether or not we are by then remarried to others. We're going to be Grandma and Grandpa, regardless. And if we are married to other people by then, so much the better! Our grandchildren will only get *more* love, *more* support, and *more* games of Go Fish.

Each grandparent (however many there are!) should have a unique and distinctive name for the children to use in addressing them: Grandma, Granddad, Nana, Poppy, Bubba, or any name that makes sense within your family unit.

To our someday grandchildren—and yours, too,

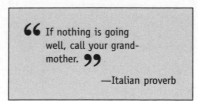

❝ If nothing is going well, call your grandmother. ❞

—Italian proverb

we hope—a divorce somewhere in the past will be ancient history, and will in no way affect the wondrous relationship that grandparents have with grandchildren, nor the harmony at family gatherings.

On death and dying

We all suffer when those close to us die. The death of an immediate family member is the most painful of all. Should your co-parent and ex-spouse die before you, please, please be there emotionally for the children. No matter what their age, five or fifty, they will need you like they've never needed you before, although their needs will vary depending on their age. You are now their only parent. Even if you had an ugly divorce and never found it within yourself to forgive your ex, you can and *should* do so now.

When Susan's father was hospitalized in a distant city in 2000 (leading to his death several days later), and Susan and her sister kept vigil in the intensive care unit, their mother called every day to check his status and lend support to her daughters. On the morning he died, Susan called her and cried with her. (Susan's mother was so saddened that she immediately left work and stayed home grieving for the next few days.) At that point, she had been divorced from Susan's dad for more than 20 years, and, living thousands of miles apart, barely saw him in that interim. Yet she grieved, and supported her daughters with genuine emotion. It was vital to her daughters during that difficult time. Interestingly, although she offered to travel to come to the funeral, Susan and her sister declined out of respect for their stepmother, who had never been fully accepted by their dad's siblings, and who would have been ignored at the funeral if their mother—his first wife—had been there. This too is an example of adjusting to circumstances within an expanded family unit, to everyone's benefit.

> 66 Death ends a life, not a relationship. 99
>
> —Jack Lemmon, actor

Your in-laws pass away

One of your ex's parents dies. Perhaps you haven't been very close to your ex since the divorce, but he or she would so much appreciate at least a call at this most difficult time. Do it. And, if you were close to your in-laws, allow yourself time to grieve, as well. Above all, if the deceased was a grandparent to your children, you will have to be the primary nurturer. Remember that your co-parent is probably in shock and may not be able to offer much comfort and support to the children during this time when they too need it.

If your relationship with your ex's family is still good, consider stepping in to assist with funeral arrangements, arranging for food for any post-funeral gathering, notifying extended family and friends of the death, etc. Again, all of this may be beyond the bounds of your particular situation. But if it is not, you can perform a valuable service to a family that was once yours, and that is still your children's extended family. In doing so, you will reinforce your children's feelings of stability and harmony, and may find that you do some healing yourself as well.

Your own mortality

No one wants to think about it, but, yes, we are all mortal. At some point, we must ponder whether we want cremation or burial, and if a burial, where. For the divorced with children, an extra factor needs to be figured into the equation: Will you and your ex be buried apart, or buried together, or at least in close proximity so that the children can visit you both? Of course, many things—such as where you are living and whether you are each remarried—will factor into the decision. But do think of the children. And, if they are old enough, you might ask them how they feel about it. As difficult as it may be to contemplate these issues and come to a decision, force yourself to do it, and then record your wishes in writing. You will save your children and your family a great deal of anxiety during their time of mourning. An example of such a written record follows.

A Sample Letter to the Family

Dear Loved Ones:

1. It is my desire to be buried in _____, unless my adult children mutually agree on an alternate location.

2. I hereby instruct my family members to purchase a casket or coffin of the following type [designate whether you wish something very simple, or something with religious symbols on it, or any other specifics that are important to you.

3. If possible, I wish to be buried in _____ cemetery.

4. I would like at least one family member to say a few words at my funeral, in addition to any clergyperson who may conduct the service. I do not have a preference as to the clergyperson who conducts the service, but if, at the time of my death, I am a member of any congregation, I ask that the clergyperson associated with that congregation conduct the service, provided he or she is willing to do so within the directives of this letter.

5. I would like my former spouse of ___ years and co-parent, _____, to be present at my funeral, and to be asked and permitted to participate in any manner needed or as desired by him (her).

6. I would like my beloved companion [spouse, or other term], _____, to be accorded the same respect and sympathies as would be shown to a surviving widow or widower, or family member, and I ask that he (she) and [former spouse] jointly lend emotional comfort and support to my children, my

siblings, my parents (if then living), and any other family members.

7. In turn, I ask that my children (if they are of adult age), my siblings, my parents, and any friends or other family, lend support and emotional comfort to [current spouse or companion] and [former spouse], separately and equally.

8. I request that pictures of the following individuals be displayed at my funeral and then placed in my casket before burial: [names of individuals, including former spouse, if so desired]. I also ask that a photo of [current spouse or companion] and me together be displayed and enclosed.

9. In the event of any confusion or questions about my desires, my family members should consult my long-standing friend, _____, for input and guidance as to what my wishes would be.

10. I hereby direct that my funeral and any final services or celebrations be conducted with dignity, at moderate expense, and in a manner which fosters harmony and comfort for all of those people closest to me. I further direct that this letter be reproduced and distributed at my funeral services.

Signed:

_____

(your signature)

Date: _____

Should you die without a clear letter of instruction to family members, they may agonize over whether to include your former spouse in the funeral. Don't make them guess what your wishes might have been. Write them a letter. Include all the information you want to include about how you want your death handled, including the role, if any, of your former spouse.

This letter should be tailored to your specific needs and desires. Again, composing something of this sort may ultimately ensure that your desires are carried out, and will provide guidance to your family members who may otherwise be confused about dealing with the competing needs of the extended family unit. It will also prevent meddlesome or ill-intentioned relatives from excluding individuals who should be part of the process.

Just the facts

- It's largely your decision how close you want to remain to your in-laws—and what you want to call them.
- Don't rush into new relationships; give yourself time to get over your divorce.
- Stepparents should adopt the "trusted babysitter" model.
- Ideally, both parents should be there for their children on milestone events such as graduations and weddings.
- A death in the family can be a time for making amends.

Post-Divorce Money and Health Issues

PART VII

GET THE SCOOP ON...
How to transfer assets ▪ On being a single
taxpayer ▪ An overview of investments ▪
Insurance considerations ▪ Making
changes to your will

Mastering Your Finances

Often the emotional challenges of divorce are so stressful and all-consuming that many other things, including matters of financial importance, get put on the back burner. It is essential that you not ignore your finances for too long. You are now a single person, or soon to become one, and as a single person you suddenly have new financial needs and require new financial strategies. Even if you weren't previously the one who handled financial affairs, you now will have to have at least a working knowledge of your money matters.

A few of the things you'll need to consider include your new status with the IRS, your will and other estate-planning documents, your bank accounts, your insurance policies, and your healthcare. That last item, healthcare, is so daunting that we're going to devote the entire next chapter to discussing it. For now, let's look at the other items.

Bright Idea

If dividing the house is part of the divorce agreement, ask a local real estate agent or two to provide you with a no-cost appraisal based on the recent sales of other houses in the neighborhood. Any agent, on the prospect of earning you as a client, will be happy to provide such an appraisal.

Transferring assets

In earlier chapters we spoke of the goal of achieving an equitable split of assets between you and your soon-to-be ex. But we haven't talked about how to actually transfer assets. In short, after the dust has settled and you and the spouse work out your deal, then come the bank forms, a probable notarization or signature guarantee here and there, possibly a complex thing called a QDRO, and a lot of attention to the tax implications of moving money.

Moving money (the easy part)

Assets held in a taxable, nonretirement account are usually not very difficult to transfer from one person to another. Let's say Robin has a money-market fund at XYZ Brokerage Firm, and as part of the divorce agreement, she must move half of the money in that money-market fund to Bob. Bob says he wants the money transferred to his checking account at the First American Bank. Robin must take the initiative and ask the representatives at XYZ to provide her with a *transfer-of-assets form*. (Many institutions will also have the form online.) Robin will probably need to provide either notarization or a signature guarantee along with the form, depending on the rules of that particular financial institution. She will also need the full name, address, and telephone number of Bob's bank, as well as Bob's account number and his Social Security number. (The IRS likes to keep track of any transfer of funds.) You have up to six years after your divorce to transfer assets before you need to worry about incurring a gift tax. After six years, any transfer of more than $11,000 to a nonspouse would incur such a tax.

Moving money (the tricky part)

Transferring money from a money market account or a savings or checking account is relatively easy compared to transferring stocks and bonds. Actually, the process is the same, but the tax ramifications make matters difficult. And we're not talking here about gift taxes, but, rather, capital gains taxes. If, for example, Bob were to transfer 500 shares of the GidgetWidget stock to Robin, he can do that by either transferring the shares themselves or cashing out the shares and giving Robin the cash. If he cashes out, *he* may incur a tax hit if he has held the stock for a long time and the stock has risen in price. On the other hand, if he transfers the actual shares to Robin, *she* will be responsible for paying a capital gains tax whenever she sells the shares. As a general rule of thumb, as the recipient of funds, you want cash; as the giver of funds, you want to transfer the securities themselves. But the rule of thumb reverses if there is a transfer of a security that has lost money. In that case, the giver benefits by cashing out (and taking a tax deduction for a capital loss). If the giver passes along the security, the potential tax deduction goes with it.

Moving money (the expensive part)

The most difficult transfer of assets traditionally has been the transfer of assets held in a tax-advantaged retirement account, such as a 401(k) or 403(b). In order to split such accounts and retain the tax benefits while avoiding possible penalties, a couple must use a legal document called a qualified domestic relations order (QDRO, commonly referred to by lawyers as a

 Bright Idea

If selling an expensive house is part of your divorce plan and the house has appreciated greatly since you bought it, you might want to sell while you're still married and divide the proceeds. A married couple can enjoy as much as $500,000 in capital gains without paying any tax. A single person gets a tax break for just half that amount.

"Quadro"). In the past, a lawyer could help you obtain a QDRO, you'd then pass the paperwork onto your employer, and that would be that. Very recent changes in the law, however, have made the whole matter considerably messier. Now, an employer has the right to charge you for such a "service," and, in some cases, those charges can run from hundreds to several thousand dollars. You need to find out from your employer whether such charges will be levied, and if they will be, that needs to be figured into the divorce negotiation.

Obviously, it is easiest to work around your job's retirement accounts and split other assets, if possible. In a perfect world, you and your ex will have roughly the same amount of money in your respective retirement accounts, and each will hold on to his or her own, without any transfers being made. If the numbers are not equal but are close, you should both work with the goal of transferring other assets and leaving the retirement accounts alone.

Not all retirement plans require a QDRO, only so-called "qualified" plans. You do not need a QDRO to split up an IRA. But there are complications there also. Contact the financial institution that holds your IRA.

You are now a single taxpayer

If you haven't dealt with taxes before—if you allowed your ex to do it all—brace yourself. Especially if you are self-employed, you'll soon discover that the complexities of the American tax system make quantum physics look like tic-tac-toe. If you know the ins and outs of the system, you'll pay a lot less than your neighbor who pulls in the same income as you do. Fair or unfair, just or unjust, that's the reality.

> 66 I'm proud to be paying taxes in the United States. The only thing is—I could be just as proud for half the money. 99
>
> —Arthur Godfrey, radio and television host

How to file taxes the year of the divorce

The law says that if you are married on December 31 of any given year, then you must file as a married couple for that year. But is filing as a married couple a good thing or a bad thing? Should you hurry a divorce to make sure that it happens by December 30? Well, of course, you should never hurry divorce, but if you're going to divorce anyway, and your decision is firm, then perhaps yes, it might make sense to get moving before year-end. At the urging of our accountant, that's what we did. But it depends on a couple's financial situation. You should ask your accountant to punch the numbers both ways to see which is best: filing as a married couple or filing as two single people. The fees for doing so should not be exorbitant, and often, some of the groundwork the accountant does would be necessary for your eventual tax filing anyway. In any event, spending some money on the accountant at this point may save you big bucks in the ultimate tax sting, so consider it money well spent. Often, what's best for one person may be detrimental to the other. But if you're going about this thing smartly, you and your soon-to-be-ex can figure out how to divide the difference, and Uncle Sam will actually wind up subsidizing your divorce.

Alimony and child support

As we discussed earlier, child support is neither taxable nor tax-deductible. Not so for alimony. The giver gets to deduct. The receiver must pay tax. No exceptions. Note that the amount of the deduction the giver takes (because he is likely in a higher tax bracket) and the amount of the tax due by the recipient can differ quite a bit. Imagine that Juan, in a 30-percent tax bracket, pays alimony of $1,000 a month to Anna-Marie, who is in the 20-percent bracket. Juan gets a deduction of $300 from his taxes, and Anna-Marie only needs to pay $200. This is something both parties need to think about at settlement time.

Investments made easy (sort of)

Remember when you were a kid and there were only three brands of shampoo? Have you looked at the shampoo aisles lately? And do you remember when you'd walk into a coffee shop and you'd simply ask for coffee, small or large? The biggest decision you had to make was whether you wanted cream and sugar.

How things have changed! For the investor today, the number of choices is overwhelming. According to Morningstar, the investment research firm, there are currently no fewer than 6,000 individual stocks, 6,200 mutual funds, and nearly 200 exchange-traded funds that Americans can choose from. And that's to say nothing of the thousands of individual bond offerings, money-market funds, CDs, hedge funds, REITS, closed-end funds, commodities, ADRs, and derivative products like puts and calls. If you've always let your ex do the choosing, you may be at a loss as to where to begin.

How much risk can you take?

The first questions you'll need to ask yourself in choosing investments is how much risk you can take, and how much risk you want to take. Risk in the world of investments is synonymous with volatility. Risk is also closely tied to return. (Have we already lost you? If so, consider hiring a respected and trustworthy financial advisor as soon as possible. See Appendix E.) It's really a rather simple formula: The more you're willing and able to see your investments go up and down, the more *potential* you have for making money. (If anyone says that you can earn sky-high returns without taking any risk, run. You are dealing

Watch Out!

If the divorce settlement left you with a good amount of money to invest, take your time. Making investment decisions while your emotions are overwrought is a sure way to make big mistakes.

with a con artist.) As a very rough rule of thumb, any money that you may need to tap into over the next six months should be kept as cash or "near-cash"—either held in a savings account, checking account, money-market fund, or short-term bond fund. Any money you won't need for at least six months can be invested elsewhere, such as a CD. For money you plan to hold for at least a few years, consider something more risky (but more likely to see a high return), such as a stock mutual fund. In general, stock mutual funds are more volatile than bond mutual funds, but in the long term they will likely make you more money. (Don't even think of buying individual stocks or bonds unless you have substantial money and know-how.)

The two cardinal rules of investing

You've heard the first cardinal rule before, as has everyone: Don't put all of your eggs in one basket. It's amazing how many people ignore that advice. Never, never, never put all of your money into any one stock or bond...or even one stock or bond mutual fund. Diversify, diversify, diversify. You should seek out different "asset classes"—that is, not only different investments, but different *kinds* of investments—that tend to go up and down at different times. A financial professional can help you to do that, or you can educate yourself by reading some of the books listed in Appendix C.

The second cardinal rule to investing is this: Keep your investment expenses low. Don't ever buy a "load" fund, don't purchase any mutual fund with management expenses of more than 1 percent (1.5 percent for international funds), and if you hire a professional to help you, shop around for one who won't charge you an arm and a leg. Ask friends or family whom they use, and interview your investment counselor just as you did your lawyer.

Do you need a professional to invest?

Most amateur investors don't do especially well. They tend to buy expensive investment products. They buy high; they sell low. They make lots and lots of money—for the brokers and fund companies—and wind up with little to show for themselves. Most people would benefit by hiring an investment advisor, but finding one who is both knowledgeable and honest and doesn't charge a fortune isn't easy. See tips for doing so in Appendix E.

Those all-important beneficiary forms

For every bank account, brokerage account, and mutual fund account you hold, you may have had the option of filling out either a beneficiary or transfer-on-death form. At the time you opened the account, if you were married and listed a beneficiary, you probably listed your spouse. You die, your spouse gets the goods. But now you're divorced. Do you still want your ex to get your assets if you die? Are you operating under the incorrect impression that once you're divorced, your ex is no longer entitled to your funds if you die? Unless you change your beneficiary forms—which many people don't—your ex could get it all. Note that you can update your will, but that won't change a thing. Beneficiary forms supersede a will.

> 66 I've seen people forget to update their beneficiary forms, and it's really awful. The former spouse gets everything. The rest of the family gets nothing. 99
>
> —Portia Carmichael, CFP, financial planner and divorce counselor

How much insurance do you need?

Whether it's life, home and auto, or disability, insurance serves to protect you or your estate from catastrophic economic loss. Now that you are divorced you might need less insurance, or you might need more. It all depends on what you have, and what (and whom) you have to protect.

Life insurance

Most married couples who have life insurance policies list each other as the beneficiary. If Pablo dies, Jill gets $50,000. If Jill

Watch Out!

Remember that when insuring against the loss of a co-parent, if that person dies you will not only lose his or her economic contribution to raising the kids, but you will also lose that person's physical presence. Suddenly, you will be solely responsible for raising the children. Perhaps you will no longer be able to work full time, and will therefore need the insurance money to make up for lost wages.

dies, Pablo collects $50,000. The purpose of life insurance in marriage is to make certain that the spouse (or spouse and children, if there are children) will be able to get by alone. As a divorced couple, you are no longer living under the same roof, but you may still be economically joined at the hip if one of you is providing the bulk of the income, and sharing with the other via alimony. If there are children, the two of you are jointly responsible for their welfare. So life insurance may be as important as ever. It makes sense for the person contributing the most to the support of the children to have a larger amount taken out on his or her life. After all, if the major source of income dries up, the more insurance will be needed to pay the bills.

Upon divorce, Jill and Pablo may wish to keep their respective policies in place, especially if they have children. As before, Jill collects if Pablo dies; Pablo collects if Jill dies. But what if Pablo no longer trusts Jill and suspects that she may cancel her policy in order to avoid having to pay premiums? If she does that, and she dies, Pablo is left all alone to support the children. He has two options. First, he can ask in the divorce decree to have it mandated that Jill continue to pay the premiums for *x* number of years. Or, the more simple solution: Pablo can take ownership of Jill's policy, and so it becomes his responsibility, not hers, to pay the premiums. Jill likewise should take ownership of the policy on Pablo's life. That way, both parties have an incentive to continue paying the premiums...each is protecting himself or herself in case the other dies. And there is no longer the need to require proof that the other has maintained his or her insurance policy every year.

Home and auto insurance

Many people who have asked me (Russell) to create financial plans for them reveal that they are woefully underinsured. Hey, you bought your house in 1985 when it was worth $100,000, and now its estimated value is triple that. Did you think of changing your homeowner's insurance policy along the way? Perhaps not. If anything happened to the house, your largest asset could literally go up in smoke. If you've just won the house in a divorce settlement, chances are it is your largest asset. Protect it. It's generally wise to insure the home for roughly the amount it would cost to rebuild the home from scratch. This is what is known as "replacement value." That might be more than the market value of the home, or it might be less. It will depend on the value of the land itself and construction costs in your area. Any Realtor should be able to give you a ballpark figure. And most insurance companies are only too happy to work with you to make sure you are adequately insuring your property.

Auto insurance is required in most states, along with minimum amounts of coverage. The minimum is just that—a minimum. Typically, the state minimums are for $15,000 of coverage. You should consider having one with far more coverage than that. A pretty standard policy these days will cover you up to $300,000 for bodily injury to any one person, or $500,000 per accident. Note, however, that these limits are for injury to persons other than yourself ("third party coverage"). You also need to understand what the insurance coverage is for *you* if you are injured in an accident that you caused ("first party coverage"), or if you are injured by another driver who doesn't have sufficient insurance ("underinsured motorist coverage"). Explore these different kinds of insurance coverages with your insurance company or agent, and stress that you want to make sure you are not only protecting your assets (in the event you injure someone else), but also protecting yourself (in the event you are hurt by someone else). If you don't feel your insurance company or agent has adequately explained these concepts to you, ask your divorce attorney whether he or she understands insurance law or can refer you to someone who does for a consult. One hour of attorney time is about all it should take to learn about these issues and determine whether you

> 66 I don't want to tell you how much insurance I carry with the Prudential, but all I can say is: when I go, they go too. 99
>
> —Jack Benny, comedian

have sufficient insurance. Whether married or divorced—but especially divorced—you can't afford to be without adequate coverage.

Disability insurance

Should you become disabled as a married person, there's someone to help catch you as you fall. Should you become disabled as a divorced person, the economic consequences can be devastating. Unfortunately, disability insurance can be very expensive. Remember that you don't need a policy that will cover 100 percent of your income. Closer to 60 percent would probably be okay. You also most likely will be able to collect something from Social Security. And, sad but true, if you're disabled you won't be jet-setting around the world, or even the country, so your cost of living should be modest. Speak with an insurance agent about this type of insurance and shop around for quotes, as prices vary greatly from one company to another. Make it a priority to secure this type of insurance as soon as possible. The expense will be lower when you are younger, and generally the premium will remain fixed at the original cost.

A word on wills

When you file a divorce action or when you and your spouse separate with an eye toward divorce, you may want to update your will. Very often married couples have wills in which each leaves his or her entire estate to the spouse. In most states, such provisions terminate automatically upon divorce, but if you have not named an alternate beneficiary, your estate may be eaten up by probate and legal costs, and the court may be drawn in to divvy up what's left. And if you're not yet divorced, but just separated, your spouse who is named as the beneficiary will still take all. Is that what you intended?

Considering the many emotional issues involved when your divorce or separation begins, it is quite understandable that you're not thinking about what would happen if you died before you were actually legally divorced. If you had a will that left all of your property to your spouse and you died before you were divorced, your spouse would inherit all of your property. Considering you would have been in the process of obtaining a divorce, other relatives or friends may have an opportunity to contest the terms of the will. However, a will generally speaks for itself, and it is often extremely difficult, if not impossible, to overturn it.

To avoid this problem, you may wish to write a new will before the divorce is final. Until you actually settle your divorce, you may not be able to address all the issues that you would ultimately like to resolve in your will, but at the very least you can write a basic one that explains your present marital situation and makes arrangements to leave your assets to someone other than your spouse. For help with this, consult a lawyer who specializes in estate planning.

Be aware that in many states, your spouse—even if you are separated, but not divorced—will be entitled to some share of the estate, what is known as a "statutory share." The rules on this vary greatly from state to state, and an estate-planning attorney will be able to advise you on the best way to make sure your intentions are carried out. Once your divorce is completed, you should pay another visit to that estate

> 66 Nothing in life is certain except death and taxes. 99
>
> —Benjamin Franklin

planning attorney and make sure your will is again updated, so your ex-spouse will no longer be able to stake any claim to your estate.

Why wait?

Although you may not be able to write your spouse out of your will while you are still technically married, in the case of a pending divorce, you may have more leeway in leaving your assets to someone other than your spouse. At the very least, by writing a new will, you will protect your assets to the fullest extent allowed by law.

Very often married couples do not have wills. When this is the case, the laws of intestacy divide their property, and most often the surviving spouse would receive most, if not all, of the property. If you do not have a will, the event of a divorce or separation should be a very good impetus to write one. In the event you should die while a divorce is pending, you do not want the laws of your state to determine whether your spouse is entitled to your assets.

Don't forget the other kind of will

Aside from your last will and testament, you should have a living will. A living will sets forth your instructions for your medical care in the event you become incapacitated, either mentally or physically. Since no one can list all possible contingencies, a living will also stipulates who will make important medical decisions for you. That person is called your "surrogate" or "attorney-in-fact," and given "power of attorney." If you already have a living will in place, it most likely gives your spouse power of attorney. But now that you are divorcing, is he or she the person you still want in that all-important position? You may want to consider your parents (if they are still vigorous), a sibling, your children (if they are grown), or another trusted individual. Or, if you have minor children and you are still on good terms with your ex, you may still want him or her to be your surrogate on these important decisions, considering that no one has as great an interest in your medical well-being as the children and your co-parent. But in any event, do not let this time pass without addressing the all-important issue of a living will.

And while you're at it, ask your lawyer to prepare a more general power of attorney document, one that gives another person power to conduct business and financial affairs on your behalf. This document does not become effective unless and until you become incapacitated, so don't worry that you're vesting another person with automatic power over your affairs. The person designated may be the same person who has your medical power of attorney, or it may be someone entirely different. You may want to consider giving that role to a family member who shows good judgment in his or her own business affairs, whereas your medical power of attorney should be vested in someone who has a strong emotional connection to you and who understands your wishes concerning long-term medical care. Most lawyers will "bundle" the living will, powers of attorney, and last will and testament together in a reasonably priced package.

Just the facts

- Transferring assets in a divorce may have substantial tax consequences.
- Insurance needs can change radically after a divorce.
- If your spouse always handled the taxes, you will have a new large responsibility after the divorce.
- Don't invest without knowing what you're investing in.
- When you and your spouse separate with an eye toward divorce, you may want to write a new will.

Chapter 18

GET THE SCOOP ON...
A look at COBRA ▪ Covering the children ▪
Shopping around for the best insurance ▪
How to save money on your medical care

Who'll Pay the Doctor Bills?

The cost of healthcare in America is nothing to sneeze at—to say the very least. In 1960, America devoted about 5 percent of its gross domestic product, the total fruit of the economy, to healthcare. That percentage is now over 15 percent—twice that of most other Western nations—and rising. Doctors, drug companies, hospitals, insurance people, and politicians all wag a finger at one another. Meanwhile, you get stuck footing the bill. And now that you're getting divorced, that bill may prove the biggest economic challenge of your future years.

Naturally, as you and your spouse divorce and divide the economic pie, you should count health insurance as a marital asset. If one of you is employed and the other is not, the employed person probably has health insurance that is at least partially subsidized, and that should count as part of his or her total income in any settlement discussions. The nonemployed person is soon to be uninsured, and that is a burden that needs to be taken into consideration in deciding what is a fair and equitable split. In some cases, it may make sense for the employed person to cover or subsidize the nonemployed ex-spouse's health insurance premiums.

Ah, but where will that health insurance come from?

Understanding COBRA

The Consolidated Omnibus Budget Reconciliation Act (COBRA) is quite a mouthful. What it amounts to is a law that says that employers with more than 20 employees who offer those employees health insurance must also offer that same insurance to employees' ex-spouses for up to three years. It sounds good, but there's a big catch: The employer doesn't have to pay for the insurance; the employer merely has to offer it. Unless you've worked out some kind of deal with your ex, you, the former spouse, are the one who'll need to cough up the payments for the insurance company. And that can be frightfully expensive.

Having COBRA is better than not having COBRA, but understand that it isn't always the best deal in town. If you are in relatively good health and take no expensive medications on a regular basis, an individual policy may be cheaper for you than paying into your ex's group plan. Some group plans have higher premiums per person because of the unique medical situations of a few members of the group, which drives up the entire group's costs.

If you are self-employed, you might want to look into getting a group plan with your local Chamber of Commerce. Or you

---

 Watch Out!

If you're using the COBRA plan, you must pay your premiums on time. If you miss a payment, your ex-spouse's company can drop your coverage automatically. Get the details from the human resources person at your ex's office or place of business.

might have one offered to you by one of a number of professional organizations. (See the upcoming section, Shopping for Health Insurance.) Look around. Don't be lazy. You might save a bundle. Remember this: If you wait three years, you may have a harder time finding affordable health insurance. Anything can happen in three years. And when negotiating your

> **66** Be careful with COBRA. You might be better off seeking your own insurance as soon as possible. Remember that in three years, you'll be older, and possibly in not-as-good health. It may be wise to shop for your own plan now rather than waiting. **99**
>
> —Portia Carmichael, CFP, financial planner and divorce consultant

divorce settlement, if part of the deal is that your ex is going to cover your health insurance premiums, make sure that will apply even if you go outside COBRA for your insurance coverage.

What about the kids?

If you and your spouse have children and the entire family was covered under your spouse's health insurance plan, the children can, of course, still be covered even though you are no longer on your spouse's policy. It usually makes sense for the children to continue to be covered by whatever health insurance plan existed during the marriage. If the plan is provided to you or your spouse by an employer at little or no cost, the two of you will need to address only the issue of who will pay the children's deductibles, co-pays, and unreimbursed expenses. However, if you or your spouse must pay for the insurance, you will have to decide who is going to foot the bills. As a general rule, like child support, parents are required to pay for the expenses of their children in the ratio of their individual earnings to the total earnings of both spouses. *Never* overlook this all-important issue when negotiating a divorce settlement.

Shopping for health insurance

After your mortgage and food, health insurance may well be your largest expense. It pays to shop for the best deal. The Internet can be a goldmine of information. Go to www.ehealth insurance.com and browse dozens of insurance companies. As a general rule, group plans are cheaper than individual plans, so you'll also want to check to see if any organizations you belong to offer group benefits. Professional groups such as your local Chamber of Commerce, teacher's union, or other organization are always a good bet, but don't forget to touch base with your alumni association, old fraternities or sororities, or social clubs.

Health savings accounts (HSAs)

HSAs are so new that few people know about them yet. But they are awfully enticing, and our guess is that they are going to be hot. Why hot? Because the HSA is a nifty way of getting Uncle Sam to help pay for your healthcare. It works sort of like a tax-deductible IRA, but the money invested gets earmarked for medical expenses. In tandem with a low-cost, high-deductible insurance policy, most people, or at least relatively healthy people, should wind up considerably ahead. The whole deal is neatly explained on the Treasury Department's Website, www.treas.gov/offices/public-affairs/hsa. Or, for those with no Web access, call 202-622-4HSA. You might also want to discuss HSAs with your accountant and your present insurance carrier.

Medicare and Medicaid

In most wealthy countries, people don't have to worry about health insurance. The government sees to it that its citizens

Moneysaver

Forty-one million Americans have neither group nor individual health insurance. Hopefully, you're not one of them. But if you are, know that many hospitals, doctors, and pharmacies will often cut you a break. But you need to ask.

have coverage. In the United States, only three groups of people are guaranteed healthcare: 1) prison inmates (we don't recommend that route); 2) the elderly or severely disabled; and 3) the destitute. Know that if you are 65 or older, or disabled so that you cannot possibly work, you qualify for Medicare. You will also qualify if you have end-stage renal disease (permanent kidney failure treated with dialysis or a transplant). For more information, go to www.medicare.gov or call 1-800-MEDICARE.

Medicaid—quite distinct from Medicare, even though the names are similar—is administered by individual states, and the eligibility requirements can be complicated. For more information go to www.cms.hhs.gov/medicaid, or contact your state government or local social service agency.

Miscellaneous and sundry ways to save money on health bills

Whether you're paying for all or only part of your medical expenses, you can very often save money, especially on drugs, by shopping smartly. Here are five suggestions:

- **Go generic.** Need a certain drug? Ask your doctor to prescribe the generic version, if one exists. It typically will cost a fraction of the brand name, and while it may differ as far as trifles such as color and taste, all of the active ingredients will be the same. It's the law.

     For the latest generation drug, there will be no generic version. But often you don't need the latest generation. A newer drug isn't necessarily a better drug. In fact, the opposite is often true. Talk to your physician. And, if you don't have a decent prescription plan, let him know that. Often doctors save their inventory of free samples that they get from the drug companies for their needy patients.

- **Price-shop for pills.** Once you know what kind of medication you want—whether brand name or generic—you can take your prescription to the local drugstore and perhaps pay through the nose. Or you can shop around. Thanks to the Internet and mail order, comparison-shopping is easy and can often save you a bundle. The National Association of Boards of Pharmacy keeps a list of U.S.-based cyber-pharmacies at www.nabp.net/vipps/consumer/listall.asp.

You might also try some Canadian outfits, such as www.mapleleafmeds.com (1-800-794-8552) or www.canadian drugstore.com (1-888-773-2698). But be forewarned that the legality of ordering Canadian drugs is in question as we go to press on this book (thanks to intensive lobbying by U.S. pharmaceutical companies), so be sure you check out the state of the law first.

▪ **Talk to a nurse.** Nurse practitioners and physician's assistants are highly trained at diagnosing and treating common health problems. In some parts of the country, you may find independent nurse practitioners (check your phone book) who will see you outside of the doctor's office. Almost anywhere, doctors' offices will have nurse practitioners and physician's assistants on staff. Either way, opening up and saying "ah" to a medical professional other than a physician will often wind up costing you less.

▪ **If you can, avoid Saturday night at the hospital.** Unless it's an emergency, *never* check yourself into a hospital on a weekend. Most hospital staffs aren't especially active on weekends, which means you'll be paying $1,200 to $2,000 a day for basically room and board. If you want a night out of the house, check yourself into a fancy hotel. You'll pay a fraction as much—and you'll get far, far better food! Then report to the hospital on Monday.

▪ **Take a hike.** Or go for a swim. Or take a bicycle ride. It doesn't matter what kind of exercise you choose, the point is to stay active, and you'll save money on healthcare. Honest. Researchers from the Centers for Disease Control and Prevention (CDC) found that people who engage in regular physical activity—at least 30 minutes of moderate or strenuous physical activity three or more times a week— tend to lower their medical bills by nearly 25 percent! So who says you can't just walk away from your problems?

If you belong to a health club, find out if your health insurance plan offers you a rebate each year upon proof that you actually went to the gym on a regular basis. Many now do, in the interest of preventive health maintenance, which the insurance companies have recognized will lower your overall health costs. If they've figured it out, so should you!

Just the facts

- Health insurance is expensive, but you can't do without it, nor can your kids.

- Through COBRA you can remain covered for three years on your former spouse's employer's insurance plan, but you'll have to pay, and sometimes using COBRA may not be right for your situation.

- Shop around for the best health insurance plan.

- Health Savings Accounts are new and worth investigating.

- Be a proactive health consumer. Look for ways to save your health-care dollars.

Glossary

alimony   Also known as spousal support. Payments one spouse makes to the other after a divorce. For income tax purposes, the paying spouse may deduct these payments and the receiving spouse must declare them as income.

annulment   To nullify a marriage as though it never existed. By contrast, a divorce terminates a legal status (i.e., marriage).

arbitration   A proceeding before an attorney or appointed court officer other than a judge that can be binding or nonbinding, as agreed by the parties. May avoid the need for a trial before a judge.

child support   Money paid by one parent to the other for support of the children of the marriage. Cannot be waived by agreement of the parties; it is an absolute obligation to support children until they reach the age of emancipation. Failure to pay may be punishable by jail time.

COBRA   Federal law mandating continued health insurance coverage for 18 months after cessation of employment or 3 years after a divorce, at employee's cost.

community property   A method of division of marital property, used in a few states. Provides that property accumulated by the spouses during a marriage is to be evenly split upon dissolution of the marriage. Contrast: *equitable distribution.*

custodial parent   The parent with physical custody of the child(ren) at any given time. Contrast: *joint legal custody* and *joint physical custody.*

defendant   One against whom a complaint is filed; the defending party.

deposition   Testimony taken by a party or witness in a legal setting, although usually out of court. Questions are asked and testimony under oath is given in response. The individual whose deposition is taken is referred to as the "deponent."

discovery   The legal process in the initial stages of the divorce, when the parties (usually through their lawyers) exchange written information, generally on issues regarding their finances, their children, and their lifestyle.

emancipation   The age at which a child is deemed to become an adult—in most states, 18. Upon emancipation, parents no longer have an obligation to financially support their children.

equitable distribution   The division of marital property in a fair and reasonable manner. The term refers to a concept used by most states to ensure that the division of property takes into account certain factors, such as length of marriage, earning potential of each spouse, and medical conditions. Contrast: *community property.*

garnishment   The act by which child and/or spousal support may be obtained directly from a delinquent spouse's employer, who in turn deducts it from the employee's paycheck.

grounds   The legal reasons, or basis, for the divorce. The modern trend is toward "no-fault" or uncontested divorce, whereby traditional grounds such as adultery are no longer considered.

joint legal custody   A modern principle that provides each parent with the opportunity to have input on all matters having to do with a child's health, education, and welfare, regardless of the party with whom the child resides.

joint physical custody   An arrangement whereby the child(ren) resides with both parents on an alternating schedule; does not have to be 50-50 arrangement.

judgment   A final order of the court that is usually monetary in nature. It can be recorded in the county of residence and will operate as a lien against assets until paid.

litigation   The process by which parties to a lawsuit (for divorce or otherwise) prepare and present their case before a judge.

liquid assets   Assets that can be readily converted into cash. Examples of liquid assets include money market funds and very short-term bond funds. In contrast, nonliquid assets such as your home or your business can't be converted into cash quickly or easily.

mediation   A process for facilitation of communication between the parties, with a goal of settling differences out of court. Generally conducted by a trained mediator, often a lawyer. Nonbinding in all cases. Contrast: *arbitration.*

motion   A legal paper filed by a party or his lawyer, asking the court for a specific form of relief or action. Generally done on an interim basis during the pendency of the divorce litigation; for example, when one party is not receiving child support or is having problems with visitation. Most courts have expedited processes for setting hearings on motions.

no-fault divorce   A term that is not used in many states, but refers to the granting of a divorce without the need for "fault"— such as adultery or abandonment—to exist as a basis.

order   A directive by the court for a party to act or refrain from acting, as in an order to vacate the family home or to pay child support. Contrast: *judgment.*

perjury   The act of giving testimony that is untruthful while under oath.

petition   A formal written request to the court. Not used in all jurisdictions. Similar to *motion.*

plaintiff   The person who files a lawsuit.

pleadings   The initial documents used in a lawsuit to set forth the parties' positions (i.e., the plaintiff's complaint and the defendant's answer).

precedent   Decisions handed down by courts in prior cases that may affect the case at hand.

prenuptial agreement   Also called a premarital agreement. A contractual agreement made prior to a marriage, by which the couple agrees in advance how they will divide assets and liabilities if the marriage is terminated. Generally upheld by the courts unless there is a showing of unfair advantage by one party over the other, or fraud, coercion, or duress.

PFA   See *restraining order.*

pro se   A Latin term meaning "for yourself," referring to a party who represents himself or herself in court, without legal counsel.

qualified domestic relations order (QDRO)   A court order allowing for the splitting-up of funds within a qualified retirement account such as a 401(k). Without a QDRO, the IRS would assess penalties and taxes.

quit claim deed   A document transferring title of property to another person, often used when one spouse is giving up interest in the marital residence.

restraining order   Often also referred to as a "protection from abuse" order, or PFA. An order by the court requiring one person to stay away from another (or multiple others, in the case of a parent and children). Generally limited to a specified period of time, unless a "final" order is rendered.

retainer or retainer fee   Money required to be paid up front to an attorney before beginning legal services. The sum paid is put into a client escrow account, as governed by all states' laws regulating attorneys. Monthly bills are then deducted until the retainer is exhausted, at which time most attorneys in divorce cases will require a "refresher" to ensure that their legal fees are fully paid.

separation agreement   Also known as a settlement agreement. A contractual agreement between spouses that can determine the disposition of property, payment of support, and custody and visitation of children, although not all separation agreements address all of these issues. A separation agreement is negotiated by the parties and their counsel, without court involvement, but will be incorporated into the final divorce decree and will become part of the terms of the divorce.

transcripts   A written record of divorce proceedings, testimony, or depositions. Transcripts often constitute a large part of the expense in divorce proceedings, as sworn testimony is recorded by a stenographer, who then charges each party by the page for the record.

visitation   The right to see children, often limited in time, place, and manner. Contrast: *joint physical custody*. Increasingly, states are granting visitation to grandparents and other close relatives as well as spouses.

Resource Guide

Divorce attorneys

www.aaml.org The official Website of the American Academy of Matrimonial Lawyers, with more than 1,500 members nationwide. A substantive resource, including the very helpful *Divorce Manual: A Client Handbook,* which gives clear advice on a state-by-state basis.

www.lawyers.com The "consumer" version of martindale.com (see next entry).

www.martindale.com The "official" directory of the legal profession, this site is fairly easy to navigate and permits you to enter specific names of lawyers or your geographic preference and area of practice to match you with lawyers in your area. This should be considered a starting point, but since the lawyers pay for the listings and are free to advertise their own specialty or area of practice, users should ask for specific references.

www.milleniumdivorce.com This Website links to lawyers who pay to have their listings on the site. A decent locator Website, but the same precautions apply as for the site above.

Mediation specialists

www.alpha-divorce.com Alpha Center for Divorce Mediation, with locations in Pennsylvania and New

Jersey. Offers mediation and advice on legal, financial, and psychological matters, all under one roof. We believe there will be many more such firms in the future.

www.divorcehelp.com   A Website that showcases a California mediation and collaborative divorce firm, but which offers links to very helpful tools even for non-California residents.

General information about divorce laws

www.divorcesource.com   A rather commercial but comprehensive divorce network for the general public. It is somewhat of a mega-site of information relating to all divorce issues. A state-by-state link is particularly useful to enable the viewer to research the specifics of divorce law in his or her own jurisdiction.

www.law.cornell.edu   Sponsored by Cornell University's Legal Information Institute. Enter a search word in the query box on this site for extensive background information on all issues pertaining to divorce, custody, support, and distribution of marital assets. Highly accurate and completely reliable, this site does not aim to help the user "do it yourself," but rather to provide solid, understandable information about the law.

Custody issues

www.gocrc.com   Originally a "father's rights" resource, this Website is the public information arm of the Children's Rights Council, an organization that, according to its own mission statement: "...works to assure children meaningful and continuing contact with both their parents and extended family regardless of the parents' marital status." This organization was founded by a father who had been deprived of contact with his children, and now works diligently for the rights to shared custody for both parents.

www.missingkids.org   Sponsored by the National Center for Missing and Exploited Children. Custody battles rarely lead to parental kidnapping, but if yours does, this site offers extensive information on recovering missing children, as well as a wealth of other information.

Child support issues

www.acf.dhhs.gov/programs/cse/index.html Links to the Federal Office of Child Support Enforcement. Generally, this site is for the experienced legal practitioner who knows what to look for, but for the highly resourceful and motivated consumer who has the time, this Website can provide useful information about each state's child support enforcement laws, support guidelines, income withholding, and more. Also links to each state's child support enforcement agency.

www.supportguidelines.com Although this site is a marketing tool of an attorney who authored a book on child support guidelines, it is nonetheless a valuable resource for anyone who wants information on child support laws in any state, and provides a child support calculator that may be helpful to those wishing to negotiate an amicable agreement. Also contains links to each state's bar association.

Financial planners

www.cfainstitute.org CFA Institute: The place to go to find a Chartered Financial Analyst (CFA), which is similar to a CFP.

www.fpanet.org Financial Planning Association: The national organization of Certified Financial Planners (CFPs).

www.institutedfa.com Institute for divorce financial analysts: A nice designation to look for, but your top candidate should have other qualifications, such as a CFP or a CFA, as well.

www.napfa.org National Association of Personal Financial Advisors: The organization for fee-only (noncommissioned) comprehensive financial planners.

www.nasd.com Go to "Broker Check" to learn about the professional background, registration/license status, and disciplinary history of the firm and the brokers with whom you're planning to do business.

Financial advice for beginners

www.financiallearning.com Sponsored by General Electric, this Website offers 60-minute, easy-to-follow courses on various financial topics.

www.investinginbonds.com Everything (sort of) you need to know about bonds.

www.investopedia.com/university/buildingblocks.asp A little bit of everything about personal finance, very easy to understand.

www.practicalmoneyskills.com Visa's Website for basic household economic skills. Good information, although it doesn't highlight the dangers of overindulging in credit cards.

www.sensible-investor.com A wonderful portal to lots of specific Websites on specific financial topics, plus some pretty good investing information on this Website itself.

Financial advice for the more experienced investor

www.indexfunds.com This site is run by a guy who is an absolute zealot about index investing (there are worse things one can be). Play with the tiny icons at the top of the home page and you will find an unbelievable library of information about wise investing.

www.moneychimp.com An excellent primer on successful investing.

Miscellaneous

www.co-abode.com A Website run by a nonprofit organization through which single moms can find other single moms to share homes.

www.divorce.lifetips.com Advice (sometimes simplistic) on everything from how to handle the death of your ex's parent, to relocation with children, to accepting that it's over.

The authors

(E-mail us at any time with questions)

Russell Wild, MBA, NAPFA-certified financial advisor, Global Portfolios

www.globalportfolios.net

E-mail: Russell@globalportfolios.net

Susan Ellis Wild, Esq., Gross, McGinley, Labarre & Eaton, LLP

www.gmle.com

E-mail: Swild@gmle.com

Recommended Reading List

Bankruptcy

Caher, James P. and John M. Caher. *Personal Bankruptcy For Dummies.* Wiley Publishing, 2003.

Children

Brown, Marc and Laurie Krasny Brown. *Dinosaurs Divorce.* Little, Brown & Company, 1998.

Neuman, Gary M. *Helping Your Kids Cope with Divorce the Sandcastles Way.* Random House, 1998.

Custody

Boland, Mary L. *Your Right to Child Custody, Visitation and Support, Second Edition.* Sphinx Publishing, 2003.

Lyster, Mimi E. *Child Custody: Building Parenting Agreements that Work.* Nolo Press, 2003.

Sember, Brette. *The Visitation Handbook for the Custodial and Non-Custodial Parent.* Sphinx Publishing, 2003.

Economizing

Cline, Elizabeth. *The Bargain Buyer's Guide 2005.* The Print Project, annual.

Appendix C

Dacyczyn, Amy. *The Complete Tightwad Gazette*. Villard, annual.

Woodhouse, Violet, Attorney & CFP, and Dale Fethering. *Divorce & Money: How to Make the Best Financial Decisions During Divorce, Seventh Edition*. Nolo Press, 2004.

Investing (for beginners)

Armstrong, Frank. *The Informed Investor: A Hype-free Guide to Constructing a Sound Financial Portfolio*. AMACOM, 2002.

Bernstein, William J. and Donald G. Coxe. *The Four Pillars of Investing: Lessons for Building a Winning Portfolio*. McGraw-Hill, 2002.

Ferri, Richard A. *Protecting Your Wealth in Good Times and Bad*. McGraw-Hill, 2003.

Investing (for beyond beginners)

Bernstein, William J. *The Intelligent Asset Allocator: How to Build Your Portfolio to Maximize Returns and Minimize Risk*. McGraw-Hill, 2000.

Ellis, Charles. *Winning the Loser's Game: Timeless Strategies for Successful Investing, Fourth Edition*. McGraw-Hill, 2002.

Gibson, Roger. *Asset Allocation: Balancing Financial Risk*. McGraw-Hill, 2000.

Malkiel, Burton G. *A Random Walk Down Wall Street: The Best Investment Advice for the New Century, Fifth Edition*. W. W. Norton & Company, 1999.

Money management

Garrett, Sheryl with Marie Swift and the Garrett Planning Network. *Just Give Me the Answer$*. Dearborn, 2004.

Warren, Elizabeth and Amelia Warren Tyagi. *All Your Worth: The Lifetime Money Plan*. Free Press, 2005.

Settlement negotiations

Margulies, Sam. *Getting Divorced Without Ruining Your Life: A Reasoned, Practical Guide to the Legal, Emotional and Financial Ins and Outs of Negotiating a Divorce Settlement.* Simon & Schuster, 2001.

Stoner, Katherine E. *Using Divorce Mediation: Save Your Money and Your Sanity.* Nolo Press, 2004.

Taxes

J. K. Lasser Institute. *J. K. Lasser's Your Income Tax 2005.* Wiley Publishing, annual.

Important Checklists

Preparing to see your attorney

Before your first meeting with your attorney, collect the following information, and if at all possible, type it up in a neat format to give to your lawyer for your legal file.

Personal data

_____ Your full name, including middle name, maiden name, and any prior names

_____ Your spouse's full name, with the same degree of completeness

_____ The date and location of your wedding

_____ Your birth date

_____ Your spouse's birth date

_____ Your address and phone number

_____ Your spouse's address and phone number

_____ Information on any prior marriages of either you or your spouse

_____ Any plans you have to revert to use of your maiden or former name (this decision may be deferred until later)

_____ Your plans, if any, to relocate

Marital conditions

_____ Length of the marriage

_____ Dates of any prior separations between you and your spouse

_____ Date on which you and your spouse separated on this occasion

_____ Information on any marital counseling you underwent, including identity of counselor, whether joint or individual, and duration of therapy

_____ Previous filings for divorce between you and your spouse

Be prepared to discuss the following issues pertaining to the reasons for dissolution of the marriage, and bring any documents which pertain to these issues: infidelity by either spouse, abuse, financial irresponsibility, or other contributing factors to the breakup of the marriage.

Financial standing and personal assets

_____ Your occupation

_____ Your spouse's occupation

_____ Any future job changes for either of you

_____ Your income (take-home pay plus income from any other source; paycheck stubs for six months or more are ideal)

_____ Your spouse's income (take-home pay plus income from any other source)

_____ Any changes expected in income for either of you (raises, promotions, better-paying job, etc.)

_____ Copies of past three years' tax returns

_____ Current value of your home, including any written appraisals (if recently purchased, your real estate closing papers should be included)

_____ List of your personal and jointly owned personal belongings, with current values of each item

_____ Amounts of money in your personal and joint financial accounts, or copies of recent bank statements (preferred)

_____ Amounts of money in stocks and bonds or copies of recent investment statements

_____ Current value and details of both parties' insurance policies, or copies thereof

_____ Listing of all joint and individual debts, or (preferably) copies of most recent statements

_____ Listing of property, money, or assets brought by either spouse into the marriage (inheritances, gifts, past divorce settlements, etc.)

_____ Alimony paid to or received by a former spouse

Data on children

_____ The full names of your children

_____ Your children's birth dates (MM/DD/YY)

_____ Information on any stepchildren

_____ Children's special needs or disabilities

_____ Children's school year and grade average

_____ Current "custody and visitation schedule" of the children, even if not formally ordered by court or agreed upon between you

_____ Any conditions specific to the children's well-being

_____ A complete list of the children's health care providers, including pediatrician, dentist, and psychologist, if any; as well as specialized providers (speech therapist, tutor, etc.)

Discovery documents

The following is a list of the items your lawyer should seek from your spouse during the discovery phase of your divorce litigation. Be forewarned that your spouse's lawyer will probably turn around and demand the same items of you, so do not ask for anything that you are personally unwilling to produce on your own behalf.

_____ Personal checking account statements

_____ Joint checking account statements

_____ Business checking account statements

(If there is a serious dispute about income and outflow, your lawyer should demand copies of all cancelled checks from the above accounts for at least a three-year period. Otherwise, in this cyber-age, it is unreasonable to demand actual cancelled checks.)

_____ Children's savings account statements

_____ Business savings account statements

_____ Partnership statements

_____ Personal loan statements

_____ Educational loan statements

_____ Loans from family members

_____ Personal credit card account statements

_____ Joint credit card account statements

_____ Business income tax returns

_____ Joint income tax returns

_____ Investment statements: IRAs, mutual funds, money market funds, etc.

_____ Retirement account information from employers

_____ Stock certificates

_____ Bond certificates

_____ Expense account statements

_____ Frequent-flier mile statements

_____ Statements of bonuses, commissions, deferred salary increases

_____ List of safe-deposit box activity/sign-in sheet

_____ List of contents of safe-deposit box

_____ Phone bill statements (including cell phone and business phone)

_____ Business phone bill statements

_____ Cell phone bill statements

_____ Journals or diaries

_____ Photographs or surveillance evidence your spouse has had made of you

Financial information and assets

You should be prepared to answer all of the following questions during the litigation process, and you should ensure that your lawyer asks these questions of your spouse:

1. What is your current occupation?

2. What is your place of employment?

3. How long have you been employed there?

4. What is your current income?

5. Has your current income increased or decreased since the start of your divorce proceedings?

6. Why has your income decreased so substantially since the start of your divorce proceedings?

7. Do you receive any bonuses or commissions from your work?

8. What other sources of income do you have?

9. What are the details of your employee benefit package?

10. Is your spouse currently covered under your employee benefit plan?

11. Are your children currently covered under your employee benefit plan? Specifically, which spouse has medical insurance for the other members of the family, and have steps been taken to ensure that it continues until the date of divorce, and that COBRA arrangements are made thereafter?

12. What deductions are taken from your paycheck?

13. What exemptions are you taking from your paycheck withholding?

14. Do you have any outstanding personal debts?

15. What are the amounts and details of those debts?

16. Have you claimed bankruptcy in the past year?

17. Have you transferred any of your assets to a third party?

18. Did you withdraw any money from the checking accounts of your children, and if so, for what purpose?

19. In what ways did your spouse contribute to your business success?

20. Did your spouse help pay for your graduate school tuition?

21. Did your spouse help you apply to graduate school?

22. Did your spouse help you study for any licensing exams?

23. Did your spouse put off his or her own education until you received your degree?

24. Do you and your spouse own a home?

25. What is the current value of the home?

26. What additions have been made to the home?

27. How would you divide up between yourself and your spouse the responsibilities for the maintenance of that home? 50-50? 60-40? 80-20?

28. Do you own a vacation home?

29. What is the current value of that home?

30. Do you or your spouse expect to receive an inheritance, and if so, what are the details thereof?

Support

1. What was your pre-separation average household monthly income?

2. What were your fixed household monthly expenses?

3. Detail your children's monthly expenses, by category and amount (day care, school tuitions, clothing, out-of-pocket medical, sports and recreational activities, etc.).

4. Detail your own monthly expenses, by category and amount (clothing, work-related expenses, transportation costs, restaurants and reasonable entertainment, etc.).

5. What is your work schedule? Is it a set schedule? Is it flexible?

Use the following checklists as guides when choosing an attorney, evaluating your finances, choosing a counselor, and gathering important documents.

Legal checklist

_____ Get referral from the State Bar Association

_____ Get referrals from people you respect

_____ Call around to prospective lawyers' offices for basic information

_____ Check out Websites of local law firms

_____ Set up preliminary interviews with lawyers (see Appendix E for questions to ask)

_____ Disclose basic information about your case

_____ Discuss legal details of the handling of your case

_____ Hire the best candidate

_____ Begin discovery process

_____ Begin filings

_____ Deliberate on alimony

_____ Deliberate on child support

_____ Deliberate on child custody

_____ Deliberate on division of assets

_____ Begin negotiations

_____ Consider the help of expert witnesses

_____ Consider mediation

_____ Consider arbitration

_____ Prepare for the trial

_____ Prepare for the final court hearing

_____ Settle up loose strings

_____ Rewrite wills

_____ Establish credit in own name

_____ Change awarded assets into your own name

Financial assistance checklist

_____ Freeze assets (credit cards, accounts, etc.)

_____ Determine values of assets

_____ Determine values of debts

_____ Divide debts

_____ Divide investments

_____ Divide pensions

_____ Determine future Social Security benefits

_____ Transfer assets

_____ Block your spouse's illegal asset transfers

_____ Form new individual accounts

_____ Sell assets for capital

_____ Decide whether or not to sell the house

_____ Compile household budget

_____ Compile income/expense list

_____ Cut household expenses as much as possible

_____ Get out of debt

_____ Evaluate financial experts

_____ Interview financial experts (see Appendix E for questions to ask)

_____ Hire a financial expert

_____ Research financial management on your own

_____ Set financial goals

_____ Evaluate investment goals

_____ Research individual investments

_____ Procure investment policies

_____ Evaluate income tax standing

_____ Collect past tax returns

_____ Collect present tax returns

_____ Hire an accountant, or...

_____ Prepare to file your own taxes

_____ Call the IRS with your tax questions

_____ File your federal taxes

_____ File your state taxes

_____ Apply for credit in your own name

_____ Get a copy of your credit report

_____ Correct credit report problems

_____ Build good credit

_____ Evaluate bankruptcy pros and cons

_____ If necessary, get a bankruptcy lawyer

_____ Evaluate do-it-yourself options

_____ Purchase financial- or tax-planning software

_____ Take financial- or tax-planning seminars or classes

Counseling checklist

_____ Evaluate counselors for yourself and/or for your children

_____ Get referrals from professional associations

_____ Get referrals from your local hospital

_____ Get referrals from another doctor you trust

_____ Look into free counseling options

_____ Call individual therapists for details

_____ Conduct preliminary interviews (see Appendix E for questions to ask)

_____ Hire a counselor

_____ Arrange a payment plan

_____ Arrange session scheduling

_____ Determine what kind of therapy you and/or your children need

_____ Determine the length of the therapy

_____ Determine whether or not to go on medication

_____ Complete therapist's detailed questionnaires

_____ Outline your/your children's biggest issues and questions to be tackled in therapy

_____ Consider group therapy as well

Documents checklist

_____ Prenuptial agreements

_____ Retainer agreement with lawyer

_____ Separation agreements

_____ Alimony agreement

_____ Child support agreement

_____ Visitation schedule

_____ Assets list

_____ Appraisals

_____ Transfer of assets

_____ Illegal transfer block

_____ Settlement agreement

_____ Final divorce decree

_____ Mediator's report

_____ Therapist's report(s)

_____ Expert witnesses' reports

_____ Restraining order

_____ Updated will

_____ Living will

_____ Power of attorney

_____ Medical power of attorney

_____ Trusts

_____ Updated credit report

_____ New budget

_____ Updated life insurance policy(ies)

_____ Updated health insurance policy(ies)

_____ COBRA forms for continuation of health insurance

_____ Homeowner's insurance policy

_____ Disability insurance policy

_____ Auto insurance policy

_____ Social Security benefits statement

_____ Change of name documents

_____ Passports

_____ Marriage certificate

Assembling Your Divorce Team

Questions to ask your attorney

When hiring

1. Have you handled cases that are similar to mine, dealing with the same issues involved (child custody, spousal support, abuse, etc.)?
2. How long have you been doing this kind of work?
3. Approximately how many of your divorce cases have gone to trial?
4. What do you charge? (Ask for a sample fee agreement and bill before retaining the lawyer.) Is your hourly rate higher for court work than it is for office work?
5. How often will I be billed? (Monthly is usual.)
6. Will you be willing to take my case to court if we cannot reach a good settlement?
7. Do you have time for my case? How heavy is your caseload?
8. Will others in your office be working on my case? If so, who are they, what are their credentials, and will I be charged a different rate for their time?
9. Do you charge for copying and postage?
10. Do you require advance payment of court costs?

11. How much should I expect court costs to be?

12. What are your office hours?

13. Can you be reached at home? By beeper? By answering service?

14. Do you use e-mail? Can I e-mail you with questions about my case?

15. Is there anything about my situation that causes you concern in terms of handling the case?

16. Is there anything I need to be on the lookout for?

17. Do you know my spouse?

18. Do you know my spouse's attorney?

19. How much input will I have in the case?

20. Will you contact me regularly regarding the status of my case?

21. What do you foresee as the outcome of my case?

22. How long do you think it will take for my case to be resolved?

23. Is there anything I can do during the pendency of my case to minimize or reduce costs?

24. Will you notify me in advance of incurring any extraordinary costs, such as for expert witnesses, private investigators, etc.?

Regarding custody and visitation

If there is a court order for custody and visitation:

1. Can my spouse and I agree to vary the terms of the court order?

2. What if my spouse violates the terms of the court order?

3. Can I withhold visitation if my spouse fails to pay child support?

4. What if my children do not want to visit my spouse?

5. How can I modify the custody and visitation order if problems arise?

If there is no court order for custody and visitation:

1. Do we have to have a written agreement for custody and visitation if we get along well and no problems have surfaced?

2. What if we informally agree to a custody and visitation arrangement, but then problems develop?

3. Will the court honor our agreement on custody and visitation?

About support

1. How soon can I start receiving support?

2. What is the easiest way to file for support?

3. Do I have to wait until other issues are settled before receiving support?

4. Is there a way to force my spouse to continue to contribute to the costs of housing, even after he/she has moved out?

5. What if he/she violates a court order for support?

6. Is there a way to process support requests or enforcement through the court without using a lawyer?

About a settlement

1. Do you feel that the settlement, as proposed, is fair?

2. What are our chances of getting a better deal if we go to court?

3. Am I being reasonable in my requests?

4. Are my spouse's requests reasonable?

5. Would you accept this offer if you were in my shoes?

6. If we are not able to settle, how long until we are likely to get a trial date?

7. How much more will this process cost me if we do not settle now?

About the trial

1. What is the general course of the trial going to be?

2. What is involved?

3. Will I be called to testify?

4. Will I be prepared ahead of time for my answers on the stand?

5. Will my spouse have to testify?

6. Will anyone else have to testify on my behalf or against my spouse?

7. What if I get nervous and answer something wrong?

8. Will you be able to help me out while I'm on the stand?

9. What should I say if I'm asked about...?

10. Can I look at any of my notes or evidence while I'm on the stand?

11. Will there be evidence used in my case? Exhibit A, etc.?

12. Will you contact my witnesses and tell them where to go and what to do?

13. Can I talk to my witnesses before the trial?

14. Can I talk to my witnesses during breaks?

15. How can I let you know my questions as the trial is taking place?

16. How should I address the judge?

17. How should I address my spouse's attorney?

18. How should I refer to my spouse?

19. Can I bring other members of my family to court to watch?

20. Should I bring the children to court during the custody phase of the hearing?

About the final divorce decree

1. When will the divorce be final?
2. What has to be accomplished before the divorce is final?
3. What documents will I receive for the final judgment?
4. When will our division of assets take place?
5. Who oversees the division of assets?
6. Can I openly date another person now?
7. When can I get remarried?
8. When can I change my name (if applicable), and how do I go about making it legal?

Questions to ask your therapist

When hiring

1. How much experience do you have working on issues like mine?
2. What kind of session schedule do you have in mind for me? Weekly appointments?
3. How do you organize your therapy? Do you employ medicine and psychotherapy, or do you just attempt to solve the problem with medicine?
4. Do you assign "homework"?
5. How accessible are you? Can I contact you via voicemail, e-mail, or cell phone if necessary?
6. What is your billing schedule?
7. What kind of payment do you accept?
8. How long do sessions last?
9. Do you have group therapy options as well?
10. What is your policy on canceled appointments?
11. Do you accept my insurance?

12. Do you belong to any professional associations or boards?

13. Do you offer individual, child, and family counseling as well?

Within therapy

1. Are my feelings normal?

2. How can I raise my self-esteem?

3. What part did I play in the end of my marriage?

4. Can you help me understand my spouse's point of view?

5. How long will these emotions last?

6. Do you have any recommended reading that I can do to change my perspective?

7. How can I learn to trust again?

8. How can I help my children cope?

9. How can I form a workable relationship with my ex?

10. How can I start to create a new identity for myself?

Russell's suggestions for hiring a financial planner/money manager

1. **Ask yourself why.** Financial planners (whose business cards may also say financial advisor, financial consultant, or wealth manager) vary widely in their practices and expertise. Most if not all planners will manage or provide guidance on investments. Others may offer counsel on everything from how to balance a checkbook and reduce debt to how to lower taxes or set up an estate plan. A few specialize in divorce. Some will work with you for a day to help you get your fiscal affairs in order. Others prefer longer-term arrangements. Take a good look at your strengths and weaknesses around money and ask yourself where you most need a helping hand.

2. **Gather names and brochures.** Start by drafting a list of potential planners. Begin close to home. Ask family,

friends, and business colleagues for referrals. You can also contact either the National Association of Personal Financial Advisors (847-483-5413) or the Financial Planning Association (800-647-6340) and ask for a referral to members in your area.

3. **Look for experience and credentials.** Just about anyone can call himself a financial planner. And just about anyone does. That's why other more standard credentials are important. A business degree such as an MBA is a good thing. Some CPAs and attorneys specialize in financial planning. In addition, over the past several years, the designation CFP (Certified Financial Planner) has become widely recognized as a mark of competency. To attain the CFP a planner must meet certain educational requirements, pass a fairly tough exam, and gain a requisite amount of practical experience. Other good credentials: CFA (Chartered Financial Analyst), ChFC (Chartered Financial Consultant), and CDFA (Certified Divorce Financial Analyst). The latter signifies that the planner has special training in divorce issues.

4. **Toss the bad apples.** A financial planner (or his employer) should be registered with the Securities and Exchange Commission (SEC) or the state's security commission. Find out by asking to see a candidate's *ADV* (advisor*) form.* Anyone who professionally gives investment advice is required to provide such a form. It will provide you with lots of interesting information about the planner and her practice, such as how long she's been in business, how many clients she has, and how much money she manages. It will also tell you about any disciplinary history for unethical conduct. Check, too, with the local Better Business Bureau, and the Certified Financial Planner Board of Standards (303-830-7500) to make sure the planner isn't prone to lapses of good judgment.

5. **Schedule an initial appointment.** After you've gathered a list of planners who look clean on paper, it's time to meet face to face. Although you're no expert in the field, you can still get a pretty good sense for whether a planner knows his stuff. Ask what sets him apart from other planners. Ask for his philosophy on money, and whether he has a clearly defined strategy for financial success. As for investing, ask how he does it, and whether his choices in investments are based on hunches or on academic research. If a planner can't answer those questions quickly and confidently, think twice about hiring him.

6. **Check out the bill.** Be clear about how, and how much, a planner will charge you. Some financial planners charge by the hour, some will charge you a percentage of your assets "under management," and others will make money off commissions from the products they sell you. Many planners who do not sell products or take commissions ("fee-only" planners) feel that they can be more objective in the advice they give you and in the investments they suggest for you. Being a fee-only planner myself, I hold that opinion. But that's not to say that you can't find a commissioned planner who is both honest and talented.

7. **Make sure you "click."** At times financial planning can get very personal. A competent planner working on your long-term financial goals should be asking you questions about your retirement dreams, health, and perhaps even the quality of your marriage and your relationship with your children and grandchildren. If you're going to be working with a planner for a long time, the two of you should feel comfortable together. Competence and honesty are important, but personality and chemistry certainly matter, too.